NO TIME FOR SILENCE

NO TIME FOR SILENCE

EVANGELICAL WOMEN IN PUBLIC MINISTRY AROUND THE TURN OF THE CENTURY

Janette Hassey

Academie
Books Grand Rapids,
Michigan
Zondervan Publishing House

NO TIME FOR SILENCE
Copyright © 1986 by Janette Hassey

ACADEMIE BOOKS is an imprint of
Zondervan Publishing House
1415 Lake Drive S.E.
Grand Rapids, Michigan 49506

Library of Congress Cataloging in Publication Data

Hassey, Janette.
    No time for silence.

    Bibliography: p.
    Includes index.
    1. Evangelicalism—United States—History—19th century.
2. Fundamentalism—History—19th century.   3. Evangelicalism—
History—20th century.   2. Fundamentalism—History—20th century.
5. Women clergy—United States.   6. United States—Church history—
19th century.   7. United States—Church history—20th century.
I. Title.

BR1642.U5H38   1986   280'.4'0973   86–13339

ISBN   0–310–29451–7

Edited by John Vriend
Designed by Louise Bauer

Printed in the United States of America

86 87 88 89 90 91 92 93 94 95 / 10 9 8 7 6 5 4 3 2 1

for
Linda and
Ruthanne Hassey,
hoping that Evangelical
churches at the next turn of
the century will joyfully welcome
all your gifts of ministry

"I tell you, if they keep quiet, the stones will cry out."

Jesus Christ

CONTENTS

ACKNOWLEDGMENTS

Special thanks to my professors—Stan Gundry, who first exposed me to the historical tradition of Evangelical feminism; Jerald Brauer and Martin Marty, who guided my research in its earliest stages; and Timothy Weber, who subsequently encouraged me to finish this project. I am deeply grateful to my parents and Paula Smith for their constant support. Finally, I am indebted to Carol Engle for countless hours spent on the computer graciously supplied by Tom Morton.

PREFACE

In 1927, the Moody Bible Institute *Alumni News* proudly published a letter containing an astounding personal account of the ministry of Mabel C. Thomas, a 1913 MBI graduate. Thomas, called to the pastorate in a Kansas church, had preached, taught weekly Bible classes, and baptized dozens of converts. She concluded her letter with praise, since she "could not have met the many and varied opportunities for service without the training of MBI."[1]

Today, because of gender, female students at MBI and other Evangelical institutions are barred from pastoral training courses. Why has such an enormous shift occurred since the turn of the century? Why do many Evangelical groups who used women as pastors and preachers *then* now prohibit or discourage such ministry? This research will analyze that provocative historical question.

At the turn of the century, Evangelical churches in America grappled with two thorny issues—theological liberalism and feminist demands for women's equal rights. Many Evangelicals responded to this first challenge by reasserting scriptural inspiration and even inerrancy. Some of these same "proto-Fundamentalists" supported equality for women in church ministry.

How could Evangelicals a century ago hold high their inerrant, verbally inspired Bible in one hand while blessing the ministry of women preachers, pastors, Bible teachers, and evangelists with the other? This study will explore that question, with particular focus on the way these Evangelicals interpreted Scripture passages. Those who endorsed women's public ministry were convinced that a literal approach to the

Bible, and especially to prophecy, demanded such leadership by women.

Why another study of women in the church? My research counters the popular but misleading claim that Evangelical feminism (that movement for women's equality rooted in Scripture and Evangelical Christian faith) is simply an accommodation to recent secular feminist and theologically liberal movements for women's rights. Rather, Evangelical feminism in America first surfaced in the mid-nineteenth century and accelerated at the turn of the century.

Recently, church historians have documented the existence of this nineteenth-century Evangelical feminism in America that mobilized women and freed leaders such as Phoebe Palmer and Frances Willard to preach.[2] These pioneering studies, focusing on women in the Wesleyan holiness movement, constitute the first step in reevaluating the historical role of women in Evangelical American churches.

By asking some new questions, this work attempts to carry on where the story of nineteenth-century Evangelical feminism leaves off. What of women outside the Wesleyan holiness sphere? What role did Bible institutes play in training women for ministry? Can the rise of Fundamentalism at the turn of the century be blamed for the increased exclusion of women from church leadership?

A graduate course paper on the founding and early years of Moody Bible Institute (MBI) first cracked my stereotype of early Fundamentalism's antithetical relation to Evangelical feminism. The last thing I expected to find in my historical research at MBI was precisely what I stumbled upon—scores of references to women preachers, pastors, and evangelists, trained at MBI and publicized in the Alumni News section of old *Moody Monthly* magazines!

As I continued my investigation of women's roles in early Fundamentalist circles, I found turn-of-the-century Fundamentalism to be neither exclusively male-dominated nor inherently antifeminist from inception. Specifically, when I examined the life and ministry of transitional Evangelical figures like D. L. Moody and A. J. Gordon or of self-avowed Fundamentalists like W. B. Riley and J. R. Straton, I discovered key leaders who saw their support of women preachers as consistent with their biblical literalism. Consequently, these findings forced me to reevaluate current historical interpretations of Fundamentalism's impact on Evangelical feminism.

George Marsden's recent history of Fundamentalism, for example, mentions key nineteenth-century Methodist holiness women and alludes to A. J. Gordon's advocacy of women's right to preach. He describes the newer Reformed holiness movement as "male-dominated" but neglects the great exceptions to that phenomenon. For instance, Marsden fails to explain how the Reformed holiness Keswick movement in Britain was then spearheaded by a woman, Hannah Whitall Smith. Smith spoke at suffrage conventions and preached regularly. Marsden does not mention that A. B. Simpson, a leader of the movement in the United States, provided equality for women at his Nyack school and in the Christian and Missionary Alliance. These examples of female leadership need to enter the discussion of women's place in church ministry.

Marsden states that Fundamentalists generally relegated women to quite subordinate roles. Marsden explains that

> when experiential emphasis predominated, the idea that Pentecost opened a dispensation when women would prophesy (as the prophet Joel suggested) might be accepted. Yet the Baconian Biblicism conflicted with such ideals due to Pauline statements about women. Apparently even in the Holiness traditions the role of women in the church declined during the fundamentalist era.[3]

Donald Dayton echoed this same idea in explaining the decline of Evangelical feminism. "As Evangelicals were more and more distanced from the abolitionist controversies, they tended to fall back into biblical literalism. The forces of "Fundamentalism" and "traditionalism" replaced the "evangelical spirit."[4]

Marsden and Dayton accurately connect abolition and the emphasis on Christian experience to wider roles for Evangelical women. These authors also conclude that biblicism (intending to take the words of the Bible literally) tends to restrict women's church ministry. Indeed, certain Fundamentalists then as now opposed women's public ministry. But many did not, and proponents of early Fundamentalism advocated women pastors and preachers as actively as the Wesleyan holiness people did.

In short, I will attempt to answer three key questions: (1) What evidence exists that women had a significant public ministry in turn-of-the-century Evangelicalism? (2) What explains this openness to women? (3) Why have women gradually been squeezed out of those leadership roles as the century progressed? My study will highlight the underside of Evangelicalism—those lesser-known women drawn to study or teach at Bible institutes, invited to preach at Bible conferences, called to local church pastorates, or asked to evangelize and lead revivals in local communities.

Examining the ministries of these Evangelical women raises several related questions. What relationships existed between liberal Protestant, Wesleyan holiness, Pentecostal, and the other Evangelical women in ministry? Early twentieth-century Pentecostalism, partly founded by women and eager to utilize female preachers and healers, constituted a Protestant subgroup distinct from Fundamentalism. Early Fundamentalists rejected the Pentecostal doctrine of speaking in tongues as the sign of Holy Spirit baptism.

How did women's home ministry compare to foreign mission work?[5] Did the experience of British and Canadian Evangelical women parallel the American scene?[6] How did Evangelical women's benevolence work relate to women's public ministry? What of black preachers at the turn of the century?[7] How did Evangelicals of that era reconcile women's typically subordinate domestic position in marriage with equality in the church? Hopefully others will continue research on the historical phenomenon of women in public church leadership.

Recent debate in Evangelical circles over women's public ministry tends to focus on biblical and theological issues without grappling with the historical questions. Asking what women and men have done in church ministry in an earlier age and why can make that theological discussion more historically informed. Though knowledge of the past does not and should not dictate the future, it helps illumine how present attitudes toward women developed. For several decades at the turn of the century, Evangelical churches did not leave all the public gifts of women in the church buried. We, in turn, dare not bury the accounts of those courageous, committed, pioneer women.

1

INTRODUCTION: TURN-OF-THE-CENTURY AMERICA

In May 1888 the graduation prize for excellence in "Homiletic Exercises" at a school in New York went to a woman. A New England Baptist pastor published "The Ministry of Women" in 1894, supporting women's preaching with New Testament exegesis. In 1901 another nationally known Baptist minister from Minneapolis warmly greeted the Thirty-third Annual Convention of the National American Woman Suffrage Association held in his church, preaching the opening sermon in support of women's right to speak from the platform in a mixed assembly. Two years later, Rev. Rosa A. Lizenby graduated from an Illinois school that prepared her for ordination and pastorates in Kansas. The 1908 constitution of a small Swedish immigrant church provided for the membership of female preachers. In 1913 Salvation Army founder Catherine Booth preached twice at a strategic church in Chicago. A union of churches in the 1920s listed thirteen ordained women with the title "Reverend" on its membership roster. In 1926 a prominent New York City Baptist pastor invited the young evangelist Uldine Utley to preach revival for five weeks from his pulpit, writing publicly in support of her ministry. In August 1929 Lottie Osborn Sheidler completed her ministerial training in the Midwest and received a Pastor's Course diploma.

Were these schools, denominations, and churches part of liberal Protestantism in turn-of-the-century America? To the contrary—each instead reveals a startling approach to women in public ministry by key Evangelical institutions and individuals. A. B. Simpson's Nyack College awarded the preaching prize to a woman. A. J. Gordon wrote "The Ministry of Women." William Bell Riley, founder of the principal organization of the premillennial wing of Fundamentalism—the World's Christian Fundamentals Association—ministered at Minneapolis's First Baptist Church where the suffrage meeting convened.[1] Lizenby and Sheidler both trained for the pastorate at Moody Bible Institute.[2] The Evangelical Free Church of America provided for women preachers in its original constitution. Booth preached at Moody Church in Chicago. The thirteen female clergy held membership in the American Conference of Undenominational Churches, renamed in 1930 the Independent Fundamental Churches of America.[3] John Roach Straton, nicknamed the "Fundamentalist pope," pastored Calvary Baptist in New York where Utley preached.[4]

If the discovery that these people and institutions were Evangelical surprises us, it would have surprised some people of that era as well. The misconception that primarily liberal Protestantism, not Evangelicalism or early Fundamentalism, provided equality in the church for women exists even in some turn-of-the-century accounts. Frederic May Holland asserted in 1892 that most women clergy ministered in liberal denominations.[5] J. T. Sunderland argued that liberal Christianity, which rejects the Bible's inspiration, can undoubtedly expect more from women. Liberals favor women's freedom, he claimed, while orthodox with their fixed doctrine do not. After praising Unitarian, Universalist, and Quaker female ministry, Sunderland wrote, "no orthodox body has opened its regular ministry to women."[6]

Ellen Battelle Dietrick concurred, naming the Universalists, Unitarians, and Quakers "the more Christ-like denominations" for opening doors to women. British liberal minister A. Maude Royden, herself unable to reconcile Paul's teaching on women with equality, found more prejudice against women in "old fashioned circles where the literalist doctrine of Scriptural inspiration still holds the field."[7]

Even some orthodox writers reiterated this relationship between liberalism and women. Victor I. Masters, for instance, interpreted the 1918 Southern Baptist decision to seat women messengers at its annual meeting as "a significant indication of a current tendency toward more liberalism."[8] These turn-of-the-century authors initiated some of the misconceptions regarding Evangelical women in public ministry that persist to the present.

An adequate examination of that ministry at the turn of the century must be placed in historical context. The purpose of this chapter is to set a historical framework, specifically highlighting the rise of Fundamentalism and development of feminism in turn-of-the-century America.

Between the founding in 1883 of Nyack College, America's first Bible institute, and the adoption in 1920 of the Nineteenth Amendment, which gave women the vote, the United States completed its transition from an agricultural society to an industrial, world-wide power. Accelerating immigration, rapid urbanization, awesome industrialization, plus the cultural impact of Darwinism transformed American life after the Civil War and prepared the ground for the Progressive movements of the early twentieth century.[9]

These important changes occurred at a time of increasing pluralism in American religion. At the turn of the century, Eastern Orthodoxy, Oriental religions, black churches, Catholicism, Liberalism, Evangelicalism, holiness churches, Pentecostalism, new groups such as Jehovah's Witnesses, and a variety of ethnic churches coexisted and competed for members.[10]

Significantly, by World War I the basic religious map of the United States was set. Since the revivals of the Second Great Awakening, the Baptists and Methodists had dominated the South. Immigrant Catholics flooded urban areas and the Northeast, while the Catholic Hispanic population expanded in the Southwest. Lutherans and Scandinavian churches populated the upper Midwest whereas Disciples of Christ grew strong across America's heartland. The three leading denominations in

the colonial era—Congregational, Presbyterian, and Episcopal—settled thinly across the nation. According to the 1900
census, Methodists comprised the largest Protestant body, with
Baptists a close second.

TURN-OF-THE-CENTURY ROOTS
OF FUNDAMENTALISM

American Evangelicalism between the Civil War and World
War I confronted the vexing problem of growing theological
liberalism. One response within Evangelicalism consisted of
that historically complex religious movement known as Fundamentalism. Thanks to current scholarship, the older view of a
socially backward, theologically stunted, and psychologically
disturbed Fundamentalist movement has given way to a more
balanced interpretation.[11]

Flourishing in the cities of the Northeast and Midwest, the
organized Fundamentalist crusade which surfaced in the 1920s
curiously combined a variety of Evangelical subgroups. Converts of the Second Great Awakening from a variety of
Protestant denominations shared a common religious and
cultural outlook, constituting the nineteenth-century Evangelical Alliance. Within that Evangelical coalition the Fundamentalist roots of revivalism, pietism, holiness, dispensationalism,
premillennialism, and Calvinist orthodoxy intertwined with a
conventional mainline conservative protest against liberalism.

Revivalism, for example, emphasized conversion as central in becoming a Christian. Pietism focused on that moralistic
impulse seeking to intensify Christian piety and purity. Though
sometimes encouraging social reform and philanthropy, pietism
also formalized a legalistic code of Christian behavior in terms
of prohibitions (i.e., no dancing, cards, theater). Leaders of the
holiness movement promoted perfectionism as the second step
in Christian experience after conversion. Princeton's A. A.
Hodge and B. B. Warfield defended the old Calvinist orthodoxy and formulated a precise doctrine of biblical inerrancy.

The system of dispensationalism intricately interpreted the
Bible by dividing Scripture into various periods (or dispensa-

tions) and divine programs—a method widely spread through the 1909 publication of the *Scofield Reference Bible*. Premillennialism expressed dispensationalism's key doctrine of the end times, advocating a literal second coming of Christ prior to the establishment of the Millennium on earth. Fundamentalism, which was more than just a new label for premillennialism, encompassed this wide spectrum of movements. It emerged from the Evangelical soil of American revivalism and pietism with an increasingly intense concern for doctrinal issues.[12]

By 1920, diverse theological, ecclesiastical, and cultural elements of Evangelicalism united to combat a common foe—Modernism. The self-conscious, militant, anti-Modernist Fundamentalist crusade began after World War I, crested in 1925, became defensive in the 1930s, and attempted to regroup in the 1940s. These fighting Fundamentalists of the 1920s protested the liberalizing scholarship of biblical higher criticism and opposed theological Modernism in the churches. They tried to counter liberalism in culture (i.e., teaching evolution in public schools) while promoting combinations of revivalistic, holiness, dispensational, and Calvinist doctrines. This coalition of defenders of the faith joined together numerous interdenominational Evangelicals in the battle for orthodoxy.

Fundamentalism was institutionalized in scores of Bible institutes, spread at Bible conferences, and crusaded through the printed page. The most influential publication effort of both major strands of Fundamentalism (dispensational premillennial and conservative mainline) occurred between 1910 and 1915. In a twelve-volume series of pamphlets entitled *The Fundamentals* (sent to over 300,000 ministers and missionaries), conservative Evangelicals tried to offer their definitive answer to liberalism.

Though committed to certain fundamental doctrines, most of the early leadership retained strong denominational ties and loyalties and therefore exhibited considerable fluidity in other beliefs and practices. Whether dispensational or postmillennial (advocating Christ's return after the establishment of the Millennium on earth), Calvinist or Arminian, anti-revival Presbyterian or pro-revival Baptist, advocates or opponents of holiness, Fundamentalists somehow agreed to disagree on a variety of issues in order to join forces on what they perceived to be the essentials.

While the Fundamentalist-Modernist controversy clearly split northern Baptists and Presbyterians, it affected and shaped numerous other denominations as well. At the turn of the century, disputes broke out between conservatives and liberals in almost every major Protestant group. Traditionalists among the Disciples of Christ and the Congregationalists opposed Modernism and in that sense contributed another branch to the proto-Fundamentalist family tree.

Certain holiness groups like the Nazarenes experienced a definite Fundamentalist leavening.[13] Methodism in general split over holiness rather than Fundamentalist doctrines, largely rejecting dispensationalism. In contrast, many Pentecostal groups embraced dispensationalism, yet diverged from a Fundamentalism increasingly critical of their approach to healing and tongues. Missouri Synod Lutherans strongly protested liberalism yet never formally joined the Fundamentalist crusade, alienated in part by the Fundamentalist practice of unionism (Christians uniting without full doctrinal agreement). Other theologically conservative immigrant churches like the Swedish Baptists and the Christian Reformed developed as Evangelical cousins to the predominantly English-speaking Fundamentalists.

The identification of institutions and individuals as Fundamentalist in the opening decades of the twentieth century proves almost as complex as defining the word in the first place. The term embarrassed Princeton's John Gresham Machen, intellectual leader of Fundamentalism. Even Moody Bible Institute expressed uneasiness with the Fundamentalist handle. *Moody Bible Institute Monthly* declared in 1924:

> We are not Fundamentalists in the sense that we have joined that association or become a part of that movement as a movement. We shrink from "movements," and as we have said before, "evangelism" is all the name we want.[14]

Given this fuzziness in terminology, I have intentionally chosen to use the term *Evangelical* in this study to describe the women found in various places on the Fundamentalist-Evangelical continuum.

TURN-OF-THE-CENTURY AMERICAN FEMINISM

A variety of social movements flourished in turn-of-the-century America. Whether advocating temperance, feminism, suffrage, Marxism, anarchism, populism, nativism, black self-help, Catholic Americanism, reform Judaism, or the social gospel— each reform movement exhibited effort to change some part of society or the whole of it.

Most nineteenth-century feminists had championed other reform movements such as abolition or temperance and were deeply rooted in Evangelical revivalism. By the turn of the century, the feminist movement encompassed a wide spectrum of advocates and reform platforms. Religious or Evangelical feminism held up religion or Scripture as woman's basis for equality. In contrast, secular or Enlightenment-type feminism of the Elizabeth Cady Stanton brand grounded equality for women in natural law or philosophy, rejecting traditional religion and the Bible as degrading to women. This feminism struck at the core of American society in its challenge to woman's traditional roles in the home, church, school, labor force, and in politics.[15]

Particularly seen to be at odds with the fight for women's rights and equality was the institution of the family, traditionally dependent on women's subordination.[16] The dramatic nineteenth-century shift to smaller families (i.e., the birth rate dropped from 7.04 in 1800 to 3.56 in 1900) paralleled other significant societal changes. The increasing number of middle-class women with both a common school education and growing leisure time on their hands opened new avenues for involvement outside the home. Yet most turn-of-the-century Americans still accepted woman's primary function as mother, her subordinate position as wife, and her idealized role as moral guardian of culture. The church traditionally reinforced these concepts, urging women to submit to God's established order.

Turn-of-the-century feminists not only differed as to basic

starting points, but they fought among themselves over purpose and priorities. Social feminists, for example, subordinated individualistic women's rights to social reform. They tried to change unjust conditions in society and stressed service to others, thereby enlarging the female sphere of action in socially acceptable directions. Equality in the public sphere often took precedence over the private sphere, with the issue of subordination in marriage temporarily laid aside. The more individualistic "hardcore" feminists, in contrast, pressed toward woman's equality with man as their central goal. Social feminists aimed at a different target—the moral reform of American life.

One branch of the multifaceted women's rights movement at the turn of the century was clearly the heir to Evangelical revival in Britain and in America. Several features of John Wesley's eighteenth-century British revival especially contributed to a new role for women in the church.[17] First, revivalism carried an implicit egalitarianism which tended to undermine traditional structures of authority. Second, the revival turned to Christian experience as central along with doctrine. Third, the revivalist leaders generally possessed pragmatic qualities. These factors helped open the doors for women to serve as Methodist class leaders.

In America, evangelist Charles Finney mirrored the Wesleyan openness to women within his Presbyterian/Congregational orbit of ministry. One of his controversial "new measures"—allowing women to speak in mixed assemblies—opened new doors for Evangelical women. Striving for female equality in one specific public arena—church life and ministry—these nineteenth-century Evangelical feminist pioneers paved the way to the pulpit for scores of turn-of-the-century women.

While professions like law and medicine began granting women equal rights in turn-of-the-century America, women also sought entrance into professional church ministry. As during the antebellum abolition crusade, most denominations faced again the thorny questions of women's proper sphere of ministry. For example, the Presbyterian Synod of Virginia established a committee in 1897 to study women's rights in the church. In spite of decades of restrictive deliverances regarding women, the perceived "current, rapid revolution regarding women's sphere" forced the issue anew.[18] Christian Golder, historian of the deaconess movement, declared the "Women Question" a leading topic of the times; Peter Z. Easton saw it as "the burning question of the day."[19] Churches grappled with three broad issues—female control of women's missionary societies, laity rights, and clergy rights for women.

Statistics illumine women's expanding role in public ministry at the turn of the century.[20] The number of professional women clergy in 1880—165 ministers or 0.3 percent of male and female clergy combined—increased to 1,787 women clergy (1.4 percent of the total) in 1920. The 1910 census significantly inserted these new semiprofessional employment categories in addition to the traditional clergy class: (1) fortunetellers, hypnotists, and spiritualists; (2) healers; and (3) religious/charity workers.[21] It listed women that year under the old system (with only one category—clergy) and under the new. Since 8,889 of the 9,574 women who called themselves "clergy" under the old system reclassified themselves "religious/charity workers" under the new 1910 system, the actual meaning of the pre-1910 term "clergy" for women was ambiguous. In any case, the number of women religious workers (who in 1910 comprised 55.7 percent of male and female workers combined) jumped to 26,927 in 1920 (65.6 percent of the total).

According to the 1890 census, over 75 percent of all female clergy were unmarried—over 17 percent widowed, almost 60 percent single. In contrast, over 75 percent of all male clergy had a wife, while 18 percent remained single and 4 percent were widowed.[22] This reflected dramatic differences in the family life of women clergy compared to that of men.

Apparently the tremendous increase of professional female clergy in the early twentieth century paralleled the more dramatic surge of females into the semiprofessional "religious work" field which women rapidly dominated. Not so obvious is what identified the two groups. Did ordination, education, form of ministry, or a combination of these factors distinguish female clergy from the religious worker? Would a female itinerant revivalist or unordained supply preacher perceive herself as part of the clergy? Whatever the title, women clergy and laity alike in unprecedented numbers stepped out into public church ministry at the turn of the century.

In 1919, M. Madeline Southard founded an Association of Women Preachers, later renamed the Association of Women Ministers. This organization, plus Southard's publication of *Woman's Pulpit* journal in the 1920s, mark the growing professionalization of some clergywomen.

Turn-of-the-century Evangelicalism resisted Modernism in culture as well as in theology. How then did Evangelicals perceive the women's rights movement in relation to Modernism? To allow a woman to vote or preach or pastor—was that not an adaptation of religious ideas to modern culture? Why did many Evangelicals of that era *not* identify women's public church ministry with the specter of Modernism as later proponents would?

A significant reversal among Evangelicals on the women's issue took place between the World Wars. Understanding the relationship of turn-of-the-century Evangelicalism to the women's rights movement may modify our conception of what its resistance to Modernism was all about. Though not calling themselves Fundamentalist feminists, many of the Evangelical leaders in the chapters to follow stood both as heirs of the nineteenth-century Evangelical feminists and forerunners of later twentieth-century Fundamentalists.

2

EVANGELICAL WOMEN AND THE EARLY BIBLE INSTITUTES

Whatever else it was in addition, the Fundamentalist movement was decidedly an educational movement; education was implicit in its overriding objective, which was the evangelization of America and the world."[1] Without a doubt, Bible institutes played an important part in shaping turn-of-the-century Evangelicalism and institutionalizing Fundamentalism. More specifically, they provided a major training ground for Evangelical women of that era who entered public ministry. Though Bible institutes first appeared in Europe and England, only in America did they take root so deeply and prosper. The early Bible institutes provided an institutional channeling of the intense late nineteenth-century spirit of revivalism and missions.

The lack of universal public education on the secondary level made college and seminary education impossible for many drawn to evangelistic and missionary service. Women confronted the additional barrier of exclusion from many schools and most seminaries because of gender. If the spheres and ministries of men and women did indeed differ greatly, one might expect them to be trained separately. Morgan Dix, rector of Trinity Church in New York City, recognized the potential leveling effect of co-education in 1883 when he declared, "The sexes ought not to be educated together, unless all distinction between them be abolished."[2]

However, simply training women and men within the same four walls did not automatically entail equality of education. In 1906, for example, the Southern Baptist Seminary in Louisville admitted thirty-five women for missionary training. Barred from taking examinations or earning degrees, these women "could attend class but not raise questions or participate in class discussions."[3] Until 1920, Congregational Hartford Theological Seminary required women who entered to state that they did not expect to enter the ministry. Even at the University of Chicago Divinity School, though admitted to classes along with men, women were encouraged to prepare for the foreign field and "pagan pastorates," not home ministry.[4]

Given this setting, the Bible institutes provided an auxiliary means of securing lay recruits to evangelize at home and abroad, enabling less-educated, less-privileged classes to train for Christian service. In addition, many women for the first time received formal biblical and theological training. Evangelicals clearly established these earliest schools primarily to train Christian lay workers, not to counter the theological growth of liberalism.

Yet later, in the heat of the Modernist-Fundamentalist debate, some Bible institutes obviously began to serve as an interdenominational headquarters for Fundamentalism. These schools established part of the bridge between the earlier premillennial and later Fundamentalist movements. They assured Fundamentalism's survival and growth, providing crucial grassroots leadership for the movement through graduates who carried Fundamentalists' doctrine and practice to local churches. According to Ernest Sandeen, no analysis of the structure of Fundamentalism can proceed very far without some understanding of the Bible institute's role.

Bible institutes constituted one form among several of turn-of-the-century religious higher education.[5] The earliest schools focused primarily on the preparation of home and foreign missionaries. They arose in the same context as schools for YMCA training and deaconess education—at first all distinct from Christian liberal arts colleges and theological seminaries. The Women's American Baptist Home Mission

Society, for instance, established the Women's Baptist Missionary Training School in Chicago in 1881, predating all American Bible institutes.[6] Even the Women's Christian Temperance Union (WCTU) realized early its need for trained workers and established the Home and School for WCTU Evangelists and Missionaries in New York City. Begun in 1890, the New York Training School educated Episcopal deaconesses in Bible, theology, church history, and missions.

Bible institutes, providing an inexpensive, flexible period of training for laity, were not alone in carrying the early Fundamentalist education banner. William Ringenberg described Wheaton College in Illinois as the leading Fundamentalist college of the early twentieth century. Founder Jonathan Blanchard had ministered in a Wesleyan Methodist church, advocating both abolition and women's rights before the Civil War. Decades later, Wheaton president Charles Blanchard helped draft the World's Christian Fundamentals Association nine-point doctrinal statement; by 1926 Wheaton adopted the nine points as its statement of faith. J. Oliver Buswell, Jr., Fundamentalist leader in the orthodox wing of Northern Presbyterianism, began his Wheaton presidency in 1925. He constituted just one of the many Wheaton supporters in the 1920s from the northern Fundamentalist leadership ranks.[7]

As at Wheaton, most Bible institutes felt increasingly compelled to express and undergird their commitment to orthodox belief with a written statement of fundamental doctrines. This assisted the Fundamentalist task of separating suspect liberal schools from safe Evangelical institutions. The eighth aim of the Baptist Bible Union clearly expressed that concern in 1925. The BBU proposed

> to approve, patronize, and support such denominational schools and theological seminaries as unequivocally show themselves to be loyal to the inspiration and authority of the Bible and all the consequent fundamentals of our Confession . . . to commend heartily the loyal Bible training schools, the Bible Institutes and Bible Conferences conducted by Christian Fundamentalists.[8]

Which Bible institutes founded before 1920 met that standard of loyalty to the Bible's inspiration and to fundamental doctrine? In 1924 *The Sunday School Times* introduced its list of forty-two "Bible Institutes That Are Sound" with this paragraph:

> No sane and intelligent person would think of unnecessarily exposing himself or others to infection from disease. Why should Christians be less careful of the spiritual health of themselves and or their children? If you or those dear to you are contemplating preparation for Christian service you will make no mistake in choosing from the sound Bible institutions listed below.[9]

Each of the schools examined in this chapter appeared on that significant list. Another compilation of explicitly "fundamental" schools, compiled for the 1930 convention of the World's Christian Fundamentals Association, appeared in *The Christian Fundamentalist*.[10] Looking finally at S. A. Witmer's historical sketch of the Bible schools founded before 1920, one can ascertain fairly precisely which institutions met the Evangelical loyalty tests.[11]

Careful examination of these endorsed Bible institutes reveals their wide denominational diversity. Emerging from a broad spectrum of Evangelical churches—Mennonite (Hesston Academy and Bible School), Presbyterian (Brookes Bible Institute), Methodist (Chicago Evangelistic Institute), Advent Christian (Boston Bible Training School), Friends (Cleveland Bible Institute), Baptist (Bethel Institute), Berean Fundamental (Denver Bible Institute), and Christian and Missionary Alliance (Nyack)—these training schools united in their core commitment to fundamental Bible education as preparation for lay Christian service. Several prominent Bible institutes (Moody Bible Institute, Bible Institute of Los Angeles, Northwestern, Philadelphia, and Gordon) affiliated at first with the founder's particular church background but quickly established a self-consciously interdenominational constituency.

When plotted on a map of the United States, the Bible institutes display their overwhelmingly common sociocultural context—the urban north, centering on the arc of cities stretching from Boston to New York, Philadelphia, Chicago, and Minneapolis.[12] Before the Civil War, Evangelical feminism had flourished geographically in the wake of Charles Finney's revivalism (New England, upstate New York, northern Ohio). Possibly in a similar fashion, turn-of-the-century Bible institutes that trained Evangelical women for public ministry centered in the northern urban centers revived by evangelist D. L. Moody.

Moody in Chicago, A. B. Simpson in New York, A. J. Gordon in Boston, W. B. Riley in Minneapolis, R. A. Torrey in Los Angeles, and C. I. Scofield in Philadelphia—these nationally prominent Evangelical leaders established or administered the six major American Bible institutes which dominated the movement and provided educational models for the others. Each man's attitude and practice regarding women's public ministry decisively affected women's roles in each school and directly influenced the church at large. The impact of their views on women set the basic parameters for women's acceptable forms of public ministry at each Bible institute.

NYACK AND THE C&MA

Approached chronologically, Albert B. Simpson (1843–1919) established North America's first Bible institute in 1883—the Missionary Training College for Home and Foreign Missions in New York City. Canadian-born, seminary-educated, and Presbyterian-ordained, Simpson accepted the call to minister in New York City's 13th Street Presbyterian Church in 1879. Burdened with the need to evangelize the urban poor and establish a missionary training school to equip laypeople for ministry, Simpson resigned his pastorate in 1881.

Simpson, inspired by Dr. Grattan Guiness's East London Institute in England, made plans for his school. Within two years, his fledgling school opened, utilizing Evangelical leaders such as A. T. Pierson and A. J. Gordon to lecture. By 1887 Simpson relocated the school to Nyack and formally organized the Christian Alliance. This society merged with his Evangelical Missionary Alliance in 1897 to form the Christian and Missionary Alliance (C&MA).

Simpson intended to create interdenominational alliances of sanctified, mission-minded Evangelical Christians, not to establish a new church. As one wing of the turn-of-the-century Reformed holiness movement, the C&MA preached a "fourfold gospel": conversion, entire sanctification, divine healing, and the premillennial Second Coming. Simpson, a major proponent of the Keswick movement, incorporated a healing emphasis normally not present in other Keswick leaders.

Simpson's theology of the Holy Spirit may have influenced his view of women. In 1911 he wrote a series of meditations in *When the Comforter Came*. One article—"Our Mother God"—expressed Simpson's unusual approach.

> The heart of Christ is not only the heart of a man but has in it also the tenderness and gentleness of a woman. Jesus was not a man in the rigid sense of manhood as distinct from womanhood, but, as the Son of Man, the complete Head of Humanity, He combined in Himself the nature both of man and woman. . . . in the Old Testament we find God revealing Himself under the sweet figure of motherhood. . . . And this aspect of His blessed character finds its perfect manifestation in the Holy Ghost, our Mother God.

A. B. Simpson gave women a prominent place in church ministry, encouraging women's participation and leadership in virtually every phase of early C&MA life.[13] In celebrating its golden anniversary, the C&MA proudly recalled that "especially in the early days of Alliance, there was a host of Spirit-filled women who labored as evangelists and Bible teachers with great effectiveness."[14] Simpson included women on the executive board committee, employed them as Bible professors, and supported female evangelists and branch officers (the early C&MA equivalent to a local minister).[15] Half of all C&MA vice-presidents in 1887 were women.

Simpson primarily emphasized overseas missions for which he vigorously recruited women. But his promotion of female service abroad affected the home front, opening doors for women at every level of school and church ministry. Nyack required women to practice preaching in chapel along with men. In fact, the May 1888 graduation prize for excellence in "Homiletic Exercises" went to a woman.[16] The experiences of Harriet Waterbury (teacher of Bible Doctrine), Mary Glover Davies of England (C&MA field evangelist), and Anna W. Prosser (C&MA Buffalo Branch president for five years) each demonstrate the early C&MA inclusion of women.[17]

In addition to Nyack, the C&MA began three other training schools before 1920 and Simpson College of Seattle in 1921. A German branch of the C&MA joined with revivalistic Mennonites to open the Fort Wayne Bible Training School in 1904. In an earlier attempt, Nyack-trained B. P. Lugibihl and his wife opened Bethany Bible Institute in Bluffton, Ohio, in 1895. Until it closed in 1901, Defenseless Mennonite revivalist J. E. Ramseyer served as principal.[18] Bethany supporters, a German-English mixture from Mennonite, Evangelical, and C&MA churches, founded the Missionary Church Association (MCA) in 1898. Under the leadership of Ramseyer, MCA president until 1944, the Bible school reopened at Fort Wayne.

Another Nyack couple, Evelyn and Richard Forrest, expanded the C&MA work in the South. Graduating in 1900, Evelyn served the C&MA as a full-time Christian worker, establishing an Alliance Branch in Oil City, Pennsylvania.[19] Richard finished at Nyack the next year and, as the first district superintendent of the Alliance in the South, organized his first branch in Orlando, Florida. In 1906 Rev. Forrest sat on the C&MA board of managers.

Richard Forrest's southern evangelistic efforts produced many converts in the coal mining camps, cotton milling towns, and southern mountain regions. The C&MA by 1911 had approximately sixty home missionaries ministering in the southern Appalachian region. Sensing the need to train some of these uneducated rural converts for Christian service, Forrest founded Golden Valley Institute in 1907 in the North Carolina mountains. The school relocated in 1911 to Georgia, marking the opening of Toccoa Falls Institute.

Toccoa Falls, though affiliated with the C&MA, advertised as nonsectarian and open to any Protestant. At the start, Forrest combined some vocational training with preparation for

Christian and missionary service. Rev. D. Y. Shultz of Fort Wayne served as first principal of this "school for the man or woman without a chance." Forrest's nation-wide speaking ministry took him to the Bible Institute of Los Angeles (BIOLA) in California and Moody Church in Chicago. His contact with Lyman Stewart in Los Angeles later assisted the school financially.

As at several other small Bible schools, information regarding early alumnae is scarce. Evelyn Forrest did join other women on faculty as a Bible teacher. All early instructors and workers at Toccoa Falls had to sign a doctrinal statement, part of which stated women's ministry to be an open question.[20] Apparently even the C&MA in the South must have encompassed workers on both sides of the women's issue.

Rev. and Mrs. J. D. Williams trained at Nyack, both taught at Fort Wayne, then founded St. Paul Bible Training School in 1916 to prepare midwestern C&MA young people for pastoral missionary, and church-related ministries. The experience of St. Paul women in public ministry mirrored their opportunities at Nyack. Women on faculty taught Bible and Greek and female students engaged in church planting. Mrs. Williams described how "girls went out in Summer Bible School work without equipment and to places where there was no pastor—no church. They would rent old store buildings, clean them up, and hold services."[21] Minister Otto Simon explained how his St. Paul-trained wife Mabel "occasionally filled the pulpit when I had a speaking engagement out of town."[22]

The Full Gospel Messenger, maintained by and devoted to the interests of the C&MA in the Northwest, openly endorsed the revivalistic efforts of female evangelists included on the list of official C&MA workers.[23] For example, after praising the heroic pioneer efforts of Margaret Houser and Sallie Botham for their revival meetings in Duluth, Minnesota, that magazine reported

> Miss Houser has done very faithful work as local Superintendent of the work at Aberdeen, S.D., and is at present engaged in a series of Evangelistic services at Sebeka, Minn.[24]

Nyack and Fort Wayne contributed to the establishment of two other institutions in addition to St. Paul. The opening in 1919 of the Lutheran Bible Institute (LBI) in St. Paul (today merged with Augsburg College) demonstrates the impact of A. B. Simpson far beyond the C&MA. Dean Samuel M. Miller explained at the first LBI commencement how

> . . . Annette Elmquist was testifying about the Lord Jesus in our midst, and she raised her appealing voice for a Lutheran Bible Institute. Having herself spent a year at a Gospel Alliance Bible School, she knew what a great influence such a school could be. But she also felt that she could not urge Lutheran young people to attend any but a Lutheran Bible School.[25]

Elmquist's zeal to establish a lay school "for intensive Bible study and for training home, foreign, and inner mission workers" flowed from her Nyack experience. Most LBI women trained for home missions, serving as parish workers, deaconesses, and church teachers. LBI's anti-revival stance eliminated women and men as evangelists, while the pastorate remained open only for Lutheran seminary-trained males.

Rev. C. W. Oyer, former Fort Wayne instructor, served as superintendent of the newly established Bible Institute of Washington (D.C.) in 1925. That school originated as a series of Bible classes initiated by Mrs. Rice I. Steele in local churches and homes. C&MA-related Midland Bible Institute trained students in Shenandoah, Iowa, from 1918 until 1923.

A. B. Simpson's utilization of women in all spheres of ministry decisively set the pace for women's rise to leadership in early C&MA schools and branches. His emphasis on sanctification and his view of the Holy Spirit as Mother God may explain part of Simpson's theological rationale for that egalitarianism. Primarily, women in church leadership correlated with his lay missionary concept—that ordinary people given basic Bible training could just as effectively evangelize primitive, uneducated tribes as the seminary-trained clergy. Once trained, ordinary women proved as capable and effective in carrying the Evangelical gospel as men.

GORDON

A. J. Gordon (1836–95) explicitly stated his scriptural understanding of women's role in the church, publishing a major
treatise in 1894 called "The Ministry of Women." That article
summarized how Gordon, using New Testament exegesis,
supported women's preaching.[26] A graduate of Newton Theological Seminary and an active abolitionist, Gordon served as
pastor of the Clarendon Street Baptist Church in Boston the last
twenty-four years of his life.

Gordon zealously advocated the deeper spiritual life,
missions, and temperance.[27] He claimed that a sanctified, Holy
Spirit-filled life, not gender, qualified one for church ministry.
Gordon contacted increasing numbers of uneducated laity,
especially women, Spirit-led to foreign missionary service. To
prepare those people previously excluded from the mission
field, Gordon—with D. L. Moody's financial encouragement
of a hundred dollars—opened the Boston Missionary Training
School in 1889.

Moody's 1887 Boston revival in a tabernacle beside
Gordon's church also contributed to the school's founding.
Moody used Gordon both at MBI as visiting lecturer and at
Northfield to chair the 1892 summer conference in Moody's
absence. The close relationship between the two leaders was
apparent from the fact that Moody held the 1895 memorial
service for Gordon at Northfield. James M. Gray, MBI dean
and later president for thirty years, taught at Gordon's school
from 1889 to 1894 and served as pulpit supply for his Clarendon
Street Church.

What impact did the early Gordon Bible College have on
women's public ministry? Maria Gordon described in "Women
as Evangelists" how Gordon's training prepared women to
"answer any call of the Spirit."[28] Yearbooks clearly documented the wide ministry of alumnae serving as preachers,
pastors, and Bible teachers. Graduate Iona Haynes, for example, reminisced in 1927 that

when the Still, Small Voice called me for definite Christian service eight years ago, I did not dream of the wonder of the way which stretched before me. . . . I have done most kinds of Church work from keeping correct addresses to preaching.

A native of Stoughton, Massachusetts, Mary Frances Macomber prepared for her church work at Gordon Bible Training School and Boston University School of Theology. In 1900 Macomber began ministry at the Wayside Mission in Stoughton. Soon the American Sunday School Association heard of her work and sent her to Maine and New Hampshire to build up churches and evangelize. She later returned to Stoughton, continuing to preach in local churches. After her 1914 ordination, she served as assistant pastor of the Stoughton Congregational Church.[29]

Both women and men received field education experience during the summer, pastoring rural churches in northern New England. These summer pastorates at Gordon prepared many women for church leadership after graduation; Marguerite Emma Tifft, for example, received a call to a Guildhall, Vermont, pastorate. Rev. Norma M. Farnham ('28) was pastor of a West Kingston, Rhode Island, church. Carolyn H. F. Scott ('26) optimistically expressed her enthusiasm and hope for women's public ministry.

I have had churches in Deerfield and Epping, NH, and also the Baptist Church in Candia Village. I am now beginning my ninth year in Candia. When I went there the church had been closed for some time, and the first year the congregation averaged 12–15. It has grown every year. . . . Women preachers are still few, but I find and believe there is a great future for them.[30]

Olive Myrtle Cudworth Eaton (1905–44) graduated from Boston University before attending Gordon Bible College, earning a Bachelor of Theology degree in 1927. She later attended Auburn Theological Seminary for two years. Married to Rev. E. Earle Eaton, pastor of the First Congregational Church of Munnsville, New York, Olive preached a number of times in her husband's absence. The Munnsville church ordained her in 1931. Her preaching load increased as the clergy couple opened another church nearby. Olive intended "to use her ordination to assist her husband in ministry and to add authority to her various activities and engagements in the field of religion."[31]

Maria T. Hale Gordon equally shared her husband's advocacy of women's public ministry and embodied those principles in her own life. She taught at the training school and led in the temperance fight as president of the Massachusetts Women's Christian Temperance Union and Boston area chair. In her defense of women's evangelistic work, "Women As Evangelists," Gordon argued that prejudice and false interpretation of biblical texts had kept women silent in the past. It was time, however, for the *real* business of women's lives—prophesying—to take precedence over housekeeping.

For Maria Gordon, Scripture's testimony and example plus the Holy Spirit's blessing on female evangelists gave women their credentials to minister. She explained woman's special suitability for public speaking in her manuscript "Women and the Temperance Movement."

> Two women of the Lord, Deborah with the Spirit of God in her heart and Jael with a hammer and nail in her hand—these were the instruments by whom the Most High turned back his enemies—and is it not possible that the Lord has prophetesses and warriors among the daughters of this 19th century? . . . There's a reason why woman can do a work in the temperance reform that none other can hope to effect. She is the greatest sufferer. . . . There's a great power and persuasion in woman's speech. Men may say that she's no logician—but it's not logic that prevails in personal importunity. . . . If logic does sometimes stir men mightily, it does so because it has been set on fire by love. . . . So those men who constantly oppose woman's public speaking on the ground as we have heard a hundred times that she "lacks theological faculty" might as well remember that it shows a great lack of logical faculty in them to put forth such an argument. . . . But above all, I applaud the woman's movement because it belongs strictly in the category of moral suasions. The religious movements must be of this kind. In our capacity as citizens, we may vote for the stringent liquor laws, but in our efforts as Christians, we must leave law for grace and resort to strictly moral measures.[32]

NORTHWESTERN

Two years after A. J. Gordon's death, William Bell Riley left Calvary Baptist in Chicago to start a forty-five year pastorate at Minneapolis's First Baptist Church—one of the largest congregations in the Northern Baptist Convention. Possibly the most important Fundamentalist minister of his generation, Riley combined the roles of educator, evangelist, editor, church politician, and social critic with pastoring.[33] His policy of militant conservatism eventually led him to found the World's Christian Fundamentals Association in 1919 and the Baptist Bible Union in 1923. Riley's wife explained how "baptized in his youth in the Evangelical fervor of a Spurgeon and a Moody, he knew no university doubts about God; he had no biological quibbles about the virgin birth; he entertained no doubts as to the verbal, plenary inspiration of the Word."[34]

Started as a Bible class of converts in his church, Riley opened perhaps the most aggressive of the Fundamentalist Bible schools in 1902. Northwestern Bible and Missionary Training School represented Riley's solution to the growing Modernism in eastern seminaries. He perceived two urgent problems—the need for premillennial indoctrination in the Northwest (in 1897 only one Minneapolis pastor reportedly believed the doctrine) and the need for pastors in small-town, rural churches (ninety of three hundred Baptist churches in Minnesota reportedly had no minister). Though a Baptist, Riley, like Gordon, self-consciously established his school as interdenominational. As evidence, a Congregationalist served as first president of the board.

How did Riley view women's public ministry? His 1901 sermon, "Woman's Rights and Political Righteousness," supplies a clue.

> I recall the first time I ever heard Frances Willard speak. She was in a small southern city, where it was regarded a shame for a woman to appear on the platform with men in the assembly. But I confess, that I went from that house convinced that so long as saloons remained to embrute women's husbands; blight women's beautiful boys; blast women's lives; and even blacken

women's souls, that every speech against it would be justified,
no matter who made up their assemblies, and would be approved
and applauded by that heavenly assembly of saints and angels
. . . when in defense of all that is true, a suffering woman feels
compelled to break the silence and speak against sin.[35]

Consistent with Riley's personal openness to women speaking
in public, Northwestern employed women preachers in its
Extension Department while alumnae preached, pastored, and
evangelized with official school recognition.

The Extension Department, for example, advertised the
ministry of Miss Playfair, open "to address Sunday or weekday meetings, church audiences . . . religious conferences or
community gatherings of any kind."[36] School evangelist Alma
Reiber ('15) joined Irene Murray to lead an evangelistic
campaign in Antigo, Wisconsin. They left "for other fields of
labor, carrying with them the highest endorsement of the pastor
and the people."[37] The evangelistic work of Miss Hauser ('16)
included pastoral care, church renewal, and preaching.[38]

Sent temporarily to carry the gospel to rural communities
and small towns of the upper Midwest, some Northwestern
women ended up with a pastorate. For instance, Claire
Weiermuller ('22) directed the summer vacation Bible school at
Esmond, North Dakota's Congregational church. But "the
people liked her so well they extended a call to her to become
their regular pastor. She has been supplying the pulpit at
Hester, N.D. in the morning and speaking in Esmond in the
evening."[39] Minnie S. Nelson ('17) traveled hundreds of miles
preaching and teaching and reestablished a northern Minnesota
church. Sadie Busse ('26) and Henriette Rodgers ('28) co-
pastored an Evangelical church in Pequot, Minnesota, which
apparently made "great spiritual progress under their leadership."[40] Busse gave out the Word while Rodgers cared for the
music.

The public service of these Northwestern alumnae, many
in full charge of a local congregation, embodied Riley's concept
of women's freedom to speak. By 1930, however, the shift
toward a hardening on that issue by other leaders at Northwest-

ern surfaced. Dr. C. W. Foley, instructor in Christian Evidences, Exegesis, and Analysis, answered the question "How are we to understand 1 Cor. 14:33–36 and 1 Tim. 2:11–12, where women are forbidden to speak or teach in the church?" Foley explained that women can speak, but with an attitude submissive to men.

> We see no reason therefore for hermetically sealing a woman's mouth in the assembly, and neither do we see any Scripture authorizing a woman to take full charge of an assembly, and occupy the position plainly assigned to the man throughout the Word of Inspiration.[41]

Ironically, the *Northwestern Pilot* printed Foley's response alongside praise for alumnae in "full charge of an assembly"!

BIOLA

Several Northwestern personnel contributed to the opening of the Bible Institute of Los Angeles (BIOLA) in 1908. Presbyterian minister A. B. Pritchard and his assistant from Northwestern, Rev. Thomas C. Horton, joined with wealthy layman Lyman Stewart (founder of Union Oil Company) to establish BIOLA. Also from Northwestern, J. H. Sammis edited BIOLA's *The King's Business* in the early years. Stewart, printer of *The Fundamentals* pamphlets, sought a stronger emphasis on the Bible in education. In 1912 he recruited R. A. Torrey from Moody Bible Institute, who served twelve years as dean. BIOLA incorporated Stewart's principles, purposing to train women and men in the knowledge and use of Scripture and in the practical work of saving and sanctifying souls. Perceiving hundreds of small churches closed or without pastors, large seminaries destitute of students, and unoccupied fields throughout the land, BIOLA's founders set out to train Christian workers to fill those gaps.[42]

Mixed and scant evidence remains regarding women's public ministry opportunities at BIOLA. N. Finn studied at MBI before joining Rev. Pritchard at BIOLA as a Bible teacher. In 1910 a corps of eight Bible Women, trained under the direction of Mrs. T. C. Horton in evangelism and service, canvassed Los Angeles. They visited homes, taught neighborhood Bible studies, distributed literature, and cared for the sick and needy.[43] Horton assigned each woman a district where, after house-to-house visitation, she taught parlor Bible classes on the fundamental truths of Scripture. Alumna Bertha E. Kirk ('22) did establish the Church of the Open Bible in Hollywood, New Mexico.[44] Whether or not other BIOLA women trained as evangelists and pastors is unclear.

A 1912 advertisement in *The King's Business* attempted to recruit BIOLA students from the following gender-distinguished categories. For training women in Christian service, BIOLA appealed to foreign missionaries, ministers' wives, women at home desiring to witness better, women of leisure desiring Bible study, those called to deaconess or to rescue or Bible class work, city and home missionaries, YWCA secretaries, and pastors' assistants. As regards preparing men, however, BIOLA sought, in addition, experienced ministers and evangelists who desired more study, prospective teachers of English Bible in colleges and conventions, college or seminary graduates wanting to supplement their education, and pastors and evangelistic preachers needing Bible knowledge.[45]

These distinctions at BIOLA between appropriate ministry roles for men and women did not surface at such an early date at Moody Bible Institute, Nyack, Gordon, or Northwestern. Could the combination of BIOLA's Presbyterian roots, West Coast location, and direct contact with excesses of some Pentecostal women in Los Angeles possibly have tempered women's opportunities? With such meager historical data, hypotheses remain tentative.

The views of R. A. Torrey (1856–1928) may have contributed to the early attitude of women's separate spheres. Torrey, head of the 1919 committee to draft the Confession of Faith of the World's Christian Fundamentals Association, clearly identified with organized Fundamentalism. In 1915, *The King's Business* published Torrey's explanation of 1 Timothy 2:12 and 1 Corinthians 14:34 regarding women's silence.[46] Scripture, Torrey asserted, allows women to teach the truth, prophesy, pray, and speak as Spirit-led. But the Bible forbids women from interrupting worship with questions or taking the place of authority in the church. His middle-of-the-road position (preaching, yes; authority, no) would eventually be transformed into hard-line Fundamentalist opposition to women's preaching as well as authority.

PHILADELPHIA

Without a doubt, the attitude toward women's ministry expressed by Philadelphia School of the Bible (PSB) founder C. I. Scofield in his reference Bible notes directly influenced the Fundamentalist wing of early twentieth-century Evangelicalism. Congregational minister Scofield joined with William L. Pettingill, an ordained Baptist, to open PSB after a 1914 Bible conference.[47] Pettingill, a consulting editor for the Scofield Reference Bible and PSB dean until 1928, also edited *Serving and Waiting* from 1911 to 1928. That dispensational, premillennial monthly journal, devoted to Bible study and the International Sunday School lessons, became the official publication of PSB.

As no pre-1920 PSB alumni information exists, one must examine the Scofield Reference Bible and *Serving and Waiting* to find clues regarding women's public ministry at PSB. Naturally, the school highly publicized and promoted its founder's Scofield Reference Bible, published in 1909. Scofield commented on Genesis 3 and the Fall that the Adamic covenant conditions the life of fallen people until the kingdom age, the thousand-year literal reign of Christ on earth that will be inaugurated by the Second Coming. For women, the fallen state included multiplied conception, sorrow in motherhood, and the headship of man.[48] Sin made necessary a headship vested in man and woman's subordination, symbolized by a headcovering. As for New Testament teaching, Scofield noted that women must keep silent when the whole church comes together.[49]

Articles by Pettingill and Scofield in *Serving and Waiting* supplement those brief notes. Asked in 1920 just how silent female missionaries and Sunday school teachers must be,

Pettingill replied that women can testify but not serve as pastor or rule as head in the church.[50] Later, he again differentiated between woman's prophecy and headship.

> Over against the words, "let your women keep silence in the churches" . . . there are the words "but every woman that prayeth" . . . which words surely imply that not all praying or prophesying is forbidden to women. What *is* forbidden to her is headship in the assembly. Let her not assume that place, nor let her be "appointed" or "voted" into it, for it is contrary to God's order.[51]

A careful reader of Scofield's notes submitted this provocative question in 1922. "On page 1016 of the Scofield Reference Bible, note 3, on the Parable of the Leaven, do you take it that Dr. Scofield meant that women should never teach doctrine? How then could they be S.S. teachers?"[52] Pettingill reiterated the distinction between serving as a Sunday school teacher and leading as a pastor or elder, an office entailing headship and recognized doctrinal authority.

Scofield summarized his view toward women's ministry in response to the inquiry, "Is it unscriptural for a woman to preach?"[53] Women can pray, evangelize, exhort, prophesy (speak to edify and comfort), and teach when not dogmatically declaring doctrine—doing all in a modest, womanly, subordinate manner. But women must not interrupt meetings, teach authoritative doctrine, or hold an authoritative position such as elder. Finally, declared Scofield, the ordination of women is an abomination. In light of such attitudes, one would not expect PSB women to be encouraged to enter the pastorate or ordained ministry.

What can account for Scofield's attitude toward women in ministry? The approach of James H. Brookes may have been influential. After Scofield's 1879 conversion in St. Louis, he became a disciple of Presbyterian minister J. H. Brookes, who pastored in St. Louis from 1858 until his death in 1897. Brookes, an outspoken dispensational premillennialist and under strong Plymouth Brethren influence, wrote the article "Woman in the Church."[54] He acknowledged woman's ability to preach and right to political vote, to deliver temperance speeches, and hold any political office. Women can even speak at certain prayer and evangelistic meetings. But for Brookes, the Bible plainly taught that women cannot speak in church, that is, wherever Christians gather for worship and instruction. Brookes also argued against woman's superior nature. His key attack, however, was this—those who let women speak in church deny the authority of Scripture.

SMALLER BIBLE INSTITUTES

The Bible institute movement in America expanded far beyond the work of these six major institutions. Credit for the establishment and spread of smaller schools across the nation lies with lesser-known clergy and laity. How did women fare in the less-prominent interdenominational Bible institutes?[55] The historical evidence is sketchy at best. In 1909, for example, several Presbyterian clergy founded St. Louis Bible Training School for Lay Workers. Renamed Brookes Bible Institute in memory of James Hall Brookes, premillennialist organizer of the Niagara Bible Conferences, this orthodox school produced forty-eight alumni between 1914 and 1933, forty-six of them females! Rev. Mrs. Muriel Inlow Olson graduated in 1927; her title may reflect an attitude at Brookes of openness toward women in the ministry.[56]

In Binghamton, New York, evangelist Rev. John A. Davis's organization of church Bible classes led to the establishment of Practical Bible Training School. Today identified as "Biblical, Fundamental, Baptistic, and Independent," Practical sent out early alumnae as ordained pastors and Bible teachers.[57] The Indianapolis Bible Institute, founded in 1911, advertised the study of dispensational truth as foundational and vital.[58] Women took an active leadership role in the early days. In 1923 all five Institute teachers were women, a woman served on the board of trustees, and another headed the Extension Department.[59]

National Bible Institute (NBI), begun by Dr. and Mrs. Don Odell Shelton in New York City in 1907, merged with

Lucy D. Osborn's Union Missionary Training Institute of Brooklyn in 1916. NBI advertised the preaching ministry of Eva Booth of the Salvation Army and noted the California revival meetings of alumna May Robertson.[60]

Clifton L. Fowler founded Denver Bible Institute in 1914, Berean African Missions in 1934, and the Berean Fundamental Churches of America.[61] After hearing D. L. Moody preach, Fowler was converted through a YMCA Bible class. Upon reading C. I. Scofield's *Rightly Dividing the Word of Truth,* he wholeheartedly embraced dispensationalism. Fowler, Denver's president from 1914 until 1937, edited the school's official publication *Grace and Truth.* Occasional editorials scathingly condemned the sins of women's bobbed hair, preaching, or teaching men.

This study of early Bible institutes reveals a multitude of ways in which women were utilized to minister and lead in turn-of-the-century Evangelical circles. What conclusions emerge from this sampling of evidence from across the nation?

My research uncovered evidence of only one smaller school—Fowler's Denver Bible Institute—that was outspokenly antagonistic to women in ministry. BIOLA and Philadelphia College of the Bible both apparently placed certain restrictions on women's public ministry. But major Evangelical schools like Nyack, Gordon, and Northwestern, along with most of the smaller institutes, provided Evangelical women with the training to preach, enter the pastorate, and teach Bible. These turn-of-the-century schools publicized preaching and pastoral experiences of alumnae and hired female evangelists in extension work.

The endorsement of women's public ministry by schools committed to a high view of scriptural authority cannot be denied. Leading the pack was Moody Bible Institute of Chicago—where documentation abounds regarding Evangelical women trained for Christian service.

3

WOMEN AT
MOODY BIBLE INSTITUTE

n 1 August 1979 the Moody Bible Institute administration published the following statement on the role of women in public ministry:

> Our policy has been and is that we do not endorse or encourage the ordination of women nor do we admit women to our Pastoral Training Major. . . . While there were women in the early church who exercised spiritual gifts, they were not given places of authority in the government of the church.

Using history as support, MBI also claimed to have maintained a consistent position through the years regarding women in church leadership. Contrary to this view, the evidence abounds that MBI has not held an unchanging policy toward women in ministry. At the turn of the century, Moody women openly served as pastors, evangelists, pulpit supply preachers, Bible teachers, and even in the ordained ministry. The school's official publication, *Moody Monthly,* listed Lottie Osborn Sheidler as the first woman to graduate from the Pastor's Course in August of 1929.[1] A picture of Sheidler in the November 1929 issue definitely confirms her sex.

Why an in-depth examination of women at Moody Bible Institute? Because at MBI one captures the flavor of what a major branch of turn-of-the-century Evangelicalism was all about. Protestants from dozens of church affiliations sought Moody's interdenominational training, though at first, Baptists, Congregationalists, Methodists, and Presbyterians predominated. The large percentage of foreign-born students mirrored the immigrant populations surrounding the Institute in the heart of Chicago. MBI attracted both the seminary-trained individual and the grade-school-educated layperson. Prospective students left New England, the eastern seaboard, and even the South and West to prepare for Christian service in the Windy City. Since the early school drew students from this diverse denominational, ethnic, geographic, and educational background, MBI provides an excellent cross section of turn-of-the-century Evangelicalism.[2]

In addition, early enrollment statistics point to the tremendous impact that MBI had on Evangelicals by training so many leaders and laity of that generation. Starting with only fifty students at the first May Institute in 1883, by 1914 the day school enrolled 837 students while 429 attended night classes and 1,567 signed up for Moody's correspondence courses.[3] Norman H. Camp concluded that by 1915, a total of 12,970 students had studied at MBI during a twenty-five-year period in the day, night, and correspondence schools.[4] By 1920, 732 female and 968 male day school students had graduated.[5]

Why such growth and success at MBI compared to other institutions? D. L. Moody's personal fame, Chicago's central location and population growth, affluent business contacts for solid financial backing, and academic rigor (Dean R. A. Torrey graduated from Yale) all contributed to MBI's rapid expansion.

Yet Moody's prominence among Bible institutes involved more than sheer numbers. In philosophy, structure, and curriculum, influential MBI stood as forerunner and model for schools across the nation.

For example, D. L. Moody's preaching at Chicago's World's Fair inspired Presbyterian minister William H. Jordan to build a Bible institute in the west-central states modeled after MBI. By 1921 Jordan opened Omaha Bible Institute in spite of local clergy opposition.[6] Across the border at Toronto Bible College in 1911, the new school secretary Rev. T. Bradley had known D. L. Moody, had pastored Moody Church in Chicago, and expressed sympathy with Moody's views and methods.[7] Another Bible institute superintendent, Howard W. Ferrin, had trained at MBI. Ferrin advanced to the presidency of Dudley Bible Institute (later named Barrington College) in 1926 and advertised "how Mr. Moody would rejoice" at Dudley's training program.[8]

Finally, I chose Moody for in-depth investigation because its early history is clearly documented and easily accessible. To their credit, the founders of MBI kept numerous and accurate records that make the telling of the following story possible.

DWIGHT L. MOODY

This study must begin with an examination of Dwight L. Moody's approach to women in public ministry. The views of Moody, world-renowned evangelist and founder of MBI, obviously had an impact on the role of women and helped to shape their spheres of ministry for decades after his death in 1899. In February 1877 Moody asked Frances Willard, famous founder and president of the Women's Christian Temperance Union, to assist him in his evangelistic work in Boston. Willard had dropped out of temperance work for a year due to strong negative reaction to her advocacy of women's suffrage. Moody, in contrast, encouraged her to preach temperance and suffrage as well as the gospel.[9] When asked to preach by Moody one Sunday afternoon, Willard wondered if that might hinder the work among conservatives. Moody retorted "it was just what they needed."[10] In her book *Woman in the Pulpit,* Willard first complained that women had been forced outside the church, to groups like the WCTU, in order to exercise their public gifts for Christ. She insisted,

> Let the church call in these banished ones, correlate their sanctified activities with her own mighty work, giving them the same official recognition that it gives men, and they will gladly take their place under her supervision.[11]

Willard clearly argued for women's total equality in the church, including ordination. She eventually resigned from Moody's team because of his complaints about her sharing a temperance convention platform with Mary Rice Livermore, wife of a Unitarian minister.

EMMA DRYER

Moody's association with another woman—Emma Dryer—eventually resulted in the founding of MBI. Born in New York State, she graduated from LeRoy College. Dryer, a strong proponent of dispensational premillennialism, influenced Wheaton's Charles Blanchard as well, convincing him of the truth of that system.[12] She served as principal and teacher at the Illinois State Normal University until 1871, when the Chicago Fire drew her into city benevolence work. As YWCA secretary, Dryer ministered to thousands left homeless by that disaster.

Introduced to D. L. Moody by mutual friends, Dryer assisted at his North Side Tabernacle, where she developed a program of Bible study, teaching, and home visitation.[13] For sixteen years Dryer encouraged Moody to start a permanent Bible training school, but his evangelistic tours at home and abroad often interrupted Moody's direct involvement in the work.[14] So he appointed Dryer to supervise the Chicago Bible Work herself, begun in Moody's church in 1873.

Dryer's ministry flourished, supported financially by philanthropists like Nettie Fowler McCormick. By 1878 the Bible Work of Chicago incorporated, with classes meeting in Farwell Hall—the YMCA building in downtown Chicago. Eventually Dryer secured a home on Warren Avenue, where her volunteers lived, worked, and studied in preparation for city ministry.

Women trained by Dryer as Bible readers (similar to BIOLA's Bible Women) and city missionaries visited the sick, distributed tracts, evangelized the poor, organized cottage prayer meetings, and established a morning school for children.[15]

The aim of the Bible work is to reach the poor and neglected of this city, and to train missionaries for Home and Foreign Fields. It is undenominational, and is the only work of the kind in this city. It was inaugurated by Mr. Moody directly after the great fire. It is under the supervision of Miss E. Dryer, and has in its constant employ from ten to twenty Bible Readers who give their entire time to house-to-house visitation, the holding of meetings and similar work.

For Dryer's Bible Readers, Scripture constituted the central focus of their ministry. These women sold Bibles, read Scripture, induced others to read, encouraged Bible study, and taught children a simple catechism whose answers were texts of Scripture. Clearly, Dryer's philosophy, training, and structure foreshadowed the future programs of MBI. She joined William E. Blackstone, Fleming H. Revell, and others at Saturday morning prayer meetings in Farwell Hall to pray for a more permanent ministry. To educate workers, in 1883 Dryer inaugurated the first May Institute, a month of intensive Bible study and practical training. When Moody formed the Chicago Evangelization Society in 1887, her work merged with it.

By 1888 students could attend a three-month Bible Work Institute. Dryer's Bible Workers' Home modeled the future Ladies' Department of MBI. The curriculum combined Bible study with daily practical field work, musical instruction, and a Swedish school—each later incorporated by MBI.

Emma Dryer parted company with D. L. Moody in 1889, and her Bible Work separated from the Chicago Evangelization Society. She explained:

> . . . only in one item, did we differ in doctrine or plans or practices. . . . Mr. Moody was opposed to the doctrine of Divine Healing, as he understood it. I favored it, as I understand it. . . . We held, in the Y.M.C.A. Bible Room, for many years, a regular Prayer-Meeting for the sick. Many were healed. . . . Mr. Moody's devotion to direct evangelization, led him to fear any measure that might possibly detract from teaching the plain, simple gospel of Christ.[16]

Even after 1889, Dryer remained temporarily on the Chicago Evangelization Society board of managers. She continued her extensive home visitation and Bible distribution under the auspices of the Chicago Bible Society. Dryer's departure does not undercut the prominence of this gifted woman in the establishment of Moody Bible Institute and in the shaping of its early ministry.

FOUNDING MBI

D. L. Moody, assisted by Willard in his revivals and by Dryer in founding a school, preached his key sermon on "City Evangelization" in Chicago on 22 January 1886. He proclaimed, "I believe we need 'gap men,' men who are trained to fill the gap between the common people and the ministers. We are to raise up men and women who will be willing to lay down their lives alongside the laboring."[17] Referring to the urban poor, Moody reportedly pled, "Give me women to work among this class of the population."[18]

With this vision, Moody then organized the Chicago Evangelization Society incorporated in 1887 "to educate, direct, and maintain Christian workers as Bible readers, Teachers, and Evangelists who shall teach the Gospel in Chicago and its suburbs, especially in neglected fields."[19] The Bible Institute of the Chicago Evangelization Society (renamed Moody Bible Institute in 1900) formally opened in 1889 with a year-round curriculum. Christian workers could study for any length of time at small expense, paying a room and board fee with no tuition.

Why Moody's desire to train men and women to fill the gap between laity and clergy? Understanding his reasons will provide crucial insight into early MBI's openness to women's ministry. To begin with, Moody and other evangelists experienced a chronic shortage of qualified Christian workers with a Bible education to assist in the inquiry room work connected with revivals.[20] In addition, a school in Chicago, unlike Moody's private academies at Northfield and Mount Hermon, could face more directly and immediately the problems of city evangelization. This twofold training—both to preach the gospel to the unevangelized and then skillfully to assist those who were new converts—enabled women along with men to first enter public ministry.

In 1900 Moody Bible Institute revised its purpose; it now read: "to educate, direct, encourage, maintain, and send forth Christian workers, Bible readers, gospel singers, teachers, and evangelists competent to effectually teach and preach the gospel of Jesus Christ."[21] Though this new statement indicates both a broadening of ministry (through music) and focus (no longer the Chicago area alone), the central thrust still remained public teaching and preaching.

To prepare for ministry, women at Moody combined intense academic instruction with rigorous practical training. Academics centered on the English Bible as the great textbook. By 1910 the Institute stood for the following beliefs—verbal inspiration, Christ's deity, the Holy Spirit's personality, humanity's lost condition, justification by faith, eternal retribution for the wicked, and Christ's second coming.[22]

Yet early MBI never intended divisive doctrinal creeds to take a prominent place. In 1911 the editor of *The Christian Workers Magazine* wrote that "the creed of the Moody Bible Institute, and of this magazine, is that of the evangelical churches in all the centuries, no more, no less."[23] Like other early Bible institutes, MBI existed primarily as a practical training school of revivalistic evangelism, not a theological bastion of Fundamentalist doctrines.

Alumnae who preached and entered pastorates credited MBI's intense program with providing adequate training. The required practical Christian work assignments for all students entailed such ministries as evangelistic tent meetings, saloon work, Gospel Wagon and Auto work, Bible readings, midday shop meetings, house-to-house visitation, tract distribution, and YWCA/YMCA work. The high standards for student life included a one-month probation for incoming students, who were then expelled if found unfit for Christian service.

Though MBI originally sought to train only laity, the number of students called to frontier preaching assignments and pastorates increased. In addition, the Institute increasingly questioned the theological soundness of many denominational seminaries. Therefore, MBI began to offer pastoral training classes, which culminated in a one-year Pastor's Course in 1922. By 1925 the three-year Pastor's Course began. At the turn of the century, the Institute provided women with the skills and motivation to enter public ministry and church leadership. *All* were enlisted (whether male or female) to reach the untouched masses at home and abroad through evangelism and missions.

WOMEN IN THE EXTENSION DEPARTMENT

In light of this general discussion of women associated with MBI, representative female leaders will now be examined in particular. In 1897 the Institute established an Extension Department to promote school interests by organizing Bible conferences, supplying evangelists for revival meetings, and providing churches with guest preachers. By 1928 the department reached an audience of nearly one-quarter million through twenty-five MBI-sponsored Bible conferences around the country. The way MBI first employed women in the Extension Department proves that at one time, MBI accepted females as evangelists, Bible conference speakers, and Bible teachers of mixed audiences.

The official publications of MBI (*The Institute Tie, The Christian Workers Magazine, Moody Bible Institute Monthly,* and *The Alumni News*) regularly advertised and recorded the work of these women. The first notice regarding Australian evangelist Elinor Stafford Millar, for instance, appeared in 1903. Millar experienced great success leading evangelistic campaigns in Canada, Ohio, Michigan, and New York. By 1 January 1912 she entered into a permanent arrangement with the Institute as an evangelist in the field, and churches received her enthusiastically. Following her Springfield, Missouri, campaign in October 1912, a Springfield leader wrote, "We have never had anyone here who has brought such an uplift. . . . We shall want Miss Millar in January 1914."[24]

In its August 1916 issue, *The Christian Workers Magazine* proudly advertised:

Our Field Bible Teachers and Evangelists:
E. Stafford Millar, Evangelist
Margaret T. Russell, Teacher
Alveretta W. Bowman, Teacher.[25]

Millar traveled with musical assistant Homer A. Hammontree in 1917, representing MBI as a summer Bible conference speaker that year.[26]

A number of Bible teachers also itinerated under official MBI auspices. The Extension Department listed Angy Manning Taylor as a Bible teacher in the field starting in 1911. She taught for five weeks at the Winona Bible School, a part of the Winona Lake Bible Conference summer program under the direction of MBI.[27] Ella E. Pohle joined the Extension Department as a Bible teacher in 1912.[28] She and Francis C. Allison also taught at Winona; later the Department sent Allison to assist the Bob Jones evangelistic party.[29]

An MBI graduate in 1906, Alveretta W. Bowman worked first as a notable Bible teacher in following up Billy Sunday's evangelistic campaigns before her transfer to the Institute staff. After successful ministry in Ohio, "the business man asked her to remain for two weeks longer and hold Bible teaching services in the evening so that they might receive the benefit."[30] Margaret T. Russell from Alabama graduated from Moody in 1915 and joined the field staff as a Bible teacher the next year. Several southern states enthusiastically received her teaching ministry, including a Texas cantonment for soldiers. The Institute endorsed her ministry with the following advertisement:

> Mrs. Russell is now available, (1) For Bible teaching work, following evangelistic campaigns; (2) To teach a circuit of union Bible classes in various cities . . . ; (3) To go into a single church for a special series of Bible studies. . . . She is able, not only to teach the Bible to all the various groups of girls and women, but has made very acceptable addresses before Young Men's Christian Associations, and is always at home before a mixed audience.

Russell resigned in 1922 after six and one-half years of teaching for the Extension Department because her own denomination, the Presbyterian Church, South, gradually claimed more of her time.[31] Former MBI student Virginia C. Williams from Austin, Texas, joined as a Bible teacher in 1922.[32]

Millar, Taylor, Pohle, Allison, Bowman, Russell, Williams—each of these gifted women received an undeniable stamp of approval by MBI in their public ministries. The Extension Department exhibited a similar attitude in relation to Catherine Booth of England, the famed evangelist of the Salvation Army. Booth made her headquarters at MBI for two months in 1913 and preached twice at Moody Church. The Institute advertised that the Extension Department would receive inquiries for her services as an evangelist.[33] In addition, MBI invited evangelist Sara E. Palmer as a guest speaker in 1919 and Congregational pastor Rev. Ada Heyse in 1919 and 1921.[34]

Would a school openly publicize such visits if it opposed these forms of women's ministry? Clearly not. From 1933 until 1945, the Institute noted Violet Heefner's campaigns, including her 1938 ordination as a Baptist preacher-evangelist.[35] Heefner's musical assistant, Anna Sudenga Larson, had attended MBI. The duo traveled from coast to coast four times, as well as into Canada, preaching and singing revival.[36] As long as Moody periodicals habitually recorded the revivalistic work of female evangelists often sponsored by MBI, readers would assume that ministry to be acceptable.

ALUMNAE

The most important display of MBI's openness to women in ministry entails the activities of alumnae.[37] Equipped at Moody with the skills needed for public ministry, female graduates served as pastors and preached in a wide range of denominations. A 1903 graduate, Rev. Rosa A. Lizenby was ordained in the Congregational Church of Wheaton, Kansas. Bertha Fogelberg graduated in 1905, received ordination in 1912, and pastored a United Brethren church. Rev. Hattie E. Alvord ministered for eighteen years as pastor of a Methodist Episcopal church in New York. A Congregational church in Chickasha, Oklahoma, ordained former MBI student Olive Pearson Patch in 1927.

Lillian D. Wickman (1888–1965) was born and raised in England, one of ten children and the daughter of express agent James Jones. Her son Wilson Wickman explains how Lillian came to the United States after finishing both public and private school in Hereford, England.[38] After living in Montana and Washington for several years, she attended MBI, graduating in 1913 from a pastor's course. Wickman spent one year after graduation studying voice and piano under Dr. George S. Schuler. In 1914 she married William Wickman on Washington Island, Wisconsin.

Wickman traveled two summers as a soloist with Chicago evangelistic parties. After an interim pastorate in Brainard, Minnesota, she began a full pastorate at the Baptist church on Washington Island, Wisconsin. Wickman served there from 1914 until 1930. For another decade she pastored the Little Brown Church on the island. Wickman was the only minister on Washington Island for most of her active ministry. In a community of approximately twelve hundred people, she bore sole responsibility for clerical duties such as visitation, officiating at weddings, and conducting funerals. She also served as music director.

In 1928 the First Baptist Church of Gloversville, New York ordained Mrs. Ellery Aldridge ('20), an evangelist, along with her husband for the New York Baptist State Convention. Florence M. Price, the only minister in her town, had charge of two churches—one Methodist, one Congregational. Mabel C. Thomas baptized nearly thirty converts at her Christian church in Kansas, while Fanny B. Mills was pastor of a Presbyterian church in South Dakota.

From coast to coast, Moody women shared their pastoral ministry in a variety of settings. S. L. Brown led a Baptist congregation in Bellingham, Washington, whereas Harriet H. Albee had charge of a New Hampshire church. Mary Isabella Bradley received a local preacher's license in New York City. In contrast, Violet J. G. Bagley ministered as a rural pastor in remote parts of Maine. A Baptist church in Eastbrook, Maine, ordained her in 1928. In the hills of Kentucky, Edna M. Dexter rode horseback to preach at four different stations. Martha Nichol had pastorates in two Congregational churches simultaneously in Nebraska.

A single minister for five years, Rev. Lydia Brock Mayos later co-pastored with her husband. She was ordained by the Congregational Church in Clay Center, Kansas, in 1902. Winnifred G. Rhoads, a pastor of the Second Baptist Church of Oshkosh, Wisconsin, received her ordination in Greenleaf, Wisconsin, in 1918. A licensed minister of the Methodist Episcopal Church, Rev. Margaret Flanigan attended Pittsburgh Theological Seminary after MBI and then became pastor of a church in Pennsylvania. The Northern Presbyterians sent Mabel S. Jones as a missionary into the Appalachian Mountains of North Carolina. She conducted the preaching services at Carmen Presbyterian Church in White Rock, calling them Bible talks "as a concession to the local prejudice against women preachers."[39]

Sometimes tragedy opened the door for women to enter the pastorate. Pattie Mather, for example, graduated from MBI in 1920 and married fellow student G. A. Eakins. After missionary work in Canada, the Eakins family settled in Sparta, Tennessee, where Pattie taught school and her husband ministered in a Presbyterian church. In April 1926, Rev. Eakins took a Presbyterian pastorate in Saratoga, Wyoming. While on vacation in August 1926, Rev. Eakins tragically died when he accidentally fell into Mammoth Hot Springs in Yellowstone Park. In late September the church employed Pattie Eakins to fill her husband's pastorate, based on her many years experience in missionary work and church ministry.

After training at Moody in 1901, Congregationalist Minnie J. Dickinson was ordained in Linwood, Nebraska, in 1904. By 1910 she served as a home missionary in Idaho, pastoring the Wright Congregational Church in Boise.[40] In addition to regular parish ministry, Dickinson traveled across mountains and deserts to remote preaching stations and mining camps. She was often the first pastor in years to reach certain violent settlements. Her evangelistic efforts touched a wide variety of people on the frontier, such as cowboys, Spanish-speaking people, and Mormons.

Women from Moody entered the evangelistic field as well as the pastorate. Virginia Healey Asher, converted in 1880 at Moody Church, began her evangelistic work in response to D. L. Moody's call for volunteers. Taught by Torrey at Moody Bible Institute, Asher and her husband William continued as evangelists with Wilbur Chapman and later, Billy Sunday.[41] Mary Jameson among the grape pickers in western New York, Anna E. Smith preaching in a tent on a street corner in Duluth, M. Theodora Auman conducting open air meetings in Vermont—each contributed to the spread of revivalism. Evangelist Eva Ludgate preached to prisoners at Joliet's penitentiary in Illinois before her ordination in 1913. Josephine Nance Kivell headed north to evangelize Canada while Bertha J. Harris and Helen Byrnes conducted evangelistic meetings in Florida.

The most publicized female Bible teacher to have studied at early MBI, Grace Saxe graduated in 1897 and subsequently taught Bible courses for those converted at evangelistic campaigns. In 1907 over fifteen hundred persons attended her first series of interdenominational Bible lectures held in Buffalo, New York. After supplying a Methodist Episcopal pulpit for a month while the pastor vacationed, Saxe conducted another Bible course in Buffalo for six months. By 1910 she traveled to Egypt to teach Bible to over six hundred young men at the American Mission College. From 1911 until 1921, Saxe assisted Billy Sunday as a Bible teacher. Whether as Bible teachers, evangelists, or pastors, these female MBI graduates symbolize the scores who ministered side by side with their brothers in public church ministries across the nation.

To supplement this record of early alumnae, there were editorials and feature articles in the Institute's publications which addressed the issue of women's ministry. Several authors openly defended women's public ministry. In 1909 J. Ellen Foster's article "Work for Women" argued that Christian ministry, not the joys of motherhood, constitute a woman's highest call.

The clearest presentation of a woman's right to preach occurred in Mildred B. Allen's "Ministry of Women in the Society of Friends."[42] Allen clearly based women's right to preach on divinely inspired Scripture. She upheld women's equality with men in church ministry as consistent with biblical examples of prophetesses, the Pentecostal outpouring of the Spirit on women to prophesy, and proper analysis of Paul's teaching on women.

In 1928 Rev. Graham Gilmer answered the question "Should Christian women speak or lead in prayer in our churches?" Yes, he replied, provided wives did not publicly teach husbands. In 1936 J. W. Newton examined "Women's Work in the Gospel," concluding that women may usually speak when doing gospel work but may never rule. William Parker's "Sex Relations in Church and State," Margaret T. Russell's "Woman's Work for Christ," and "Mother's Day— By Whose Authority?" also argue against woman's governance of the church.[43]

To summarize, the articles consistently defended women's public ministries of teaching, preaching, and evangelizing. From World War I on, a few authors did argue against woman's right to govern or rule church affairs. Apparently the first traces of restriction involved female pastors whose position entailed church rule. However, official Moody Bible Institute policy allowed a woman to graduate from the Pastor's Course as late as 1929.

In light of all this historical evidence, it is obvious that Moody Bible Institute at the turn of the century trained and motivated women to publicly minister in Evangelical churches and applauded such efforts. MBI leadership may not have explicitly encouraged women to preach, pastor, or seek ordination, but their implicit endorsement of women in those authoritative roles for over forty years cannot be denied. The Institute in that era cultivated rather than buried the public gifts of Christian women. Their ministry, centered in the small towns and rural areas of the Midwest, constitutes a vital legacy in the history of the American Protestant church at the turn of the century.

James Findlay writes that Moody Bible Institute "made important contributions to the life of the city of Chicago and to the shaping of twentieth-century American Protestantism."[44] In 1891 Rev. Ada C. Bowles argued for women's ordination in "Women in the Ministry" and used MBI as her example of the new equality for women.

> The new departure in methods has also an important illustration in the city of Chicago, where, under the leadership of D. L. Moody, gifts . . . have been received for a theological school and home, to be conducted under the auspices of the Chicago Evangelical Society, which is open to both sexes under the same terms.[45]

MBI exhibited for at least the first four decades of its hundred-year history a clear commitment to the equal training and utilization of women along with men in church ministry.

This case study of Moody Bible Institute provides the clearest documentation of a turn-of-the-century Evangelical institution outside the Wesleyan holiness camp that actively promoted public church ministry for women. Moody stood unequivocally in the vanguard of schools which rejected theological liberalism and higher critical approaches to Scripture. None questioned MBI's commitment to a verbally inspired, inerrant Bible. Consequently, Moody Bible Institute at the turn of the century stands as an appropriate educational symbol of the paradox of "Fundamentalist feminism."

4

DENOMINATIONAL APPROACHES TO WOMEN IN MINISTRY

The public ministries of turn-of-the-century Evangelical women must be viewed against the backdrop of the roles of women in various Protestant denominations. Whether or not to ordain a woman often related to particular ecclesiastic theories of ordination.[1] Ordination, the way one is inducted into the office of ministry, meant different things to different people. Traditional Roman Catholic doctrine explained ordination as a sacramental commissioning of a priest to pronounce absolution and celebrate the Mass. Protestant ordination, on the other hand, set apart a minister to preach the gospel and shepherd the flock.

Does God call women along with men to be ministers? This question is but one aspect of the larger one regarding women's subordination to men. Opponents of women's ordination often contended that God gave men alone authority to rule in church, just as husbands govern in the family. In actuality, a Protestant or Catholic view of ordination was not as decisive in settling the issue as was one's understanding of the male-female relationship.

Behind all this lay the foundational theological question: Is God more like the male than the female of the species? From a Roman or Anglo-Catholic perspective, God's eternal *son* became a *man,* not a woman. Therefore, Christ commissioned men, not women, to represent God in the church. The all-male apostolate conclusively bars women from ordained ministry. An ordained female minister can no more stand in the place of God than could the incarnate Second Person of the Trinity have taken female form.

Protestant opponents of women's ordination based this restriction not so much on the nature of God as on the nature of woman. While not so blatantly charged with inferiority as in previous centuries, women still were different. Inherent differences in females disqualified them from church leadership and also gave them a subordinate role within marriage.

But doctrines of ordination did not settle the issue, as cultural circumstances frequently overrode theology. Though a theoretical possibility among turn-of-the-century Southern Baptists, women's ordination remained unheard of. Similarly, small-town, midwestern Congregational parishes called women to their pulpit much more than prestigious urban churches in the East. In this era American Protestant women experienced a mixed bag of opportunities—from new-found freedom to growing marginalization.

The Universalist Church ordained its first woman— Olympia Brown—in 1863. By 1900 over seventy-five ordained women served Unitarian and Universalist churches. This freedom contrasted with more limited roles for women in mainstream denominations. The Methodist Episcopal, Presbyterian, Lutheran, and Episcopal denominations simultaneously restricted and expanded women's church service and leadership in that era. Often barred from clergy and lay rights, women moved to create their own separate organizations such as missionary societies.

Unfortunately, the current association of women's freedom to minister with this mainstream or liberal Protestantism and linkage of restrictions on women with Fundamentalism can distort the turn-of-the-century picture. Additionally, Protestant groups in the Evangelical camp a century ago may have since shifted toward Liberalism. A careful analysis of turn-of-the-century literature reveals Evangelical women preached and entered pastorates more frequently than assumed today, in numbers often lacking in mainstream churches. Fundamentalists were not inevitably the ones to oppose women's ordination.

This survey of denominational approaches to women in ministry has two major purposes: first, to uncover the stories of Evangelical women who publicly ministered around the turn of the century; second, to place those personal experiences in broader ecclesiological and cultural contexts, thereby evaluating reasons and trends.

METHODISTS

We begin our survey with Methodists, who comprised the largest Protestant body in late nineteenth-century America. Especially concerned with religious experience, Methodists did not divide along Modernist-Fundamentalist lines as did turn-of-the-century Baptists and Presbyterians. Rather, churches split primarily over holiness doctrines. While the liberal cause became more pervasive in the parent Methodist body of the North, Methodist holiness churches retained a strong Evangelical stance. The wide use of female preachers and pastors in holiness circles differed strikingly from restraints placed on Methodist Episcopal women.

A glimpse at five Methodist groups exemplifies the wide spectrum of approaches toward women held by Protestants of that era.[2] Each also highlights key factors which tended to encourage or impede women's public church ministry. Methodist Episcopal, South, opposition to women grew from basic cultural and regional attitudes. In the North, Methodist Episcopal ambivalence toward women partly paralleled increased routinization of charismatic-style leadership. Methodist Protestants modeled how a stress on lay leadership could give impetus to female leadership. The United Brethren typified the influence of revivalism in freeing women to preach. Finally, particular focus on the doctrine of the Holy Spirit opened doors for women in Methodist holiness denominations.

The Methodist Episcopal women in the South faced the greatest obstacles to public ministry. There the controversy centered on laity rights. Belle Bennett's recommendation before the 1910 General Conference to grant women lay rights met defeat.[3] Still denied membership to quarterly, annual, and general conferences, Methodist laywomen consequently had no voice or vote in the government of their church. Laywomen's right to vote came in 1918 and partial clergy rights only in 1939, when northern and southern Methodists merged along with the smaller Methodist Protestant Church. Finally, in 1956 Methodist women gained full clergy rights with the accompanying right of pastoral appointment.

Official Methodist Episcopal policy in the North toward women in ministry often shifted from decade to decade, while the actual practice of individual congregations occasionally diverged from the stated regulation. In the mid-nineteenth century, for example, Methodist Episcopal women had served as revivalists, itinerant preachers, and local supply pastors. The church granted its first woman—evangelist Maggie Newton Van Cott—a license to preach in 1869.[4] A decade later the 1880 General Conference not only refused Anna Howard Shaw and Anna Oliver's requests for full ordination in addition to their local preaching licenses, but rescinded all women's preaching licenses.[5] Shaw left the denomination that year and received ordination from the Methodist Protestant Church.

In protest against the domination of the Methodist Episcopal Church by bishops and clergy to the exclusion of the laity, Methodist dissidents had formed the Methodist Protestant denomination in 1830. Methodist Protestant women founded their own Woman's Foreign Missionary Society (WFMS) in 1879 which gave impetus to women's increased leadership roles.[6] By 1894 four WFMS women were the first to be elected to the Annual Conference, and women's ordination was fully sanctioned that year. This relatively small, struggling denomination took progressive steps regarding women while the Methodist Episcopal Church hardened on the issue.

Why the difference? William T. Noll suggests that the smaller Methodist Protestant denomination possibly needed the leadership of all its gifted members, women included, to grow. In contrast, the successful Methodist Episcopal Church could more easily afford to restrict women's ministry. But what of other denominations equally desiring growth, but barring women from the pulpit in spite of need? The Methodist Protestant focus on lay leadership, given a female lay majority, helped as well.

In 1919 the Methodist Episcopal Church finally gave local preacher's licenses back to women and ordained them as local elders by 1924. Lack of General Conference credentials still barred Methodist women from regular pastorates. From 1880 until 1919, the countless Methodist Episcopal women who publicly ministered did so apart from official church recognition. Many channeled their efforts through the women's foreign and home missionary societies or deaconess work.[7]

Jonnie Jernigan's experience symbolized the channeling of Methodist women called to preach into more acceptable parachurch structures. Raised by Methodists, in 1900 Jernigan described her call to God's work and her parents' opposition. She explained how "any suggestion to them that a woman might be called of God to preach, was promptly pronounced un-Methodistic, so I kept the longing a secret from everyone."[8] Since the Methodist church in America would not let her preach, she decided to go to China. Yet she wondered why the church would let her preach in China but not in America.

The Methodistic, German-speaking United Brethren Church, with its Reformed origins, emerged from early nineteenth-century revivals of the Second Great Awakening. Revivalism pushed for conversion (which was the crux of Christian faith), creating a milieu in which many women could function as "soul-winners." Women, though often not ordained or permitted seminary education, could still effectively preach revival.

The United Brethren granted Lydia Sexton a quarterly Conference license to preach in 1851. Women gained full licensing and ordination at the 1889 General Conference. As a result, the church ordained ninety-seven women between 1889 and 1901.[9] Key United Brethren officials wrote in support of women's ministry. Henry Adams Thompson, for instance, edited *The United Brethren Review*, and in 1914 in *Women of the Bible* he earnestly advocated equal opportunity for women.

Another factor contributed to United Brethren women in ministry. Union Biblical Seminary opened in Dayton, Ohio, in 1871 and admitted women on equal terms with men.

> The measure was opposed by some who were reluctant to see the seminary taking an anomalous position among institutions of its kind, and who held to a modern application of the words, "But I suffer not a woman to teach." But the wisdom of the provision was vindicated. . . . Since the founding of the school thirty-two women have been admitted to study, and eleven have regularly graduated. The results of the experiment have been so satisfactory that the question of admitting women to the full privilege of the seminary courses has ceased to be an open one.[10]

The Second Great Awakening also produced the Evangelical Church (of German Lutheran background). In contrast to the United Brethren, Evangelicals resisted the licensing and ordination of women. Even regarding women's missionary societies, the Evangelical Church resisted women's efforts while the Brethren encouraged that development. When the two bodies merged in 1946 to form the Evangelical United Brethren Church, the phenomenon of women preachers and pastors among the Brethren virtually ceased.

METHODIST HOLINESS CHURCHES

Holiness churches comprised the Methodist groups most open to women's turn-of-the-century public ministry. Just as conversion could serve as a common denominator in leveling sexual differences, so too the experience of sanctification in holiness circles could function as an equalizer. The Holy Spirit's second work of grace, not necessarily ordination or education, properly qualified a person to preach.

The Free Methodists, for example, began licensing women as local preachers in 1873, and founder B. T. Roberts wrote on behalf of women's ordination. The church opened North Pacific Evangelistic Institute in Portland in 1918 to train both women and men.[11] The Church of God (Anderson, Indiana) organized in 1881 and founded Anderson Bible

Training School. This denomination so encouraged women in ministry that one-quarter of its leaders in 1902 were women.

The Wesleyan Methodist Church, founded in 1842 on abolitionist convictions, promoted equality for women as well as blacks. In 1848 the first woman's rights convention at Seneca Falls, New York, gathered in a Wesleyan Methodist chapel. Wesleyan minister Luther Lee delivered the sermon "Woman's Right to Preach the Gospel" at the 1853 ordination of Congregationalist Antoinette L. Brown, America's first fully ordained woman.[12]

Local Wesleyan conferences had freedom to license and ordain women, except for a temporary ban on ordination (1887–91). Throughout the Modernist-Fundamentalist debates of the 1920s, Wesleyans and other Methodist holiness groups definitely leaned in the Fundamentalist direction. Wesleyan Houghton College in western New York, for example, identified with the World's Christian Fundamentals Association in 1930, revealing its Fundamentalist sympathies.

Seth Cook Rees founded the Pilgrim Holiness Church, which merged in 1966 with the Wesleyans. His 1897 *The Ideal Pentecostal Church* listed equality for women as one of fourteen ideal church qualities. According to Rees, "no church that is acquainted with the Holy Ghost will object to the public ministry of women."[13] He included his own wife Hulda as co-pastor and co-evangelist in his ministry. Rees's Pilgrim Bible College in Pasadena, California, also identified with the WCFA in 1930. Half a century ago, a denomination could promote Fundamentalism while equally advocating women's public ministry.

The original constitution (1894) of the Church of the Nazarene outrightly stated women's right to preach; Nazarenes ordained women by 1908. The Salvation Army, founded by Catherine and William Booth in 1865, arrived in the United States from England in 1879. Chicago operations began in 1885 and blossomed into the greatest center of Salvationist activity in the country.[14] The Army admitted women to all ranks of leadership, including those with authority over men. By 1896 over 1,000 of 1,854 American officers were women.[15]

Booth's daughter Evangeline served as American commander from 1904 until 1934. She viewed the women's movement as the direct fulfillment of the gospel of Christ. "In the Salvation Army we see, as it were, the summation of the women's movement, her equal status with man in social and spiritual and intellectual responsibility."[16] Maude Ballington-Booth held joint command with her husband over the American Volunteers, an Army offshoot.

The lives and ministries of two women—Dr. Iva Durham Vennard and Dr. D. Willia Caffrey—exemplify the obstacles faced by many turn-of-the-century Methodist women called to preach and the relative freedom provided by the holiness groups. Born in 1871, Vennard joined a Methodist church in Illinois after conversion and in 1890 graduated from the Illinois State Normal University.[17] She taught school temporarily and organized a local Women's Christian Temperance Union.

Since the Methodist church did not ordain women preachers, at first Vennard also disapproved. She called her recently begun evangelistic work "speaking" not preaching. When Vennard joined the Methodist deaconess order, she hoped for a musical or social work ministry. Instead, the Deaconess Home in Buffalo assigned her to conference evangelism in 1895. Soon Vennard preached nationwide as deaconess-at-large.

Vennard grew increasingly critical of deaconess training that emphasized social service and institutional/clerical work to the neglect of spiritual and evangelistic preparation. After the Woman's Home Missionary Society rejected her proposal for an evangelistic training school, Vennard opened Epworth Evangelistic Institute in 1903 in St. Louis. Local male Methodist ministers accused her of training women preachers under the guise of deaconess training. They encouraged Vennard to leave theology and evangelism to the male clergy, replace her revivalistic evangelism with the nurture of religious education, and give up her holiness emphasis.

Vennard refused to compromise on her commitments to evangelism, holiness, and theological preparation for women. She traveled north and founded the Chicago Evangelistic

Institute in 1910 to send Spirit-filled people into the ministry and promote scriptural holiness. Women trained at Vennard's school did more than help the poor, sick, and young—they served as preachers, evangelists, ordained elders and deacons.[18]

D. Willia Caffrey (1880–1975) graduated from Chicago Evangelistic Institute in 1917 and after the ban on licensing was lifted, received her Methodist license to preach in 1920.[19] Born in Louisiana and confirmed Episcopalian, Caffrey like Vennard initially opposed women preachers as unbiblical. She experienced conversion during a Methodist prayer meeting in 1896. Caffrey's subsequent sanctification delivered her from the southern prejudice against blacks but not from deeply engrained opposition to women preachers.

After graduation from the Chicago Training School for Methodist deaconesses in 1902, Caffrey was sent to Wisconsin as an evangelist. She complained, "I can't preach; that is a man's job."[20] Finally, Caffrey yielded; if God wanted her to preach, she would obey. That choice led to six decades of evangelistic preaching, spreading scriptural holiness throughout the nation and abroad. Caffrey was ordained deacon in 1924 and elder in 1929. Her attendance in 1943 at the National Association of Women Preachers typified the radical change in her thinking regarding female preaching.

The Methodist holiness groups self-consciously provided major leadership roles for women, whether quietly opening pulpits for women preachers or vocally demanding women's ordination. Many turn-of-the-century Evangelical women called to publicly minister found a willing reception in holiness churches. The newly formed Pentecostal denominations continued this practice in the early twentieth century, often employing Spirit-baptized women as pastors, evangelists, and healers.

BAPTISTS

By the early twentieth century, Baptist churches had grown so rapidly that they surpassed the Methodists and became America's largest Protestant denomination. Roles for women in Baptist circles differed as widely as among Methodists. Theoretically, any local church could license or ordain a woman. Baptists, like Congregationalists and Disciples, defended the individual authority of each individual congregation to govern its own affairs. In practice, opportunities for these women often depended on geography, theology, and necessity.

Though Baptists in the southern Bible Belt constitute the cornerstone of Fundamentalism today, the real core of the movement emerged from the urban North in the early twentieth century. Though American Baptists in the North now may lean in a non-Evangelical direction, until the 1920s both Modernists and Fundamentalists coexisted uneasily within the same denomination. Since anti-Modernist Baptist women openly became preachers and pastors, early Baptist Fundamentalism was not inherently antifeminist.

Like the Quakers, Baptists had a longer tradition of utilizing women to lead than most other denominations. In America at the end of the eighteenth century, women preached in Free Will Baptist churches; the denomination licensed Clarissa H. Danforth to preach in 1815. In 1878 the Free Will Baptist College in Hillsdale, Michigan, employed minister Ellen C. Copp as principal and opened its theological department to women. These Baptists, strong in the North and especially northern New England, fully ordained Anna Bartlett in 1886. By 1898 nine licensed and seventeen ordained women served Free Will Baptist churches.

A pivotal change in American culture occurred when women first gained access to higher education, and this propelled them into many male-dominated professions, including the ministry. As theological seminaries began to admit females, women could finally train on an equal footing with men. Experience (Perie) Randolph Burdick, the first woman ordained by Seventh-Day Baptists in 1885 in Hornell, New York, exemplifies this phenomenon in Baptist circles. Describing her call to the ministry, Burdick closely linked her seminary enrollment with her license to preach.

> I do not think that I inherited any tendency toward the Gospel ministry. No church influences helped me to decide the vital

question, for my home church, during my girlhood and early womanhood, was in West Virginia, where people felt that "women as pastors do not succeed, and it is not wise to encourage young women to prepare themselves for the ministry." The church of which I was a member felt yet more strongly and believed "it would be wicked for a woman to try to preach." In the spring of 1882 when the church of which I was a member heard that I had decided to enter the Theological Seminary at Alfred, they licensed me to preach. This was a little more than three years before my ordination. It now seems to me that the strongest influence which led me into the ministry was the spirit of God. From my earliest memory I had an intense longing to tell people about the Savior and his love, and I was almost rebellious because I was not a boy, for then I could preach. These feelings never left me entirely and they were greatly intensified at my conversion when I was about six years of age. The influence of my consecrated and self-denying parents, who always began each meal with thanks and kept a well-used family altar did much in leading me to heed the voice of the Holy Spirit. During my college life at Alfred, President Allen and Prof. H. C. Coon greatly assisted me in deciding the question, although they did not know until I had made the decision that I ever entertained the idea of entering the ministry. Rev. S. D. Davis, of West Virginia, was the only person who spoke to me about it. He gave me excellent advice and encouragement. For over twenty-five years my longing to enter the ministry was a profound secret between myself and God. Though I am but a weak worker, I have the consciousness that I am in the work which my Saviour has called me to and if I fail it is not because God did not call me into the work, neither is it because I am a woman, but because I am not faithful to the commission given to me, a commission which Christ gave first to Mary at the tomb.[21]

Two immigrant Baptist churches also encouraged women to preach and minister. Analysis of each reveals additional reasons why Evangelical Baptist pulpits often opened to women. Revivalist, pragmatic German Baptists utilized women preachers since that "modern method" seemed to work. When the German Baptist Brethren Church split in 1883, revivalist leader Henry R. Holsinger (called "Modernist" by the Old Order conservatives) formed the Brethren Church. These reform-minded, "Bible Only" German Baptists used any modern means such as revivalism to aid the church. Brethren churches widely supported the temperance crusade as well.

The Brethren immediately confronted the question of women in church leadership. Holsinger supported women preachers; and at both the district and national levels the Brethren Church encouraged women as pastors and evangelists. In 1890 Mary Melinda Sterling became the first ordained Brethren woman.[22] After ordained minister Laura Grossnickle spoke on "Woman's Work in the Church" at the 1892 General Convention, delegates voted to extend to women equal privileges with men. By 1915 the number of female Brethren ministers peaked.

The Swedish Baptist General Conference also employed women as preachers and evangelists at the turn of the century. Reflection on the ministries of two Swedish Baptist women— seminary professor Esther Sabel and pastor Minnie S. Nelson— shows that certain women who first sought overseas missionary service found openings at home instead and that not all women in ministry necessarily sought ordination.

The life of Esther Sabel dramatically illustrates the freedom for gifted women to speak and lead in Swedish Baptist circles. Born in Chicago in 1893 to Swedish-born parents, Sabel experienced conversion as a teenager. She was baptized in 1909 and joined a Baptist General Conference church.[23] Sabel experienced equal opportunity to lead in her church young people's society.

> My first "sermon" was "preached" at a young people's meeting when I was 16. Our entire church meetings were then held in Swedish, even Sunday School. I wrote out my "sermon" on John 4 in English, then translated it into Swedish and memorized it. I stood on one foot behind the pulpit to control my trembling.[24]

Sabel never struggled over woman's right to speak in church; Paul's statements on women were never an issue for her. She had her parents' approval of anything she did as a servant of the Lord.

In her late teens, Sabel attended noncredit evening courses at MBI. From 1916 to 1920, she majored in Latin and Greek at the University of Chicago. Sabel graduated with a Ph.B. (Bachelor of Philosophy) at the top of her class, earning the Phi Beta Kappa key as well as special honors. To study the Bible in preparation for expected missionary service, she attended MBI day school for one year (1920–21).

Since the Swedish Baptists had no foreign missions board of their own at that time, Sabel applied to the American Baptist Missionary Society, but could not leave for the foreign field because of poor health. In 1920 the society's Women's Foreign Board sent Sabel to Newton Theological Seminary for two terms, where she studied religious education. Waiting for recovery, Sabel taught and served as principal at a Minnesota high school from 1920 until 1922.

When Bethel Seminary added a Bible and Missionary Training Department in 1922, the school felt Sabel had just the preparation to head up that program.[25] Sabel accepted the invitation and taught at Bethel from 1924 until her retirement in 1958. She taught courses in Bible, Greek, and Christian education and attributed Bethel's openness to her administrative and teaching ministry to the school's president. Dr. Hagstrom had no objections to women doing any service for the Lord. On her sabbatical in 1949, Sabel earned the Master of Religious Education degree from Southwestern Baptist Seminary.

In addition to teaching, Sabel preached many sermons in local churches.

> I never preached in any but Baptist churches except on one occasion when I had to stand below the pulpit in a Lutheran church. . . . I never faced any opposition to my preaching. The opposite was true. One time when the Pentecostals were active in a certain district in Minneapolis, the members of one of our Conference churches were confused over the teaching on the Holy Spirit. The pastor said "We'll have a week of teaching on the Holy Spirit." I was asked to be the first speaker on Sunday morning. I spoke on the Personality of the Holy Spirit. After the service, I joined the crowd leaving the church and an elderly gentleman said to me, "What did you think of *that* preacher? She

beat any man I ever heard preach." Another man said, "She *is* the
preacher." The elderly gentleman looked at me again and said "I
didn't recognize you with a hat on." It was at a time when we
were wearing hats that came down low over the forehead and I
had taken mine off before I entered the pulpit.

Though never ordained, Sabel was encouraged in that
direction.

My pastor wanted very much that I be ordained, but I had no
desire to be, and I have always felt a man should head up the
affairs of the church. However, I was certified by my church in
Minneapolis in the hope that I could get a minister's reduction in
train fares when I was asked to be the speaker at camps in
Washington and Oregon. I felt this certification was equivalent
to the ordination of a male preacher as far as railroad fares went.
However, the railroad said I would be entitled only if I "wore a
peculiar habit."

Like Esther Sabel, Swedish Baptist pastor Minnie S.
Nelson was prevented from missionary service overseas because
of illness. Beginning in 1920, she labored on the home front.

Thief River Falls and Clearbrook, Minnesota, Great Falls,
Montana, and Iron River, Michigan, were my pastorates during
fourteen years. I also supplied Henning and Cook, Minnesota,
each for three months. God has opened many other doors of
service for me, too. My pulpit has often been the radio, street
corners, country schoolhouses, taverns, jails, hospitals, and
hundreds of homes. . . . I have had the privilege of speaking at
dozens of state WCTU rallies and Baptist conferences, and at one
of our General Conference sessions. . . . When I couldn't go to
the Philippines I determined to give my own beloved country
my best. Had I a thousand lives, I'd give them all to God. . . .
Resurrecting dead churches, uniting divided ones, repairing
church property, paying old church debts, strenuous travel and
speaking engagements—these do not make for an easy program
but thank God for the Ebenezer stone![26]

Just as the Methodist Episcopal Church in the South
restricted women more than the northern church did, so did
Baptists in the South. The immense shock of civil war and

subsequent disruption of traditional southern culture entrenched conservative values even more deeply into society and church. Many Southern Baptists saw biblical teaching on female submission and inferiority as clearly as they had seen the subjection of black slaves to white masters.

Southern Baptist women who desired to preach or pastor faced enormous opposition. The 1885 Convention changed the word "members" to "brethren" in the constitution to reflect its exclusion of women delegates.[27] Only in 1918 did Southern Baptist women gain laity rights. Some southerners blamed new worldly fads like women preachers on the North. An 1892 *Biblical Recorder* editorial urged Southern Baptist churches to refuse the use of their buildings to *all* women speakers, no matter how good the cause.[28] John A. Broadus, professor and president of Southern Baptist Theological Seminary, fanned the opposition to women's public ministry with his influential pamphlet "Ought Women to Speak in Mixed Public Assemblies?"

Hardshell Baptists, with their strength in the South, typically demanded total silence for women. Advocating an ultrapredestination, antimissionary theology, these Baptists saw no need for female or male evangelistic preachers, since God would save the elect apart from human assistance. For other Baptists, negative reaction to female activism in the abolition, woman's suffrage, and temperance movements reinforced their opposition to women in the pulpit.

Southern Baptist leaders overwhelmingly restricted the female public role to singing in the choir and public testimony. Baptists base membership on conversion and baptism, and traditional practice required new believers to relate their personal testimony of conversion before the congregation. This public action of women in worship constituted an important exception to the silence standard. In addition, as female involvement in missions grew, so did opportunities to speak. Whether a foreign missionary gave a field report or mission society leader appealed for funds, each took a step toward woman's participation in public worship. Overall, "order and respectability kept women silenced and seated in worship nearly as effectively in the twentieth century as scriptural prohibitions did in the nineteenth."[29]

In stark contrast, American Baptist churches in the North ordained dozens of women in the first quarter of the twentieth century. Regionalism greatly influenced a church's decision to choose a female minister. Baptist congregations in the North and South might confess an identical doctrinal creed and theory of ordination. But within distinctive cultural frameworks, these churches could radically disagree on issues such as slavery or women's place.

Licensed preacher and foreign missions promoter Helen Barrett Montgomery (1861–1934) represented the wide opportunities available to some Baptist women in the North. Montgomery taught Bible classes around Philadelphia for over forty years, was elected president of the Northern Baptist Convention in 1910, attended the Baptist World Alliance in 1923 as a delegate, and translated *The New Testament in Modern English* published in 1924.[30]

Northern Baptists generally supported women's preaching ministry but expressed ambivalence regarding ordination.[31] Nevertheless, at least fifty women were ordained between 1903 (the first year a woman's name appeared in the American Baptist Yearbook ordination list) and 1929.[32] Undoubtedly, dozens more pastored and preached in Baptist churches as licensed ministers or without official recognition.[33]

The brief sketches and occasional quotations of six ordained Baptist women which follow can provide valuable insight into the training, pastorates, and ministerial experiences of these pioneer female clergy. Each one highlights various factors which enabled women to assume church leadership.

Emma J. C. Park

Emma Park attended Boston University Medical School in preparation for medical missionary work in Ramapatnam, India. After returning to the States, she recruited missionaries for ten years, then pastored for six. The Baptist church in Bellingham, Massachusetts, ordained her in 1919.[34] Written in

1929, four years before her death, Park's autobiography, *The Fool and I*, revealed the progress of her ministry and the personal side of her experiences as a female pastor. According to her account, the lack of trained male pastors in many small churches created a vacuum into which experienced women could sometimes step.

[CHAPTER I—PROLOGUE]

The Fool and I have wandered together through this vale of tears and laughter for lo, these many years. . . . More than five years we toiled together in India, where I had the honor of being the first medical missionary sent out to that land by our Women's Baptist Foreign Missionary Society. More than ten years we journeyed in our native land, speaking and working for recruits for the task that ill health forbade us to resume. Three happy summers were spent in the green hills of Vermont, ministering to a tiny Union Church that could only have services for only a few weeks in the summer; six years we toiled together in a little church in Massachusetts, where again I had the honor of being the first Baptist woman ever ordained in that staid and steady State.

[CHAPTER XV—IN THE VERMONT HILLS]

I have referred before to the unsatisfied Christians that I found on every side in my travels. More and more during my ten years of deputation work the desperate spiritual hunger of the average Christian was borne in upon me . . . the desire grew in me to be able to help them. In a great many places especially such as that little church in Indiana, where they could have only irregular services, and that too often from totally untrained men, how I longed to stay two or three weeks. . . . And so, when Mr. Park and I went up into the hills of Vermont one summer for the sake of his health, and they asked me to take charge of the tiny little Union Church there, I dared to undertake it. . . . I knew that their previous supplies had been young men of no training, and little education, though they had been earnest Christians, and it seemed to me that perhaps my experience would offset any qualifications that they had had beyond mine . . . my sermons, if they could be called that, were practically Bible Readings and expositions, and how that isolated little flock grew. . . . Their custom was to have a service each year, at the close of the season, when an ordained minister would come from the nearest large town, who preached, administered the Lord's Supper, and baptized. . . . This experience in Vermont gave me courage when many years later, after Mr. Park had won his release, and there were younger and fresher workers in the deputation field, and after some years devoted to an aged and helpless mother, there came an opportunity to serve one of the needy churches in Massachusetts . . . there might be for me a few years of the work of feeding Christians for which I had so longed.

I had no thought except to get a license to preach, and serve as stated supply. But the State Convention strongly advised ordination, which I had never considered for a moment; and my feeling, was strong that, having no special training for the ministry, it would be wrong to seek ordination.

But the State Convention argued that my experience had been some training, and also, that as there was no other church in Bellingham, where I was expected to go, it was only fair that the village should have someone authorized to marry and to bury, and to administer the ordinances. They also argued that both my own standing and that of the church in the community and the Association would be better if I were placed more nearly on a footing with other pastors.

After much prayerful thought I consented, and was ordained in September, 1919, the first Baptist woman ever ordained in Massachusetts. And the church which was my first and only pastorate has a record well worth noting. . . .

Preparing for ordination, I was led to question again, most seriously, just what the duty of a pastor was. . . . The great effort, from Genesis to Revelation, seemed to be to make His people understand God and His love toward men.

[CHAPTER XVI—THE WOMAN OF IT]

Our femininity of course excited curiosity and comment. . . . Pumping water is harder and slower than turning a faucet, and when one woman, no longer youthful, has to do the housekeeping, write two sermons a week, and prepare for a weekly prayer meeting, there is no surplus of time or strength, especially if one attempts to do any of the pastoral work that is needed. . . .

And as the church, like so many of the little country churches, was very largely made up of women, sometimes they gloried in the fact that they had a female pastor. For instance, when one of those dear women came up at the close of a service, and gave me a loving kiss, saying, "There! I couldn't do that if you were a man!" Or when one came to the parsonage in trouble, and poured out her heart, and finally laid her head on my shoulder and wept it out, and said, "Oh, I am so glad you are a woman, and I can come to you as I would to my own mother!" . . .

Our first appearance at the Association meeting was somewhat of an ordeal . . . but I never encountered the slightest hint that I was an unwelcome member of the ministerial brother-and-sister-hood. . . . But can we ever forget our first administrations of the ordinances? . . . And baptism! We had never planned to administer that. . . . I turned to the longsuffering secretary of the State Convention . . . his reply was that unless I was physically unable to do it, he thought it would be far better for me to take the duty, which of course belonged to me as pastor . . . with many misgivings, I did so, and baptized all the candidates of the whole pastorate, excepting when strength, or lack of it, forbade.

[CHAPTER XVII—DIVERS EXPERIENCES]

. . . The experiences detailed were as unusual in their character as a female pastor in a Baptist pulpit at that time . . . we found it hard, not only at first, but always, to officiate at a marriage, and never did I pronounce a couple man and wife, without secretly wondering what business it was of mine to do so. . . . At one time we had in the church and congregation Scotch, English, Swede, Irish, Armenian, French Canadian, Hollanders, a family with a Russian father, and a mother from Poland, and a few Americans!

[CHAPTER XVIII—ASHES FOR A GARLAND]

. . . To the extreme modernist I fear that might be an acceptable answer, but it did not pass in Bellingham. . . . And at the conclusion of six years, our health began to fail again . . . we wrote our resignation. . . . In the six years, the church had accomplished much, and would have more than doubled its membership if there were not necessarily a constant moving away of young people as soon as their education is completed.

Helen Hyde Carlson

In 1920 the Paris Baptist Church in Paris Hill, Maine, ordained Helen Hyde Carlson. Her son, a teenager during Carlson's years of ministry, described her background and training. Her biography symbolizes the impact of the YWCA and WCTU in training female church leaders.

She studied to become a missionary at the American Baptist Training School (I think that is the correct name) in Chicago from which she was graduated in 1900 at age 25. She was sent then to Swatow (now spelled "Shantou"), on the south China coast, and served there as a missionary until December, 1904, when she and my father were married.

My mother was widowed in 1907. She thereafter served as a secretary to a Methodist minister in Syracuse, NY; as a Young Women's Christian Association worker (I don't know in what capacity) in Syracuse; as general secretary to the YWCA in Charleston, SC between 1913 and 1916; as a YWCA general secretary in Little Falls, NY, for a year or two; as a paid worker for the cause of woman suffrage in New York State, and as a speaker and worker for both the Anti Saloon League and the Women's Christian Temperance Union in the years between 1917 and 1919. She went to the Paris Hill pastorate in May or June of 1919. In 1926 she became minister of the Baptist Church in Greene, Maine and, about 1929 or thereabouts, minister of the Baptist Church at Owl's Head, Maine. During all of those years she was a State of Maine official of the WCTU. In the 1930s she worked, briefly, in Franklin Roosevelt's old National Youth Administration in Maine (a by no means well-paid job). She headed the Maine branch of United China Relief after the Japanese bombarded Shanghai and bombed the inland cities during the 1930s.

You asked whether church people were "receptive to her as a woman." Yes, it seemed to be that they were. I can remember no indications of prejudice or dislike—but, of course, I was only a teen-ager in those years. But, frankly, I do not recall any instances of open hostility; instead, the church people seemed very fond of my mother.[35]

Gertrude Teele

At a meeting in Boston's Park Street Church, Gertrude Teele first sensed God's call to missionary service. Her life typifies the interrelation between home and foreign missions service. At times, ordination of female missionaries could be accepted but not ordination of women pastors at home.

Teele entered Gordon Bible College in the autumn of 1917 to prepare for her ministry. One summer at the end of her junior year, the Presbyterian board sent her to Saskatchewan, Canada, as a preacher/missionary. She recalled the rigors of her first home missions preaching assignment.

> My field consisted of some twenty square miles on which were located three schoolhouses, which were used for services on Sundays. I was provided with a horse, buggy, and saddle, and had many splendid rides over the prairies. Each Sunday I drove eighteen miles to the services and stopped for the night at the last place, Prairie hill, starting back the next morning and visiting in the homes of the people, seldom arriving at my boarding house until the end of the week. Leaving for home on the first of October I had learned the answer to my question. I did want to go to the mission field more than anything else in the world.[36]

The First Federated Church of Hudson, Massachusetts, ordained her as a Baptist minister in 1921, inviting Gordon Bible College president Nathan R. Wood to the ceremony. Teele sailed to Burma in August 1921 to engage in city, evangelistic, and social service ministry.

Grace M. Brooks

In 1919 Grace M. Brooks began her twenty-eight year pastorate of the Georgia Plain Baptist Church in Georgia, Vermont. At the turn of the century, small rural churches too poor to support a married male minister could sometimes afford a single woman. Brooks's pastorate gives us a picture of such a situation.

Purported to have remained in a single church longer than any other female pastor in the Northern Baptist Convention,

Brooks also held the claim of being the first female pastor in Vermont. H. Hale Nye, a parishioner in her church and Brooks's guardian in her last years of life, provided a glimpse of her ministry.[37]

> Perhaps I know as much about Rev. Miss Grace Brooks as anyone. . . . During the time which Miss Brooks was the pastor of the Georgia Plain Baptist Church we had very few active members. Often in the winter there were 8 or 10 of us at church during the winter and the services were held around the woodburning stove in the vestry. . . . She was well accepted by the State Convention and paid dues if that is the right term to the Baptist Minister and Missionary Board. . . . She was in a nursing home. . . . When her regular pension did not meet her full needs I wrote to the M. and M. Board and they sent additional checks.
>
> She received a very small salary but fortunately she lived in St. Albans, Vermont, with two lady friends who had some income. She drove a car and brought a quarter of the congregation to church often. Georgia, Vermont, is a dairy farm area. . . . I believe that Miss Grace Brooks was the best person . . . I ever knew.

Katherine M. Leonard

In 1924 the Austin Square Baptist Church of Lynn, Massachusetts, extended the call to Katherine Leonard to serve as pastor of their church on a three-month trial basis.[38] In April that year the congregation requested that the Salem Baptist Association call a meeting to examine Leonard for ordination. The next month the church voted to retain Leonard as their pastor indefinitely. The 1925 American Baptist Yearbook listed Leonard as recently ordained. Until 1931 local church records listed her as a member.

Significantly, the Austin Square Baptist Church left the American Baptist Church in June 1952 and joined the Conservative Baptist Association, clearly indicating the church's theological stance. The present Austin Square Church's constitution provides for the licensing and ordination of men only; only males can serve today as pastor, elder, or deacon. Yet the church records from 16 November 1923 documented the church vote to license Mrs. Atwood to preach, as well as the frequent reference to Leonard's pastorate.

I conclude the discussion of Baptist women with Leonard because her story represents countless others that may never be told. These events at Austin Square Baptist Church picture for us the rise and decline of female pastors in one Fundamentalist circle.

CONGREGATIONALISTS

Especially in the urban Northeast, many Congregational churches and seminaries embraced theological liberalism in the late nineteenth century. The denomination's Kansas City Declaration of 1913 sharply contrasted with new Fundamentalist creeds. But given its congregational church polity, individual parishes particularly in the Midwest could and did remain committed to Evangelical principles. A Fundamentalist leader like ordained Congregationalist Reuben A. Torrey of Moody Bible Institute represented this conservative wing.

The First Congregational Church of Butler and Savannah in Wayne County, New York, holds the distinction of being the first church to fully ordain a woman in the United States— Antoinette Louisa Brown in 1853. The denomination ordained at least seventy-five more women before 1920.[39]

Why did these churches utilize women? Reasons which applied to northern Baptist women also fit the Congregationalist scene at times. Another possibility relates to unique opportunities for single women and ministers' wives. The following sketches of four ordained Congregational women point to such factors. Women in ministry encountered not only larger societal and theological concerns but also deeply personal ones, such as decisions to marry or not.

Mary E. Drake

Mary E. Drake aptly illustrates the Evangelical women around the turn of the century engaged in team ministry with a spouse.

She and her husband Andrew established Congregational churches in Esmond, Iroquois, Osceola, and Petrodie, South Dakota, during the 1880s and 1890s. Rev. Andrew Drake had trained at Oberlin College before arriving with his family to homestead in South Dakota. Andrew and Mary, both widowed, married in 1884. They first lived in a one-room house, burning hay for fuel. The Congregational Home Mission Society supplied the Drakes with money to purchase a horse to pull their buggy. Via horse and buggy, they drove to preach at a church in DeSmet and to schoolhouses miles away where no churches existed. Often combatting the rain and cold, these pioneer church planters held meetings in stores, sod houses, and dugouts.

In 1894, a year before Andrew's death, Mary Drake wrote her autobiography, *Fanny*, from the viewpoint of their horse.[40] One excerpt described the organization of the Drakola Congregational Church in 1884.

> One Sunday afternoon, they drove me 16 miles to Lake Thompson. I heard them telling about organizing a church there. By this time, I knew what he meant. I supposed, of course, there would be a house there of some kind, but they drove away beyond everything to a little claim shanty 14 by 15 ft. square. When we drove up there were a great many teams there already, and people from all over the prairie from 6–16–20 miles distant. They all shook hands and were very glad to see each other. They could not all get in the shanty. Presently a wagon drove up with an organ that had been brought four miles. The horses could hear every word they had to say, and it was great fun for us. I heard them say there were 18 members in the new church. They prayed and sang and had an enjoyable time as they always did.
>
> After the meeting was over, master and mistress (Mr. and Mrs. A. J. Drake) were in the buggy again. I heard mistress speak of the people being nice refined folk. Many of them had spoken of coming from Oberlin, Ohio. "Oh, yes" master said, "A number of them are graduates from the college there. That is the kind of people we have in South Dakota."
>
> We went home with some of them and stayed all night. They were relatives of my master, a brother (George W. Drake) and a sister (Mrs. Wm. Westervelt) and nephews and nieces. The

sister's husband, William Westervelt, was pastor of the church without any pay either. What a good time they did have in their little bits of unfinished houses. We had too, our good time, with plenty of oats and hay and good beds up to our knees in hay. My owners always managed that for me. Often mistress came out herself to see I was well cared for.

In 1890 the Congregational Church in Iroquois ordained Mary Drake. She also served actively with the DeSmet Women's Christian Temperance Union.

Juanita Breckenridge Bates

The daughter of a Methodist minister, Juanita Breckenridge Bates (1860–1946) pictures for us how singleness and marriage could impact on the ministry involvement of Evangelical women. In her case, marriage in 1893 resulted in a rather abrupt resignation from the pastorate.

Bates grew up in Illinois, graduating from Wheaton College in 1885. She taught for several years before entering Oberlin Theological Seminary. In 1891 Bates completed her three-year course, the first woman to receive a Bachelor of Divinity degree from that school. The Congregational Church licensed her to preach in 1890, and Bates's two-year pastorate in Brookton, New York, culminated in her 1893 ordination. After her marriage that year, Bates resigned from her position. In her personal correspondence from 1872 until 1893, Bates revealed three key issues that she personally grappled with.[41] First, she sought approval to enter theological school; second, she searched for a pastorate; third, she pursued ordination.

Amelia A. Frost

For some women, entrance into a pulpit or pastorate came partially by way of their husband's ministry. Disabled or deceased male ministers were sometimes succeeded by a spouse. In 1890 the Congregational Church of Littleton, Massachusetts, called George B. Frost as its pastor. When his health failed, forcing a leave of absence, the church installed his wife Amelia A. Frost as associate pastor in 1893.

In 1894, over doubts of some of the Ecclesiastical Council about ordaining a woman, the church ordained Frost. She convinced the Council of the clarity of her call and of biblical authority for the step she was taking, quoting Acts 2, "Your sons and daughters shall prophesy." Frost, the first ordained Congregational woman in Massachusetts, was installed as full pastor in 1895 and ministered in Littleton until 1901.[42]

Alice May Coombs Robinson

Because there were too few ministers to fill all the pulpits on the frontier, gifted women were more likely to share pastoral responsibilities with their husbands in circuit-riding style. For example, Alice May Coombs Robinson (1862–1910) and her husband William H. Robinson jointly ministered at the First Congregational Church of Palermo, California. In one of the earliest ordinations for women in the history of California, the Palermo church ordained Alice Robinson as an evangelist in 1896. The Robinsons later pastored the First Church in Oroville, California, which included several mission projects. From the First Church they served three other Congregational churches and one Presbyterian church. In addition to her local church ministry, Alice Robinson worked as the California WCTU state evangelist.[43]

DISCIPLES

Modernism divided the Disciples of Christ as it did Presbyterians and Baptists in the North. The Disciples or Christian churches had developed from three separate secession movements between 1790 and 1810. Like Baptists and Methodists, Disciples exhibited a wide range of practices regarding women's ministry. In 1883 the denomination debated whether three missionary wives should be ordained along with their husbands. Clara Celestia Hall was the first Disciples woman ordained for home ministry in 1888. Barbara Kellison's 1862 pamphlet "Rights of Women in the Church" expressed the general Disciples' acceptance of women in church leadership.[44]

To prepare for church ministry, many Disciples women attended Bible institutes. After training at MBI and Toronto Bible College, Marjorie Constance Bristow of England was ordained in 1914 by the Christian Church in Pembroke, New York.[45] Alma Lauder studied at BIOLA before returning to her home church in Moscow, Idaho, for ordination in 1929.[46]

Not all, however, accepted women's pulpit ministry with open arms. Ordained by the Church of Christ, Mary Lee Cagle of Alabama had first decided to preach to the foreign heathen. "To go out in this country as a woman preacher, would mean to face bitter opposition, prejudice, slanderous tongues."[47] Belle Reid Yates, for example, faced some of that hostility. After gaining public speaking experience through Women's Relief Corps travels, she served the Grenola Christian Church in Kansas for eighteen years after her 1913 ordination. In Oklahoma she continued her preaching ministry.

> One Sunday at Vertigris, I walked in just as the superintendent was closing Sunday School. He stopped, looked at me and said, "I will not stay in the house with a woman preacher or one who wears a silk dress." I walked to the front and taking hold of my dress, asked, "Shall I take my dress off?" This broke the tension and they asked me to stay.
>
> At one place in Oklahoma, an old Baptist preacher arose and said, "No woman can preach in this house for Jesus Christ said the women should keep silent." This about caused a riot by the half-breeds who had invited me there. I quieted them and took for my text, "Let the women keep silent in the churches." At the close of the longest sermon I ever preached, the old brother and several of his hardshells came forward and thanked me. They said they never understood it before.
>
> In this sermon, she held: "We must look the truth straight in the face and measure God's children by the standard of fitness and not by moss-grown, moth-eaten traditions of creed and breed."[48]

QUAKERS

The Society of Friends provides a good example of a denomination essentially identified with liberal Protestantism today, but

which encompassed a vocal Holiness-Fundamentalist wing in
the late nineteenth century. Clearly, the Fundamentalist convictions of certain Quakers did not alter their traditional openness
to women's ministry.

Quakers have historically provided the greatest role for
women in public church ministry. In seventeenth-century
England, George Fox's wife, Margaret Fell, wrote the tract
Women's Speaking Justified, the first such document written by a
woman. In colonial America virtually all women preachers
belonged to the Society of Friends.[49] Until the late nineteenth
century, Quakers utilized preachers but hired no pastors.
Believing God alone can ordain a person, Friends still today
record rather than ordain ministers.

The development of separate Quaker meetings for men
and women led to growing discrepancies in equality. By the
mid-nineteenth century, some American Quaker women were
excluded from administrative leadership and discouraged from
public speaking. Most quietistic Quakers criticized the radical
abolition stance of a preacher like Lucretia Mott.

Though quietist Friends dominated the movement until
the 1880s, an Evangelical wing that stressed programmed
ministry, missions, and education was on the rise. Opposed to
growing religious liberalism among Quakers, these Evangelicals identified with Holiness and Fundamentalist causes while
maintaining woman's right to preach.[50]

Revivalistic and holiness campaigns among Quakers
constituted a radical, controversial departure from traditional
quietistic Quaker practice. The convictions of Evangelical
Quakers found expression in an 1887 doctrinal statement
parallel to later Fundamentalist creeds and from 1905 to 1914 in
the journal *The Evangelical Friend.* By 1927 these "radical"
conservatives formed the Association of Evangelical Friends.

Evangelical Quaker Bible institutes opened in the wake of
revival and holiness movements. In 1892 J. Walter Malone
organized the first school—Cleveland Bible Institute.[51] In
Whittier, California, local Evangelical Quakers opened the
Training School for Christian Workers in 1899 after the
National Holiness Association evangelist Joseph H. Smith led

revival.[52] The school advertised that instructors believe and teach sanctification as a second definite experience after conversion.[53] Mary A. Hill served as first president of the training school that supplied much of the leadership for the Evangelical Quaker movement in California.

The 1918 stated aim of Kansas Central Bible Training School, the forerunner of Friends Bible College, reflected the revivalistic, holiness, and biblicist emphases of these Quakers.

> Our aim is not to give a so-called advanced theological education, but primarily, to teach the English Bible and train Christian workers for the Lord's vineyard. Our work includes a two-year preparatory course. . . . Our work is for those members of our church who feel a definite Divine call to the service of the Lord, and who feel a need of due preparation for that service. We therefore seek to secure for each student the most perfect Christian experience possible, including thorough regeneration, entire sanctification, and a vital, personal acquaintance with God. We hold strictly to the Bible as the Word of God, and aim to secure such skill in handling it as to enable our graduates to be soul winners.[54]

The existence of Bible-believing, Evangelical Friends who endorsed women preachers at the turn of the century provided other Protestants an important example when facing the question of women's public ministry.

MENNONITES

As among the Quakers, part of the Mennonite church identified with the Fundamentalist and Bible institute style of Protestantism around the turn of the century. Evangelicals among the Anabaptist Mennonites had contributed to the founding of Fort Wayne Bible College. A graduate of Fort Wayne in 1911, Catherine Niswander ministered as a home missionary for the General Conference Mennonite Church.[55] In 1914 she began city mission work in Chicago which enlisted the support of many Mennonite students at MBI. Niswander was sent to Portland in the 1920s to start a church. Not only did she do all the preaching at first, but she instructed her Mennonite congregation in the dispensational truths of Christ's second coming.

After years of preaching and evangelizing in New York City, Mennonite Ann J. Allebach (1874–1918) asked to be ordained by the General Conference. The newspaper claimed that her 15 January 1911 ordination in Philadelphia's First Mennonite Church was the first of a woman in that denomination. Allebach's pastor Rev. Schantz preached that "while Paul's instructions on silence were specific to the Greek culture, the vision that 'yet are one in Christ, neither male or female' was the vision for the future generations."[56]

In 1909, Evangelical Mennonites opened Hesston Academy and Bible School in Kansas.[57] Women involved at Hesston in the early decades reportedly preached, taught Bible, pastored churches, and received ordination.[58] Like the Evangelical Quakers, these Bible-believing Mennonites endorsed women's public church leadership.

ADVENT CHRISTIANS

In an intriguing way, the rise of premillennial theology among nineteenth-century Protestants added a new argument in support of women preachers. Based on Joel's prediction in the Old Testament that women as well as men would prophesy in the "last days," many premillennialists at first interpreted the increase of women preachers in a favorable light, as a clear sign of Christ's soon return.

The Advent Christian Church perceived of women's ministry just that way. This denomination organized in the 1860s, an heir of the early nineteenth-century Millerite movement.[59] The constant expectancy of the Lord's immediate return deterred early Adventists from founding permanent educational institutions. However, needing to prepare ministers and train laity, the Advent Christians opened the Boston Bible School in 1897.[60] Its primary stated objective in 1902 was to "promulgate Bible Christianity." From the start, women took pastoral courses along with men to prepare for ordination. The first school catalogue openly advertised its position on women under the heading "Both Sexes."

As there is no sex in sin or salvation, there should be none in citizenship, education, or gospel labor. "In Christ Jesus there is neither male or female." . . . If young *men* need special training for Christian activity, no less do the young women. Are there not fifty in New England and the Middle States who have heard the divine call to "*prophesy* in these last days?"[61]

Like the United Brethren denomination, the Advent Christian Church encouraged women to enter the pastorate through both publications and education. Pamphlets such as Beulah Mathewson's 1873 "Woman from a Bible Standpoint—Do the Scriptures Forbid the Public Labor of Women?" supported women's ministry via Scripture. The Advent Christian Church ordained Anna Eliza Smith in 1866. Born a Quaker, Smith converted to Adventism and helped organize the Union Female Missionary Association, which included Adventist preachers.[62] Smith paved the way for many other ordained Advent Christian women.[63]

Debate continues whether Ellen G. White, founder of the Seventh-Day Adventist Church, ever received ordination credentials in the 1880s.[64] In 1895, White wrote in the Adventist *Review and Herald* that women called to minister to sick, young, and poor should be set apart by prayer and laying on of hands. The number of women in denominational leadership peaked in 1915, the year of White's death.

PRESBYTERIANS AND LUTHERANS

With their historic emphasis on a seminary-trained clergy, Presbyterian, Episcopal, and Lutheran churches alike largely excluded women from the pastorate by limiting seminary education to males. The traditional Episcopal opposition to women clergy was expressed by an Anglican minister in 1917 who claimed "a woman is incapable of the Priesthood, even as a man is incapable of motherhood."[65]

Significantly, revivalistic churches like the Cumberland Presbyterians tended to utilize women to a greater extent in leadership than the anti-revival groups. The Cumberland Presbyterians, for instance, split from the Presbyterian Church in the early nineteenth century over its revival and Arminian emphases and waived the traditional educational requirements for the ministry. The denomination voted in 1892 to ordain women elders as needed. Two years later the General Assembly split on the question of full ordination; only female lay evangelists received official recognition.

Ordained by the Church of Christ, Mrs. E. J. Sheeks first heard a woman preach at a Cumberland Presbyterian camp meeting.[66] Cumberland Presbyterian Louisa M. Woosley carefully marked all biblical references to women and from her notes wrote *Shall Women Preach? or, The Question Answered* in 1891. The Session called Woosley to conduct church services for an absent pastor. The Nolin Presbytery subsequently licensed her to preach in 1888 and ordained her the next year. Throughout four years of preaching and open air meetings, Woosley delivered 912 sermons and recruited 500 new members for the church.[67] Eventually, opposition from some Cumberland Presbyterians pushed her to join the Methodist church.

The Cumberland Presbyterian Church represented the exception to the rule among Presbyterians. In the North an 1872 resolution forbade women's teaching or preaching in the pulpit as well as their licensing and ordination. When Presbyterians split over Modernism, neither wing formally advocated female church leadership. Some southern Presbyterians connected the "woman question" with the "negro question." They argued that if blacks followed the females' lead and stepped out of their proper sphere, family and society would be destroyed. Not until 1956 did the northern part of the United Presbyterian Church grant women full clergy rights; the southern church followed in 1964.

Turn-of-the-century Lutheranism was essentially unscathed by the Modernist turmoil. Rather, these Protestants faced problems of immigration, church consolidation, and confessional controversy. Lutherans after the Civil War debated the more limited controversy of women's lay right to vote in church. In 1889, F. P. Mayser argued that "voting is one of the strongest and most effective ways of governing (ruling) in the church, and if done by women, it is clearly in violation of the original and fundamental order established at creation."[68]

In contrast, another Lutheran—Ernst P. H. Pfatteicher—held that women's right to vote was a matter of justice and expediency, not Scripture. "The Lutheran Church can remain just as conservative during the Twentieth Century as she has been in this century, yet consistently hold to the rights of women as congregational voters."[69] Theodore E. Schmauk supported woman's right to vote plus her right to study theology, though not her public right to teach it. The Missouri Synod continues to restrict women's freedom to minister today, although since 1970 the Lutheran Church in America and the American Lutheran Church ordain women.[70]

INDEPENDENT FUNDAMENTAL CHURCHES OF AMERICA

In the wake of Modernist-Fundamentalist conflict, groups of conservative Christians began to leave existing denominations and form new associations. In 1923, Robert Lee Kirkland invited other Midwest ministers who opposed Modernism and denominationalism to convene in Arnold Park, Iowa.[71] From that meeting, the American Conference of Undenominational Churches (ACUC) emerged. After a 1930 meeting at Cicero Bible Church in Chicago, the name switched to Independent Fundamental Churches of America (IFCA). Regarding women in public ministry, several crucial changes occurred between 1923 and 1930 in this Fundamentalist organization.

In 1923, women who met the general requirements were accepted into full membership by the American Conference of Undenominational Churches. The ACUC usage of "his or her" in the constitution reflected this openness. Women chaired ACUC committees and spoke at conventions. By 1930, 13 of 174 members were ordained women with the title "Reverend" and were serving as pastors or pastors' assistants. Though the ACUC itself did not ordain any women on record, it openly welcomed to its membership women previously ordained.

In its first major constitutional change, the Independent Fundamental Churches of America in 1930 eliminated women from membership. Only male delegates could represent affiliated churches and vote; female leadership at the national level came to an abrupt halt. Eventually women's efforts were channeled into strictly women's auxiliary groups. The concept of a female pastor both ordained and Fundamentalist began to fade. New institutions like the IFCA formalized women's subordinate role.

This survey of women's role in turn-of-the-century denominations has attempted to investigate how women were used as ministers and leaders, especially in Evangelical churches of that era. Though many women may have trained at interdenominational Bible schools, these students invariably left to serve in specific denominational contexts. Several conclusions can be drawn from the preceding evidence.

Most importantly, this overview begins to reveal factors that undoubtedly contributed to openness toward women in church leadership. First, the relative freedom for women in the holiness wing of Methodism points to the influence of theology, especially one's doctrine of the Holy Spirit, in opening doors for women. Secondly, the wide divergence of practice among Baptists (generally more restrictive in the South) illustrates the impact of regionalism on Evangelical feminism. Next, the preaching ministry of some Cumberland Presbyterian women represents the powerful force of revivalism in changing traditional roles for women even in Presbyterian circles. Finally, the surge of women into Congregational pastorates at the turn of the century exemplifies the impact of form of church government on opportunities for women.

The Evangelical Free Church, an immigrant denomination formed in the 1880s, combined many of these factors. Revivalist in spirit, congregational in church government, premillennial and "Bible-only" in theology, concentrated among pietist Scandinavian immigrants in the upper Midwest region—the Free Church provides an appropriate case study of an Evangelical denomination which utilized women as evangelists, Bible teachers, and pastors.

5

WOMEN IN THE
FREE CHURCH

n June 1983, the Committee on Ministerial Standing and its subcommittee brought the following proposal to the General Conference of the Evangelical Free Church of America (EFCA). "It is recommended that ordination be reserved for the preaching/teaching pastors only. This will be restricted to males."[1] The General Conference tabled the vote on this recommendation for another year. Due to the variety of positions currently espoused, the Free Church has yet to issue an official statement on women's ordination as it enters its second century. The evidence to follow demonstrates the early Free Church's openness to a public ministry for women—including preaching, pastoring, Bible teaching, and even ordination. The relevance of church history to the current EFCA discussion on women highlights the crucial importance of knowing and understanding one's Evangelical heritage.

Why such a detailed focus on a relatively small immigrant church? First, because the Free Church influence within modern Evangelicalism extends far beyond its own denominational boundaries. Trinity Evangelical Divinity School, a Free Church institution in Deerfield, Illinois, attracts Evangelical students from a wide spectrum of Protestant denominations. As one of today's leading Evangelical seminaries in terms of size and credibility, Trinity is training a significant segment of tomorrow's Evangelical leadership.

Second, the waves of immigrants so critical in shaping turn-of-the-century American society likewise influenced American Evangelical religion. In 1890 over 10 percent of the more than nine million foreign-born Americans came from Sweden, Norway, and Denmark. Between 1891 and 1920, one million Scandinavian immigrants arrived in America.[2] In 1880 one of every five ministers was foreign-born, including 598 Swedish and Norwegian clergy.[3] By 1890 that number rose to 1,323 clergy, including 18 women.[4] These Scandinavian women joined the English, Germans, and Canadians as the leading ethnic groups supplying foreign-born female clergy. A study of turn-of-the-century Evangelical women stands incomplete unless integrated with the contributions of immigrant women.

FOUNDING THE FREE CHURCH

An exploration of the relationship between the Evangelical Free Church of America and home-grown Evangelicalism begins with the intriguing saga of nineteenth-century Scandinavian Free Church movements. These grew out of the "Readers" revivals in which lay Bible readers conducted worship in private homes. These Scandinavian revivalists critiqued the dead orthodoxy of some Lutheran pastors and sought a regenerate church membership. Aided by Swedish-American evangelist Fredrik Franson (1852–1908), revival spread. His efforts in Denmark and Norway led directly to the formation of local mission societies.[5] The separatist groups which emerged by the close of the nineteenth century stood "free" from Lutheran state church control; these dissenters provided the impetus for the Free Church in America.

Swedish, Danish, and Norwegian immigrants from Free mission societies in the homeland naturally brought their religious convictions and practices with them to America. Other Scandinavians converted after arrival. A combination of Lutheran, Congregational, holiness, and premillennial influences all helped to shape the earliest Free Church congregations. In 1884 a small group of believers in Boston joined for fellowship and constituted the first Norwegian-Danish Evangelical Free Church in America. By 1909 eastern and western groups merged to form the Norwegian-Danish Free Church Association.[6]

Similarly, the first Swedish Evangelical Free Church organized in Chicago in 1880. The election of John Gustaf Princell (1845–1915) as executive committee chair at a prophetic Bible conference in 1884 marked the formal beginning of the Swedish EFCA.[7] Princell, a former Lutheran minister, had led dissenting Swedes to form a mission group known as the Ansgar Synod. He eventually left that denomination along with other premillennialists to join Franson and the Free Church group.

These founders clearly shared the intense prophetic interest of later Fundamentalism. The 1884 conference claimed that "all were on fire for the saving of as many souls as possible, and in as short a time as possible."[8] The voice and champion of these premillennialists was the Swedish religious newspaper *Chicago-Bladet,* first published by John Martenson in 1877.

In addition to promoting Bible conferences, the Scandinavians also established a Bible institute to train Free Church ministers and laity, with courses open to both men and women. In 1910 a Norwegian-Danish Bible Institute opened in Rushford, Minnesota, since an earlier tie with Chicago Theological Seminary had dissolved. In 1897 the first Swedish Bible course started in Chicago, incorporated as the Swedish Bible Institute in 1901 and led by Princell. In 1915 the school functioned as the Swedish Department of Moody Bible Institute, becoming autonomous in 1926.[9]

The Norwegian-Danish and Swedish schools merged in 1945 as Trinity Seminary and Bible Institute. In 1950 the two denominations joined to form the Evangelical Free Church of America. The educational cooperation between the Free Church and Moody Bible Institute for over a decade symbolizes the close relation of the EFCA to English-speaking Evangelicalism.

Though sharing similar prophetic views with the dispensational wing of early Fundamentalism, the Scandinavian immigrant group maintained certain distinctives. Whereas typical Fundamentalists adhered to certain doctrinal "fundamentals," the early Free Church displayed its reluctance to adopt any written creed. The 1908 Swedish constitution simply stated that "this organization accepts the Bible, both the Old and New Testaments, as the Word of God, containing the Gospel of salvation for all men and the only perfect rule for teaching, faith, and life."[10]

While native Fundamentalism developed theologically in response to liberalizing tendencies in American Protestantism, the Free Church at first grappled more with controversies within their immigrant community than with issues of the larger culture, such as evolution or biblical criticism. Viewed often as radical rather than conservative by the Scandinavian state churches, the Free Church people blended their own native traditions of pietism, revivalism, premillennialism, and biblicism.

In essence, the Free Church marked a protest against the inclusive parish system of a relatively rigid Scandinavian Lutheranism.[11] The immigrants fought anything in the new country that reminded them of these practices. In spite of ethnic differences, and separated by language, Free churches at the turn of the century constituted a significant element in American Evangelicalism.[12]

FREDRIK C. FRANSON

In light of this history, we can now investigate the role Free Church women played in public ministry at the turn of the century. Without a doubt, Fredrik Franson led the way in opening doors for women preachers. Swedish-born Franson emigrated to America in 1869, experienced conversion in 1872, and by 1875 was elected secretary by the Swedish Baptist Nebraska Conference.[13] Franson studied D. L. Moody's revivalistic campaigns and launched his own aggressive, interdenominational evangelistic career in 1877.

After joining Moody Church in Chicago in 1878, he organized several new churches including the first four Evangelical Free churches in America. In his analysis of the apostolic church, Franson saw local congregations, not synods, occupied with sending out evangelists, not calling pastors. With this for a model, Franson stressed the responsibility of all God's children, male and female, to preach and testify about Jesus.

In 1881 Franson co-sponsored and prepared papers for the Scandinavian Premillennial Conference in Chicago. He returned to Europe that same year, leading revivals in Germany and Scandinavia. Franson advocated the premillennial eschatology of Moody, whose translated sermons made Moody a Free Church hero overseas.

Franson spearheaded the legal breakthrough on aggressive, interdenominational evangelistic work in Sweden. He pioneered the concept of intensive Evangelist Courses to give lay workers several weeks instruction in the Bible. Though his first course in 1884 in Oslo was originally designed for men only, eleven of forty students were women since Franson's "own reservations in this matter have been lifted."[14] To maintain the revivals, Franson founded a variety of mission organizations, including the Scandinavian Alliance Mission in 1890, known today as The Evangelical Alliance Mission (TEAM).[15]

Franson's revival, missions, and premillennial concepts spread through a variety of publications written in Swedish and German and were later translated into English, Norwegian, Finnish, and Danish. From 1890 until his death, Franson focused primarily on urgent world-wide missionary advance led by itinerant evangelists.

Franson's close association with D. L. Moody, the Salvation Army, and A. B. Simpson's C&MA partly explains his outlook on women preachers. His commitment to Alliance principles and personal friendship with Simpson resulted in a formal relationship. Franson promised to recruit two hundred Swedish missionaries for China and by 1893 the Swedish C&MA field opened in northern China. *The Christian Alliance and Missionary Weekly* often included reports about Franson's mission work. He occasionally led revival in Alliance houses, where all had the freedom to speak.

Franson held meetings Salvation Army style at a time of

debate over Salvationist methods among Free Church leaders. In 1890 a German preacher wrote *The Salvation Army and the Work of Swedish Evangelist Franson Briefly Illumined According to the Holy Scriptures*.[16] Just like the Army, Franson enlisted female evangelists to spread the gospel.

An article on "Franson and the Work of Women Evangelists" in *The Free Churchman* described Franson's impact.[17]

> Among the followers of the freedom from sin "movement" it had been common that even women preached. But when normal conditions came back, the work of women evangelists began to stop. Among free church preachers there were those who were opposed to it in principle. Then Franson came in the year 1900 to Finland again. It became even more clear to him that in Finland the women were the most suitable to pioneer the way for the gospel. He told how in Norway the work of women evangelists had stopped for lack of order and in order to avoid that, the Union of women evangelists was founded. Since then, the Union has supported some evangelists mostly in East-Finland. But the local groups of the Union had greater importance for the work of the free churches. They became like some kind of circle of sisters among the free congregations and you can compare them to the YWCA in the Lutheran church.
>
> The idea of women evangelists won success among the district missions. The district missions . . . supported preaching in the countryside. . . . At first they used only men, but where it was short of preachers, they began to support even women. It soon became more common that women worked as evangelists and some district missions have during many years had only women evangelists.

As the leading proponent of women's public ministry among the Free Church pioneers, Franson received some criticism for including women on his evangelistic team and sending out women preachers. He answered critics with his pamphlet "Prophesying Daughters."[18] Franson based his rebuttal on the public prophecy of women predicted in Joel 2 and fulfilled in Acts 2. His pamphlet, published in several languages, had far-reaching influence. Franson's biblical defense of women preachers gave impetus to the Free Church women who emigrated to America.

PUBLIC MINISTRY OF WOMEN

The American scene reflected the earlier Scandinavian practice of enlisting women to help spread revival. Evangelist Catherine Juell of Norway, Franson's helper in Denmark, was "probably the foremost Christian worker among all the women of Scandinavia."[19] Gerda Karijord, an outstanding preacher, revived Norwegian fishing villages. Famous evangelist Amanda Karlsson ministered in Sweden. A group of female evangelists sent by the Danish Free Church were exposed to the Salvation Army's views on women's ministry while studying in England. The Danish Mission Covenant leaders wrote that "whether one is a man or a woman is no longer an issue. On the basis of this the Danish Mission Covenant makes no distinction between man and woman."[20] A Scandinavian pastor wrote in 1895 that "the Salvation Army and the work of women preachers is a phenomenon of the present times."[21]

Early openness to women related directly to the Free Church style of ministry and concept of church growth. Frequently, new congregations often started as mission churches through the work of independent evangelists, often in tent meetings. Lay preachers frequently led early revivals, downplaying the need for advanced training when one was Spirit-led. This suspicion of higher education and prejudice against an educated clergy had existed at times in Scandinavia. Frank T. Lindberg described how "the need for ministers was not so great in those days as we could all thank and praise God."[22]

At the turn of the century, few Free churches had permanent, full-time pastors in residence. Most preachers served as itinerant missionary/evangelists. These revivalists usually traveled in pairs, often one preaching and the other singing. The early circuit riders received no salary.[23] The Free Church paralleled the Methodist camp meetings with its mission meeting. Organizers invited any and all local preachers to participate in these revivals, which were usually held Thursday through Sunday. Given this setting, the early Free Church first channeled the energies of its gifted women into *home* missions work as evangelists and preachers, and only later shifted the female ministry to the foreign field.

From 1885 to 1891, for example, Ellen Modin evangelized the Mormons in Utah. Her revivals often followed the Salvation Army style of singing and testimony. Modin later opened a school in St. Paul for female preachers to rest and study. Their qualifying for clergy fare on the railroads was an important stamp of approval and provided access for ministries across the nation. Alma Olson supplied a pulpit in Orland, California, while the history of the local Free church in Kimbro, Texas, lists Anna Johnson and Ida Anderson as previous pastors.[24] Grace Skow Paulsen taught Bible on the first faculty of the Bible Institute in Rushford, Minnesota.

Early Evangelical Free Church of America records list the names of nearly fifty ordained women evangelists and pastors. In addition, women initially were ordained for overseas mission work until commissioning began to replace ordination for both male and female missionaries by 1930.[25] Della Olson, through her research in the original church documents, writes that "the participation of women in preaching and teaching had a high period just before and after the turn of the century.[26]

SUPPORT FOR WOMEN'S PUBLIC MINISTRY

Rationale supporting women's ministry came in many forms. The pragmatists declared that female evangelists served a good purpose in winning souls to Christ. The 1934 authorized history of the Swedish Evangelical Free Church of America, *Golden Jubilee,* clearly endorsed the early public ministry of women for this reason.

> Women workers were in great demand for a few years. It seemed at the time that this mode of work would become permanent. One or more churches even called women as pastors. Other churches desired and called none but women to conduct revival meetings and mission meetings. None but women were thought of or welcomed. However, this movement disappeared after a few years. It went as it came, with surprising suddenness. But it served its purpose. Many souls were brought to Christ through

the movement; and scattered groups of Christians here and there were greatly strengthened. It seems to have been one of God's emergency methods for that day. As such it had its place and its value. During the past twenty-five years few women workers have labored in our home fields, although a goodly number have gone out into the foreign fields.[27]

Rev. N. C. Carlson, Free Church evangelist, gave a similar rationale in his autobiography, *Life and Work in God's Vineyard*. Later, when faced with opposition to his support of female revivalists, he wrote that "it makes no difference who God uses in His rescue operation. . . . For me it is unimportant whether God uses a man or a woman, a Lutheran or a Methodist, Quaker or Baptist, a member of the Free Church or another denomination—just as long as people do not die in their sins."[28] While some were arguing about who had the right to preach, souls were being saved. As convincing practical evidence, God blessed the female revivalists to the salvation of many.

In addition to this pragmatic argument, early Free Church leaders believed that the Bible, properly interpreted, supports a public ministry for women. Franson's pamphlet provided the key document. The *Chicago-Bladet* reported views of Free Church leaders at an 1888 Bible Conference. Question number nineteen of the conference asked, "Does God's Word permit a woman to preach, participate in all Christian work and have the right to a voice in the affairs and decisions of the congregation?"[29] Of the twelve respondents reported, nine supported and three opposed women's ministry.

Princell, considered the founder of the Free Church by many, exegeted the Bible passages which seem to forbid women preaching. He concluded that Paul is not making a general rule for all women, but a specific command not to interrupt someone's speech to ask a question. The instructions were correct for the customs of the day, similar to statements about foot washing and braided hair. According to J. P. Falk, a woman leading a holy life has a right to preach. A. A. Anderson argued that if it was acceptable for women to preach in biblical days, it should be so in our time. J. F. Long used John 4 to justify women preachers. J. W. Stromberg argued that the first person to preach the resurrection of Christ was a woman. A. Nordin found Old and New Testament evidence supporting women preachers. Joseffson believed women could prophesy or preach. A. Peterson agreed, and A. Anderson desired the spirit of muteness to flee from both men and women. These nine Free Church pioneers rested their beliefs squarely on the Bible as they saw it.

Obviously, unanimous support for women's ministry never existed, and its opponents likewise had their rationale for women's subordinate role. At the 1888 conference, C. Sandquist stated that Jesus never sent out women to preach publicly or be missionaries. Ed Nelson wanted women silent in church "not that women lack ability but because of the fall she has been given a subordinate role."[30] A. P. Rosin believed that women were unable to keep things in perspective when permitted to speak in church and therefore should be silent. Even Princell, though supportive of women preachers, hedged a bit in limiting women from administrative positions of directorship.

In 1889, P. P. Waldenstrom visited the United States from Sweden and was distressed by the number of women preachers. He wrote an article called "Regarding Preaching by Women" and used a Pauline argument to advocate female silence in the church. His supporters in the Swedish Mission Covenant followed his lead and for several decades opposed women's ordination.[31] More structured ecclesiastically than the Free Church, the Covenant Church employed women as missionaries and parish workers but not as pastors. Ironically, the Evangelical Covenant Church formally began the ordination of women in 1976, whereas the Evangelical Free Church of America has yet to make women's ordination official policy.

The autobiography of Free Church evangelist Frank Lindberg revealed his opposition to women preachers. He first blamed Franson and his writings for starting the activity of women. Then August Davis, president of the Scandinavian Mission Society, procured clergy fares for women on railroads so the movement went forward dramatically, until "at least fifty were on the field."[32] Lindberg admitted the spirituality and talent of some women. But if God needed to use women to save souls, it signaled an indictment against the male preachers who had fallen so far away spiritually that God could no longer use them. Lindberg saw no support in the Bible or church history for women's public ministry; female fields of service were distinct from male spheres. In his final attack, he claimed that the ministry of men who support women will inevitably suffer.

OFFICIAL FREE CHURCH DOCUMENTS

The official documents of the Free Church in the early days generally supported women in public ministry and their ordination, though some statements were ambivalent. In 1894, Lindberg claimed that only men were eligible to be in a ministerial association. Yet the 1897 conference in Joliet included women in an association of preachers, evangelists, and church workers among Scandinavian Free Church believers in Illinois and surrounding states. The bylaws stated specifically that "the association has not considered itself justified in denying membership to women evangelists who have been called by a local congregation."[33] Once again, the Free Church congregational principle of the local autonomy of each church necessitated this openness to women. The bylaws stated that the names and addresses of women should be listed separately and designated whether ordained or licensed.

Free Church women trained for the ministry at Bible institutes. The 1897 conference extended an invitation "to warmhearted Christian young men and women with reasonably good gifts and ability to preach the Word of God" to become students.[34] The 1909 articles of incorporation of the Danish-Norwegian Bible Institute in Rushford, Minnesota, included this aim—"to fit young persons of either sex for general missionary and evangelical work."[35]

The committee that drafted the 1908 constitution for the incorporation of the Swedish Evangelical Free Church of America intended that men and women be equal in the church. They tried to avoid misunderstanding by always following "he" by "she" in parenthesis. For example, they wrote that "every preacher who becomes a member of this organization shall hold this membership so long as he (she) lives and works in full harmony with its principles."[36] Christina Carlson, Ellen Modin, Amanda Nelson, Carrie Norgaard, Hilma Severin, and Amanda Gustafson were among the earliest ordained Free Church women, some ordained at an annual conference meeting and some in a local church.

The rules for ordination approved in 1925 applied to both men and women. They state that "a candidate for ordination shall request a reference from the church of which he or she is a member."[37] In the 1933 Yearbook, the last one printed only in Swedish, Article XIV of the constitution dealt with "Ordination of Preachers and Missionaries" and included the phrase "*han eller hon*" ("he or she").

CHANGING FREE CHURCH PRACTICE

The ministries of Josephine Lind Princell, wife of Free Church founder J. G. Princell, again exemplify woman's freedom in the early Evangelical Free Church. A close friend of Frances Willard, she became superintendent of the Swedish department of the WCTU in 1894 when the Princells moved to Minneapolis to pastor the Swedish Temple. "Whenever her husband was absent, Josephine preached and held services in their church."[38] In addition to preaching, she also taught occasionally in Free Church schools.

Della Olson attributes the decline of the practice of ordaining women in the Free Church to three factors. First, the Free Church shifted its practice of ordaining male and female missionaries to commissioning them. Apparently, as the form of service rendered overseas enlarged to include workers trained in medicine, education, agriculture, construction, and mechanics as well as Bible teachers and evangelists, commissioning replaced ordination.

Second, the Free Church shifted its emphasis from home missions to overseas missionary service for women. Even Franson, while recruiting foreign missionary volunteers, found the greatest response among women. Possibly Free Church women began to find greater liberty to publicly minister overseas than at home as the denomination institutionalized.

Third, the ratio of women to men in Free Church ministry declined as men became more available as evangelists and pastors. The Free Church began as a lay movement. In the shift from mission societies led by the laity to organized churches with full-time salaried pastors, men consequently could enter a more secure ministry position and also support a family. Women in such a setting more likely served a local church as a parish visitor rather than as pastor.

With this documentation in view, are current Free Church opponents of women's ordination in keeping with the historical tradition of that church? No simplistic answers will do, given the complexity of the situation historically. The Free Church ancestors in Scandinavia, whether male or female, had no options, since ordination outside the state churches was forbidden. Then as immigrants came to America, licensing and ordination became necessary to perform many ministerial duties.

One thing is clear from the historical records—enough women in the Free Church movement at the turn of the century ministered as revivalistic preachers, evangelists, and pastors that their presence became an issue. Two of the key leaders of the movement—Franson and Princell—wrote in public support of women's preaching ministry. The Free Church ordained some women, and the Swedish Free Church constitution as late as 1934 explicitly provided for an ordained woman. Obviously, opposition to women's ordination in the EFCA is not at all in keeping with at least this segment of the historical tradition.

Of four institutions which mutually supported each other as well as women preachers at the turn of the century—D. L. Moody's Bible Institute in Chicago, A. B. Simpson's Christian and Missionary Alliance, Fredrik Franson's Free Church, and the Salvation Army—only the last today maintains its historic commitment to freedom for women in public ministry. One hundred years ago the Free Church recruited women with warm hearts and preaching abilities to train for ministry. Today the Free Church still seeks warm hearts but discourages female preaching.

That a church once so supportive of women preachers and pastors now might possibly exclude them is somewhat ironic. As with women at Moody Bible Institute or in Christian and Missionary Alliance churches, women in the Free Church could publicly minister in the 1880s in ways labeled unacceptable or unbiblical by the 1980s. Nevertheless, most Free Church pioneers were open to the ministry of women in any area. They let a congregation decide for itself whether to call and ordain a female or a male minister. Beyond that, they took a public stand for those convictions by recognizing a woman's ordination at the conference level.

6

EVANGELICAL FEMINIST BIBLICAL EXEGESIS

At the earliest women's rights conventions in mid-nineteenth century America, Oberlin graduate Antoinette Brown outspokenly advocated women's equality by answering scriptural attacks with her own biblical defense.[1] However, at conventions in 1852 and 1853, Brown's resolution that the Bible supports women's equality met defeat. Tired of theological debate, the women's rights movement shifted in a more strictly political direction. But rejection of Brown's proposal could not quell the dispute in the churches over whether the Scriptures constituted women's foe or friend in the fight for equality.

Rev. George Francis Wilkin wrote *The Prophesying of Women* in 1895 for two reasons—he found apparent discrepancies in Scripture on that subject, and Christians were divided according to the two kinds of texts.

> The old and conservative view, or that which favors silence, is backed by a greater array of critical scholarship. But there is a very strong and growing popular conviction favorable to the opposite opinion—that the Word of God gives women a right to speak in public.[2]

The early nineteenth-century abolitionists had supplied the turn-of-the-century proponents of women's public ministry with the first example of a form of feminist biblical exegesis. Abolitionist Sarah Grimké illustrates that first appeal to Scripture for women's right to speak in *Letters on the Equality of the Sexes* (1837). Suffrage advocate A. J. Grover optimistically predicted in 1870 that Bible interpreters would be compelled to change their conclusions on the woman question as they had been forced to do on the slavery issue. By the turn of the century, Evangelicals found these new liberating conclusions regarding women's role in some standard reference books as well as in more popular works.

To historically examine the Evangelical feminist biblical exegesis of passages concerning women's public church ministry, I have chosen ten representative documents written by Evangelicals committed to the authority of Scripture. By comparing and contrasting these publications, which spanned almost seventy years (1859–1926), we can begin to understand the type of literature published in Evangelical circles which helped open doors for women to minister. Thanks partly to the circulation of these books, pamphlets, and articles, Evangelical women who preached and pastored understood their public ministry to be consistent with their commitment to Scriptural authority.

Historical analysis of what Evangelicals and early Fundamentalists *said* about the Bible (their doctrine) must be balanced by examining what they *did* with particular texts (their practice). Belief in God's Word as authoritative and inspired characterized the Evangelical doctrine. Growing numbers of Evangelicals stressed concepts of inerrancy to counter Modernist attacks on Scripture. Using the tools of biblical higher criticism, Modernist interpreters chipped away at biblical authority and purported finding myths, legends, and historical errors in place of supernatural events.

One tradition of radical feminism used these exegetical methods in its support of women's equality in the church. For example, Elizabeth Cady Stanton's *Woman's Bible* avoided the problem of harmonizing biblical texts by simply eliminating any passages not in keeping with her feminist views. In contrast, each of the authors in this chapter rejected the

Modernist approach to Scripture and defended biblical authority.

What authors do *not* write about is sometimes as significant as what *is* addressed. No document in this chapter touched the theological issue of whether female ministers could appropriately represent Christ. Such debates took place within Roman Catholic or high church traditions where ministers functioned as priests in a sacramental role. Evangelicals, on the other hand, defined minister as pastor/preacher, not priest. The central debate around the turn of the century was whether women should preach. For some the argument shifted to ordination.

PROMISE OF THE FATHER

Phoebe Palmer (1807–74) wrote *Promise of the Father* in 1859 to defend the call and need of women to speak in public. Palmer's life symbolized the link between John Wesley's Evangelical revival in Britain and the American holiness movement. Wesley's preaching had convicted Palmer's father, who later emigrated to New York City. Converted as a child, Palmer joined a Methodist church and on 27 July 1837 experienced entire sanctification.

Phoebe Palmer attributed her usefulness in the church to two things—her transforming experience of holiness and the loving aid of her husband Walter. Though Palmer was never ordained or licensed to preach, Rev. J. L. Gilder appointed her to be a Methodist class leader, the first woman ever to hold that position in New York City.[3] Palmer quickly rose to prominence along with her husband as a lay revivalist on the Methodist camp meeting circuit. Her sermons, Bible studies, and writings spearheaded the mid-nineteenth century perfectionist revival and rallied Evangelicals in pursuit of holiness. However, Palmer at times caused division as a woman in a traditional male role.

Primarily an advocate of holiness, Palmer exhibited a bibliocentricity throughout her writings. She taught that the Holy Spirit witnesses primarily through Scripture in objective ways. Palmer's "God said it, I believe it" approach presented holiness through "naked faith" in the "naked Word of God."[4] As to exegesis, she claimed that "the scriptural way of arriving at right Bible conclusions is by comparing scripture with scripture."[5] Palmer insisted that literal renderings not oppose common sense. By severing a passage from its "explanatory connections," Protestants' traditional doctrine of women's silence constituted a relic of popery.

As sanctified women felt compelled by God to speak, they often found themselves forced to buck established church order. When Palmer and others stood up in defense of one church woman's right to speak, an elder in the congregation asked Palmer to put her views in writing and make them public. Palmer's response, *Promise of the Father,* used a variety of arguments in support of women's ministry. Palmer pointed to church history, especially to Wesley and the Methodists, who licensed women to preach. She blamed the "iron hand of Calvinism" for choking the voice of feminine witness for Christ.

Palmer's major thesis and starting point, however, was biblical. She asserted that the gift of the Spirit promised by the Father arrived at Pentecost and was received by both men and women; yet, she said, the church had neglected this specialty of the last days. Palmer explained 1 Corinthians 14:34 ("women should remain silent in the churches") in the context of disorderly debates—only disruptive women must not speak.

Palmer wanted women to preach because God called them and the results were beneficial—to the speaker, the church, and the world. Once sanctified, there is nothing a woman cannot do. "If man can enlighten and instruct, woman can do more; she can warm and melt in penitence the dead and frozen sensibility of the sinner."[6] Palmer complained that two-thirds of the talent of the church lay smothered. Though women must not usurp authority over men and teach dictatorially, they may speak under the influence of the Holy Spirit, as that assumes no personal authority over others. Palmer made the point repeatedly that it is not immodest or unfeminine for a woman to preach. She lambasted pious men who "imagine that they are doing God a service in putting a seal upon lips which God has commanded to speak."[7]

Palmer did not desire a change in the social or domestic relation between men and women. Her book reiterated the traditional view of male headship grounded in creation. In summary, the *Promise of the Father* by Palmer argued not for the right of woman's ordination, pastoral charge, or legislative administrative authority, but for the right of women to preach Christ when so led by the Holy Spirit.

Phoebe Palmer's ministry and writing directly affected the next three authors. Catherine Booth heard Palmer preach during a British evangelistic tour and received encouragement for her own public ministry. Frances Willard professed sanctification during a Palmer revival, while B. T. Roberts experienced conversion through her ministry.[8]

FEMALE MINISTRY

After hearing Palmer preach, Catherine Booth (1829–90) was appalled to read a local minister's violent attack (based on Scripture) on Palmer and other women preachers. Booth responded with a letter, expanded and published as the pamphlet *Female Ministry* in 1859 and lengthened in 1861 to *Female Teaching; or, the Rev. A. A. Rees versus Mrs. Palmer, being a reply to a pamphlet by the above gentlemen on the Sunderland Revival*. Inspired by Palmer's revival preaching, Booth overcame her own reluctance to speak, confessing before her husband William's congregation her own divine call to preach. Booth soon traveled all over England conducting revivals. The Booths broke from the Methodist church and established a London mission which later became the Salvation Army. The Army advocated equality of the sexes from its inception, admitting women to all ranks of leadership.

In her pamphlets, Booth broke no new hermeneutical ground in her scriptural support for women's ministry. Rather, she quoted from *Promise of the Father* and closely paralleled Palmer's reasoning and exegesis. For Booth, the Bible urges rather than restrains women gifted and called by the Spirit to

preach. She said that taking two passages (1 Tim. 2:12 and
1 Cor. 14:34) as the key to the rest of Scripture was backwards
and was motivated by a fear of the loss of male clerical
supremacy. Context combined with simple common sense
enables Scripture to be harmonized. According to her, only a
false translation of the Bible prohibits women's preaching.
Booth claimed that:

> If commentators had dealt with the Bible on other subjects as
> they have dealt with it on this, taking isolated passages, separated
> from their explanatory connections, and insisting on a literal
> interpretation of the words of our version, what errors and
> contradictions would have been forced upon the acceptance of
> the Church, and what terrible results would have accrued to the
> world.[9]

Booth followed Palmer's explanation of 1 Corinthians
14:34 and 1 Timothy 2:12 and stressed the wearing of veils, not
preaching, as the real issue in the Corinthian church. She took
1 Timothy 2:12 ("I do not permit a woman to teach or to have
authority over a man") a step further by saying that Paul was
simply prohibiting a woman's right to preach when one's own
husband imposes silence. Though advocating that woman's
subjection to her husband was grounded in Creation, Booth
concluded that "the ameliorating and exalting provisions of
Christianity all but restore her to her original position."[10] The
law of love in marriage extracts the sting of the curse recorded
in Genesis 3.

Echoing Palmer, Booth judged a woman's divine call to
preach according to Jesus' standard—her fruit. The multitudes
converted and sanctified through women's preaching confirmed
a gifted woman's right and indeed obligation to preach. Booth
blamed opposition to woman's preaching for the church's
failure to spread the gospel to the countless millions without
Christ. Optimistically, Booth predicted that, in time, women
would be allowed to speak freely—that change brought about
by common sense, public opinion, and the blessed results of
female preaching.

WOMAN IN THE PULPIT

Methodist Frances Willard (1839–98) not only heard the Palmers preach but in 1865 experienced sanctification under their ministry. Born into an abolitionist home, Willard continued the family tradition of Evangelical social action as she founded the Women's Christian Temperance Union.[11] Willard attributed her thoughts on women to two coeducational schools—Oberlin College in Ohio and Northwestern University (including Garrett Biblical Institute) in Evanston, Illinois. After holding positions as a teacher and college president, Willard combined suffrage advocacy with her national temperance work. Though temporarily ministering as an evangelist with revivalist D. L. Moody, Willard's first love was to enter a Methodist pastorate.

Though never ordained herself, Willard wrote *Woman in the Pulpit* in 1888 to defend women's ordination. It was published in the midst of Methodist controversy.[12] The 1880 General Conference had denied women's ordination, withdrew preaching licenses from those women previously accredited, and prohibited Willard from speaking to the assembled delegates. In 1888 Willard attended the General Conference as one of the first five duly elected female local lay delegates. But after vicious debate, the women were denied seats. Willard later threatened to withdraw from the denomination.

In quoting both Palmer and Booth, Willard displayed her familiarity and reliance on their writings. Yet *Woman in the Pulpit,* written almost thirty years later, illumines new issues beginning to surface and reflects a shift of emphasis. First, Willard exposed in-depth the inadequate biblical exegesis of opponents of women's public ministry. Second, she strongly advocated women's ordination. Third, she rejected the concept of the wife's subordination in marriage implicit in both Palmer and Booth. Finally, Willard criticized noninclusive language, complaining that preachers rarely refer to the women of their audiences.

Willard defined exegesis as scientific interpretation of the Bible—a human process which increases in accuracy as the

gospel more deeply permeates the world. Willard contrasted
two extremes—absolute fidelity to literal exegesis (i.e., women
cannot sing in church; Paul condones slavery) and "playing fast
and loose" according to personal opinion (i.e., women can wear
gold or pearls). She identified her own approach with the
"progressive school of exegesis." This method of harmonizing
texts compared Scripture to Scripture and incorporated common sense. Willard herself chartered seemingly restrictive
Pauline passages side by side with liberating ones. She found
close to forty biblical texts in support of women's public
ministry and only two in opposition (1 Cor. 14:34 and 1 Tim.
2:12)—"and there not really so when rightly understood."[13]

In chapter 7 of Willard's book Professor Townsend
reiterated Willard's approach to exegesis. He advocated common sense when an absolutely literal interpretation of one text
forces another to contradict. He concluded that "a practice
prohibited in one sentence and regulated in another [i.e.,
women's prophesying], by the same author [Paul], shows either
variability in opinion, or else an intended limitation in the
original prohibition."[14] In *Woman in the Pulpit*, Willard chose
the second option. The first view—that Paul's teaching on
women entailed just his fallible personal opinion—gained
support among many outside the Evangelical camp.

Explaining specific texts, Willard paralleled Palmer and
Booth as to 1 Corinthians 14:34. Paul's prohibition of babbling, interrupting, immoral, uneducated first-century women
from speaking did not affect devout, intelligent American
churchwomen. In fact, women's moral superiority and holiness
especially authorized them for ministry. While Palmer and
Booth stressed the lay preacher's rights, Willard focused on
ordained women in the pulpit. She also blamed the theory of
women's subordination on the one-sided male interpretation of
the Bible. In Genesis 3:16 ("he will rule over you"), God
declared male dominance over women but never approved that
sinful relationship.[15] Willard urged women to enroll in theological seminaries so that women scholars could share in both
translating and interpreting the Scriptures. Otherwise, male bias
would continue to keep women from the pulpit.

ORDAINING WOMEN

B. T. Roberts fought for women's ordination within the Free Methodist denomination as Willard had in the Methodist Episcopal Church. Converted under Palmer's ministry, Roberts split from the Methodist church in part over the issues of slavery and holiness, founding the Free Methodists. He argued for women's ordination at church councils in the 1860s, presenting a resolution to the 1890 General Conference which failed. In this context, Roberts wrote *Ordaining Women* in 1891, basing his arguments primarily on Scripture.

Roberts charged that Bible-based objections to women's equality with men rest on a wrong translation of some passages and a misinterpretation of others. He explained that:

> The present position of the churches is not only wrong, but inconsistent. They concede to women too much, if Paul's words restricting her are taken literally; they concede too little, if these words are to be understood to harmonize with the rest of the Bible.[16]

Roberts insisted on the place of reason (i.e., Willard's common sense) for interpreting passages within their context.

More than the previous authors, Roberts emphasized the parallels between slavery and the women's issue. Staunch defenders of slavery considered that institution God-ordained. Did not biblical examples of slaves and Paul's teachings constitute a universal, permanent principle of slave subordination? Likewise, ardent advocates of women's subordination interpreted Paul's instructions on women as equally permanent and universal. Roberts argued that just as opponents of abolition who appealed to the Bible were so greatly mistaken on slavery, so too were the opponents of women's ordination.

Like Willard, Roberts pushed for women's ordination, the church's recognition of one's authority to preach and gift of ministry. "If she is called of God to this work, and this is evident to the church, then may the church separate her to this work by ordination."[17] Since authority to govern resides in the church, a woman does not usurp authority when given that right at ordination. To permit women to preach but forbid ordination, Roberts argued, contradicts the Great Commission, which directs those who evangelize others to baptize their converts. Therefore, he advocated the ordination of female revivalists as well as pastors.

To support his case, Roberts answered Old Testament and New Testament objections. The joint dominion given both sexes in pre-Fall Genesis was restored by Christ's redemption. Taking Galatians 3:28 ("There is neither . . . male nor female, for you are all one in Christ Jesus") as his key text, Roberts found all other passages dealing with women harmonized. In 1 Corinthians 14:34 and 1 Timothy 2:12, Paul directed his local, temporary prohibition to women abusing their liberty. Roberts insisted that female deacons in the Bible constituted a clerical order rather than a subordinate lay position. He joined Willard in support of egalitarian marriage and in opposition to subordination of the wife based on Genesis.

Roberts held that since women constituted two-thirds of all Protestants, barring them from spreading the gospel according to their ability had resulted in an incompletely evangelized world. Appealing to church history, Roberts contrasted the poor, persecuted early church, which allowed women to minister, with later wealthy, popular Christianity, where women were set aside. Roberts's Free Methodist tradition of identification with the poor (i.e., they replaced "pew rental" with "free pews," accessible to all classes) and persecuted (i.e., slaves) likewise fit his liberating attitude toward women.

Palmer, Booth, Willard, and Roberts each represent Methodist-related biblical exegesis from an Evangelical feminist viewpoint. Distinctive themes emerge from an analysis of their writings. To start, each author's view of Scripture contributed to feminist conclusions. Accepting the Bible as true and without contradiction, these Methodists saw exegesis partly as the task of harmonizing seemingly contradictory passages. After tracing passages about women through the Bible, they concluded that the vast majority, properly translated (without male bias) and seen in context, support women's ministry. Bible verses that seem to contradict actually harmonize, since so-called prohibitions were really only intended to silence disruptive women.

Not only did Scripture harmonize, but it also fit common sense. This principle of inherent logic was applied to women's roles. Does it make sense for the Bible to prohibit women preachers when ministry needs are so great, and educated, gifted women are skilled public speakers? How illogical to bar women from American pulpits yet send them abroad to enter foreign pulpits.

Though agreed on these two principles of Bible interpretation, the four authors reveal a distinct development of doctrine. In three areas, Willard and Roberts went beyond Palmer and Booth. First, Willard and Roberts pressed for egalitarian marriage, not the wifely submission taught by Palmer and Booth. Using the same principles—common sense and lack of contradictions—male rule in marriage was neither logical nor consistent. It came as a result of sin and not from God. Common sense said that if modern women are achieving equality in other realms, why not also in the home?

Willard and Roberts also outspokenly advocated women's ordination, whereas Palmer pushed mainly for lay women's right to preach. This difference paralleled that regarding marriage. Palmer rejected female rule both in the home and in the church. Willard and Roberts's push for ordination went beyond just the right to preach, as ordination bestowed authority to govern.

Roberts's book forcefully set forth a further shift by drawing parallels between slaves and women. Roberts could not separate the biblical interpretation of the one from the other. If Paul actually commanded female subjection, he also demanded that slaves remain in bondage. But if the true gospel message brings release to the enslaved, it carries freedom to women as well.

THE MINISTRY OF WOMEN

During the same decade that Roberts wrote *Ordaining Women,* A. J. Gordon, a Baptist, also wrestled with the issue of women's ministry. Gordon, who opened his own Clarendon Street Church pulpit to women, attended a convention where conservatives forbade a female missionary from speaking. Gordon, well aware that women on the foreign field did much more in the way of public ministry than give simple missionary talks, responded by writing "The Ministry of Women" in 1894. Given two options—either justify women's ministry by Scripture or modify their work to harmonize with the Bible— Gordon proceeded to scripturally vindicate the preaching of female missionaries.

Close colleague A. T. Pierson wrote of Gordon's approach to Scripture.

> Dr. Gordon was not among those who doubt either the inspiration or infallibility of the divine Word. He believed that it was essentially inerrant. When he found difficulties or discrepancies, instead of distrusting the accuracy of the divine oracles, he rather suspected the accuracy of his own understanding.[18]

Criticized by some Baptist contemporaries for his premillennial doctrine, Gordon defended his eschatology as true to the plenary inspiration of Scripture.[19] Through *The Watchword,* Gordon as editor attacked higher criticism and the new theology. Approach the Bible with the personal conviction that Scripture is infallible, he advised, and contradictions disappear. Gordon tempered the Princeton view of Scripture by his concern for revival and missions, injecting a subjective quality minimized by the Princeton school.[20]

Gordon's first principle of exegesis was to consider Scripture texts in their canonical order (i.e., start with Genesis, not 1 Timothy!).[21] He emphasized the importance of context— consider a text in the light of the entire biblical teaching, prophecy, cultural practice, and contemporary history to find its true meaning. The Holy Spirit in Paul cannot contradict the Spirit in the prophets. Gordon stressed

> . . . the value of experience as an interpreter of Scripture. The final exegesis is not always to be found in the lexicon and grammar. The Spirit is in the Word; and the Spirit is also in the Church. . . . To follow the voice of the Church apart from that of the written Word had never proved safe; but, on the other hand, it may be that we need to be admonished not to ignore the

teaching of the deepest spiritual life of the Church in forming our conclusions concerning the meaning of Scripture.[22]

Gordon carefully critiqued the biases of biblical translators and commentators influenced by Paul's "supposed law of silence for women."

Gordon asserted that Joel's prophecy ("I will pour out my Spirit on all people. Your sons and daughters will prophesy. . . ." [2:28]), repeated by Peter in Acts ("This is what was spoken by the prophet Joel. . . ." [2:16]), was fulfilled at Pentecost and brought equal privileges to women. In the present dispensation of the Spirit, female prophecy is not the exception but the rule. Interestingly, Gordon made no appeal to the Old Testament prophetesses, who represented exceptional cases in the old dispensation. He interpreted 1 Corinthians 14:34 in the tradition of Palmer—Paul prohibits disorder and interrupting questions. Clearly no Scripture forbids women's prayer and prophecy in public church assemblies.

Gordon admitted increased difficulty in exegeting 1 Timothy 2:12. In the context of 2:9–10, Paul exhorts *how* women should adorn themselves while praying publicly. But can a woman teach and govern? Gordon presented two possibilities. First, 1 Timothy 2:12 refers to married women in the private sphere, i.e., a submissive wife must not authoritatively teach her husband. Second, it forbids women's ordination and prohibits a female elder or pastor from teaching publicly or governing. Gordon, unsure as to the most accurate exegesis, suggested that if God limited women's teaching or governing, God grounded that on natural impediment and not on lack of spiritual gifts. Either way, public prayer and prophecy (fervid exhortation drawn from Scripture and experience) imply no exercise of authority and therefore are undebatable issues.

Gordon linked every great spiritual revival in church history with women's public ministry. Observing God's obvious blessing of women preachers, "many thoughtful men have been led to examine the Word of God anew, to learn if it really be so that the Scriptures silence the testimony which the Spirit so signally blesses."[23] Just as God revealed to Peter in a vision the inclusion of Gentiles in the church, God provided a present sign of the times through the vision of missionary women preaching in heathen lands, to convince this generation that "there can be no male or female."[24]

PROPHESYING DAUGHTERS

Fredrik Franson shared premillennial, revival, and missions concerns similar to Gordon. Like D. L. Moody, Franson included women on his evangelistic team and sent out women preachers. In 1889 Franson and his evangelistic team led revivals in Germany, held evangelist courses in Berlin, and founded the German Alliance Mission. In response to local criticism of his advocacy of female evangelists, he wrote "Prophesying Daughters." Subtitled "A few words concerning women's position in regard to evangelization," the article opened with quotations of Joel 2:28–29 and Acts 2:15–18. Franson tied women's evangelization to Christ's second coming, an event delayed until the "full count" of God's bride was complete. In a world crying for more workers to enter newly accessible missionary fields and reach the millions of lost heathen, why should women, who constitute two-thirds of all believers, be prohibited from preaching?

Faced with that soul-searching question, Franson proceeded to explore biblical passages referring to women's position. He concluded that Scripture overwhelmingly supports women's public evangelization and found it remarkable that two passages (1 Tim. 2:12 and 1 Cor. 14:34) could be made to contradict the rest. He labelled as heretics those who grounded a doctrine on one or two passages in the Bible, without reading the references in their context.[25]

Franson began his exegesis in Genesis 3, grounding female assistance in spiritual matters in creation. Jesus illustrated the importance of women evangelists in his own ministry. Like Gordon, Franson refuted the objection that women's extraordinary ministry seen at Pentecost ceased with the end of the apostolic age. Explaining 1 Corinthians 14:34, Franson described a church meeting where believers discuss differences of opinion. Paul in that context prohibits married women with believing husbands from asking inappropriate questions. If a wife's view opposed her husband's, that could reveal lack of submission. Franson followed Palmer, Booth, and Gordon in their view of the husband's headship and wife's submission.

Franson interpreted 1 Timothy 2:12 in a unique way. Since Paul based his prohibition of women teachers on natural creation, only in the natural, earthly, family relationships are women limited. The Bible bases women's freedom to teach in spiritual matters in the new creation, into which some wives enter first before their unbelieving husbands. Franson then vacillated; he hypothesized that women may be forbidden to teach. But the church must never silence women gifted as apostles (missionaries), prophets, evangelists, shepherds, or miracle workers. Franson never mentioned ordination, though he did outspokenly oppose the concept of strictly women's meetings.

In his conclusion, Franson warned missionary women on furlough against publicly defending women's preaching. Still uncertain what the teaching prohibition really meant, Franson feared the women might appear as teachers concerning questions of dispute.

> It is enough that they themselves have assurance in their own hearts of the Word of God, that they have the right to evangelize and don't need much discussion of the subject. If mission houses or churches are for the time being closed to them, they should take that from God, for it will help them to come to those places where the needs are the greatest.[26]

Although Gordon wrote from a Baptist perspective and Franson from a Swedish Free Church context, both shared such similar concerns that we can appropriately evaluate them together. As for hermeneutics, both stressed the principles of harmonization and common sense. Gordon in particular spoke of an inerrant Bible. With his constant emphasis on the Holy Spirit, Gordon taught that not only must Scripture harmonize with Scripture, but God's Word must jell with God's Holy Spirit. The Bible cannot forbid what the Spirit blesses, he argued. The positive results evident from women's ministry must correlate with biblical interpretation.

Gordon and Franson argued from a perspective not found among the Methodist authors. As premillennial dispensationalists, they interpreted women in the pulpit as an essential sign of the end times—not an exception but a rule of the present dispensation. World evangelization, a pivotal prerequisite for the premillennial return of Christ, demanded the utilization of female preachers.

GOD'S WORD TO WOMEN

Like hundreds of other Evangelical women in turn-of-the-century America, Methodist medical doctor and reformer Katharine Bushnell (1856–1946) sensed God's call to China as a missionary. Born in Illinois, Bushnell graduated from Northwestern University in Evanston and earned her M.D. at Chicago Medical College. In 1885 she began working in the social purity department of the Women's Christian Temperance Union. An activist, Bushnell started the Anchorage Mission in Chicago for abandoned women. She exposed white slavery in Wisconsin lumber camps as well as governmental control of prostitution in India.

When Bushnell sensed the Spirit's urge to preach abroad, she promised obedience on one condition: that God prove to her that Paul did not forbid women preaching. She sought the assurance that the Spirit's call was consistent with Scripture. A scholar of both Hebrew and Greek, Bushnell studied the Bible and commentaries in depth. After years of research including work in British libraries, Bushnell recorded her results in a Bible correspondence course for women. She sought to strengthen other Christian women called to witness for Christ by assuring them that the Word of God harmonized with the call of God.

Urged to put her mimeographed lessons together in print, Bushnell in 1919 published in book form *God's Word to Women—One Hundred Bible Studies on Woman's Place in the Divine Economy*.[27] Bushnell's book emphasized the inconsistencies between what theologians thought Paul taught regarding women and what close examination of the original Hebrew and Greek actually revealed.

Bushnell regarded Scripture as God's infallible Word, rejecting higher critical theories such as the documentary hypothesis in Genesis. Holding a high view of the Bible, Bushnell found no contradictions between science and rightly translated Scripture.

> While we in no wise question the authority and inviolability of the original text of the Bible, we hold that the present English translation of Genesis 3:16 . . . is erroneous, and *proved incorrect* by the ancient versions. Therefore the interpretation . . . based on the erroneous translation, is incorrect.[28]

The church must either change its interpretation of Paul or its present treatment of women, otherwise it acts inconsistently and defiles biblical authority. Bushnell claimed that Christian women's equal status in the church changed only as Jewish rabbinical teaching began to influence Bible translation.

Bushnell considered the original text and not English versions of the Bible inspired, infallible, and inviolable. Since Jewish rabbis who held contempt for women added uninspired vowel points to the Hebrew texts centuries after the original autographs, modern exegetes can freely amend the scribal mistakes. Yet Bushnell decried the destructive Old Testament textual critics who went beyond vowel points to manipulate inspired consonants. She devoted three chapters to explaining how "Sex Bias Influences Translators"; until women trained in the original languages begin to translate, she maintained, the world, church, and women would all suffer. In Lesson 46 Bushnell described "Needless Apologies for Paul's Logic." She critiqued expositors who support women's ministry appealing to Paul's faulty rabbinical logic, thereby attacking the Bible's inspiration.

For Bushnell, spiritual experience combined with Hebrew and Greek scholarship revealed Scripture's true meaning. She bowed to no authority (whether Talmudic or Christian) as final but the Bible, illumined by the Spirit. Interpret the Bible by what the Bible says, she urged, not by what people say. Significantly, Bushnell perceived the fundamentals of the Christian faith at stake in the issue. As she watched the church offer no defense to critics who attacked the entire Bible viciously and successfully on the "woman question," Bushnell herself took on the challenge.

Three characteristics of *God's Word to Women* immediately distinguish it from the previous writings. First, Bushnell extensively examined women's role in marriage as well as in church ministry. Second, she exegeted Old Testament passages in depth, devoting the first twenty lessons to explore Genesis 1–3. Third, Bushnell utilized Hebrew and Greek in such a way that her book became more than a popular exposition easily understood by church laity.

According to Bushnell, Genesis 1–3 pictured the woman as equally responsible to rule the earth, yet equally guilty in sin. Bushnell's translation of Genesis 3:16—"thou art turning away to thy husband, and he will rule over thee"—stood central to her argument. She charged that Genesis 3:16, the most serious mistranslation in the English Bible, lay at the root of the misinterpretation of Paul's words. God predicted, rather than commanded, that as Eve sinfully turned from God to her husband, he would consequently rule over her.

Like Willard and Roberts, Bushnell defended egalitarian marriage with Scripture. Since Christ, the woman's coming Seed, would mean Satan's doom, Satan would try to hamper the woman through painful childbirth and her husband's rule. Bushnell described the ordinary rabbinic and Christian view— that God's curse on woman demands male rule—as cruel, immoral, and contrary to the plain teachings of Scripture.

According to Bushnell, since no punctuation marks were used in the Greek text, translators have had to insert them, often in such a way that Paul's teaching is entirely obscured. For example, she summarized four current attempts to harmonize 1 Corinthians 11:5 ("every woman who prays or prophesies") with 1 Corinthians 14:34: (1) Paul's command to silence had only local Corinthian application; (2) Paul changed his mind; (3) Paul forbade babbling, not prophesying; (4) Paul prohibited asking questions.

Translating the passage with different punctuation, Bushnell rejected each of these hypotheses, concluding that Paul in 1 Corinthians 14:34–35 gave not his own view, but quoted the false Judaizer position. Priscilla's arrival at Corinth provided the Judaizers with an occasion to attack women's public prophecy, which Jewish oral law prohibited.

In other circumstances, Paul allowed women to teach. He instructed Timothy that women who come to learn should be taught, but in quietness due to the danger of Nero's persecution.

Bushnell was the only author to deal directly with the issue that Paul in 1 Timothy 2:13–14 seems to ground his prohibition of female ecclesiastical authority in creation. How could such a theologically based prohibition be only local and temporary? Bushnell explained that Adam, developed in the natural world first, had more maturity than Eve. Being younger left inexperienced Eve more vulnerable to deception.

In her view, Paul does not argue in 1 Timothy 2 that a willful sinner (Adam) makes a better leader than a deceived person (Eve). Rather, he teaches that in times of trial (so severe under Nero that women feared rape) "an inexperienced and immature person should not be put at the rudder of a ship." Paul's phrase "then Eve" reflects optimistically that women, under the influence of Christianity, will reach full social development along with men.

Bushnell based her theology of women on Christ's atonement, not on the Fall.

> Expositors of the Bible will never be able to understand, or to set forth a clear, consistent, correct interpretation of the Word of God as regards women until they abandon, once for all, the attempt to found the . . . status of Christian woman on the Fall, and found it, as they do man's . . . status, on the atonement of Jesus Christ.[29]

Not only *may* woman preach, she *must* preach and teach.

> When the world is mangled and bleeding to death, starving and rotting in social corruption, while male ministers of the gospel are as frequently discrediting Christ, in their pulpits, as honoring

> Him, as frequently attacking the Bible as explaining it, —in such
> an age as this is it pertinent to ask the question whether women
> have any right to keep silent?[30]

Echoing Gordon, Bushnell exposed the inconsistency of
premillennial advocates who in effect delay Christ's return by
hindering women's freedom to evangelize. Women who choose
to publicly minister hasten the day of Christ's second coming.
Bushnell charged that churches which silence women in effect
silence the Holy Spirit.

THE MAGNA CHARTA OF WOMAN

Two problems hindered widespread circulation of Bushnell's
God's Word to Women: first, Bushnell's in-depth, technical
scholarship, which went over the heads of many untrained
laypeople; and second, the book's prohibitive cost. Consequently, Jessie Penn-Lewis sent out Bushnell's message in
simpler form as *The Magna Charta of Woman,* published in 1919
with Bushnell's permission.[31]

Penn-Lewis (1861–1927) was born in South Wales and
nurtured in Calvinistic Methodism. Converted as a teenager
and sanctified at age thirty-one, she traveled throughout the
United States, Canada, India, Russia, and Scandinavia as a Bible
teacher. She founded *The Overcomer,* a journal devoted to the
pursuit of the deeper Christian life. Penn-Lewis's Evangelical
reputation is apparent as she contributed an article on Satan to
The Fundamentals publication.

In addition to summarizing Bushnell's research, Penn-
Lewis contributed certain of her own concepts. She clearly
emphasized the valuable role of scholarship in her introduction.

> It is not enough for a woman to say "I must leave such matters to
> better scholars than I; but in the meantime I will teach or preach,
> because I know the Spirit prompts me to do so." [But] a woman
> who is called to preach is likewise called to an understanding of
> the Word which will agree with that inward voice.[32]

She interpreted woman's emancipation as one of the great
"epoch-making results of the Great War." The subsequent

challenge to the Bible, i.e., that Scriptures are out of date in guiding modern women, touched the deep issue of biblical authority.

In her first three chapters, Penn-Lewis simplified Bushnell's teaching on the 1 Corinthians 11, 1 Corinthians 14, and 1 Timothy 2 passages. Chapter 4 explained Genesis 3:16, chapter 5 examined misunderstood words (subjection, headship, deacon), and chapter 6 recounted women's status through history. Penn-Lewis chose 1 Timothy 2:15 ("women will be kept safe through childbirth") as her magna charta of womanhood and the complement to the Genesis 3:15 promise ("he will crush your head"). With the woman thoroughly deceived and victimized in Eden, God provided woman's salvation through the childbearing of Christ. Christ's virgin birth, culminating at Calvary and crushing Satan's head, constitutes the great event of the world for women.

THE BIBLE STATUS OF WOMAN

Lee Anna Starr frequently quoted Bushnell's work in her own book *The Bible Status of Woman* published in 1926.[33] Ordained by the Methodist Protestant Church, the same denomination to ordain Dr. Anna Howard Shaw in 1880, Dr. Starr ministered as a local pastor and temperance leader. Skilled in both Hebrew and Greek, Starr comprehensively examined the Scriptures to determine women's status within marriage as well as in the church. Starr wrote convinced that "the prejudice of the past has obscured the teaching of God's Word concerning the status of women and her rightful place in the divine plan."[34]

Bushnell and Starr, with their emphasis on the family *and* the pulpit, contrast with the others who focused primarily on women's preaching and ordination. Gordon, for example, called Joel's prophecy realized at Pentecost the magna charta of the Christian church. "Your daughters shall prophesy" crystallized the biblical argument for proponents of women's preaching. Starr, however, chose 1 Timothy 2:15 as her women's emancipation proclamation, Penn-Lewis's magna charta verse. These authors, in addressing the broader questions of women's status in Scripture, focused their attention on biblical doctrines of the Creation, Fall, and redemption.

Starr found the source of women's second-rate status in mistranslations, misinterpretations, and misapplications of the Bible, not in Scripture itself. "Not the Bible, but religious hierarchs, have effected the subordination of women."[35] Starr refused to apologize for biblical passages on women or to reject them as outmoded. She opposed interpreters who reconciled Paul by attributing his views to his early rabbinic teaching.

Starr rejected modern destructive criticism and its view that certain passages were interpolations. She reasoned that "if one redactor may slash the Sacred Text because it perplexes him, others may do likewise. The result would be a mutilated Bible."[36] Since the Holy Spirit cannot contradict himself, she explained, when two passages conflict, one must be uninspired or misinterpreted.

In chapter 14, Starr summarized her two basic exegetical rules. First, Paul must harmonize with Christ and the prophets; therefore, his two problem passages (1 Cor. 14:34 and 1 Tim. 2:12) must accord with other Scriptures. Otherwise, inherent biblical contradictions invalidate the theory of inspiration. Second, Paul must himself be consistent in those passages with his other writings and his own church practice.[37]

In the first half of her book, Starr surveyed the Old Testament teaching on women and reached conclusions similar to Bushnell's. In discussing the New Testament, Starr quoted Gordon frequently. Controversy over women's position in the church centered on one main point—whether Paul's instructions were local or general in application. Starr classified instructions regarding women along with foot washing, church trials, and the holy kiss—as local, temporary customs.

In contrast to Bushnell, Starr exegeted 1 Corinthians 14:34 as Paul's view, not the Judaizers' position. In dealing with a lack of orderly worship, Paul silences only disturbances.

Starr presented two interpretations of 1 Timothy 2:12. First, a wife must not publicly teach her husband in a church assembly, since that was considered a cultural outrage in that era. Second, since the New Testament differentiates between preaching and teaching, Paul allows preaching but forbids teaching. Teaching in the Jewish tradition entailed controversy, disputative questions and answers, and authoritative decisions. Women consequently were not to teach men in that Jewish manner. After examining the two options, Starr found the first better supported. She held that 1 Timothy 2:12 illustrated Paul's principle that Christians should obey Roman laws and conform to customs when not in conflict with conscience. To keep from offending unbelievers, Paul prohibited wives from teaching husbands as a matter of expediency.

The books by Bushnell, Penn-Lewis, and Starr shared some common denominators. Written by Methodists, each appeared after World War I and was contemporaneous with the fierce Fundamentalist controversy. Each author self-consciously and specifically decried modern destructive criticism of the Bible. Dismayed that "modern" women might reject Christianity as a whole because of supposed biblical teachings on women's subordination, Bushnell and Starr sought to correct that misunderstanding in an intellectually viable way.

Earlier works, intended for a lay church audience, had appealed consistently to common sense. Bushnell and Starr, on the other hand, targeted a more educated readership, contending that technical Greek and Hebrew scholarship was essential for proper interpretation. This reflects a new turn in the theological debate over women's roles.

DOES THE BIBLE FORBID WOMEN TO PREACH AND PRAY IN PUBLIC?

In the same year that Starr published *The Bible Status of Woman,* John Roach Straton wrote his pamphlet *Does the Bible Forbid Women to Preach and Pray in Public?*[38] We conclude our analysis of feminist exegesis with Straton, for he more than any other author in this chapter espoused militant Fundamentalism. His article proves conclusively that a commitment to both biblical inerrancy and women's public church ministry were feasible.

Trained at a Southern Baptist seminary, Straton began his pastorate at Calvary Baptist Church of New York City in 1918.

He outspokenly represented the Fundamentalist camp in the Northern Baptist Convention. Straton assailed higher criticism from the pulpit and press, in 1922 founding the Fundamentalist League of Greater New York and Vicinity for Ministers and Laymen. From 1924 to 1925 he served on the executive committee of the Fundamentalist Baptist Bible Union, and he edited *The Fundamentalist* magazine until 1926.[39] Along with William Bell Riley, Straton personified the Baptist Fundamentalist wing of Evangelicalism.

Straton advocated suffrage for women as they, morally purer than men, could help improve politics.[40] Controversy broke out when Straton welcomed evangelist and extemporaneous Bible teacher Uldine Utley to preach in his pulpit.[41] Straton had heard Utley preach at a Florida Bible conference and invited her to Calvary to lead a five-week revival in the autumn of 1926.

Some conservatives, especially Southern Baptists, were unhappy with Straton's stance. His critics charged that allowing a female to preach constituted a denial of biblical authority and a "flagrant violation of the clear teaching of the Scriptures." Straton wrote his pamphlet to refute that criticism. He also specifically urged support for Utley's upcoming revival at Calvary so that the gospel might reach the largest number of people possible. Apparently the message got out—Utley's revival ended with 10,000 at Madison Square Garden.

Straton's exegetical principles mirrored those of previous authors. The interpreter must start with the whole trend of Scripture to get the big picture before exegeting one or two isolated verses. Also, texts must be examined in their historical, social context. Since the Bible's general teaching presents women's right to publicly preach and pray, the few texts which seem to contradict must teach otherwise. The Holy Spirit cannot direct women to prophesy in one place, then forbid that action in another. Also, Paul's actions in regard to women's public ministry must coincide with his inspired writings.

Using these interpretive principles, Straton grounded his support of women's preaching squarely on the doctrine of the Holy Spirit. He viewed Joel 2 and Acts 2 as "absolutely determinative in connection with the question of women speaking in public." Who dare forbid a woman from prophesying, Straton argued, when Joel predicted it, Peter under inspiration declared it fulfilled, and she, Spirit-filled, is commanded by God to prophesy?

As to specific texts, Galatians 3:28 declared the abolition of sex distinctions for the born-again. Straton applied 1 Corinthians 14:34 locally, Paul regulating women's speaking in view of the shameful, degenerate Corinthian setting. The type of teaching forbidden in 1 Timothy 2:12 was that which usurped authority. In a unique interpretation, Straton suggested that Paul commanded only the unregenerate women to keep silent in the assembly whereas the converted, whether female or male, may freely teach and preach. Straton also taught the necessary headship of men, based on Genesis. Remaining uncommitted in his personal view on ordination, Straton remarked that some women preachers decline ordination because of their headship concept.

Straton concluded his pamphlet with the argument from experience. No one, he asserted, can hear Uldine Utley preach and deny she is Spirit-led. In his final pages, Straton personally defended Utley's character and ministry. Through this pamphlet and other sermons, articles, and letters, Straton attempted to get Utley's preaching accepted elsewhere at real cost to himself.

CONCLUSIONS

In 1895, Dr. T. T. Easton, a Southern Baptist, in "The Bible on Woman's Public Speaking," argued mistakenly that not *one* New Testament commentator favored women's speaking. Apparently Easton had insulated himself from commentators like Dr. Adam Clarke, quoted extensively by the seven authors in the Methodist tradition.[42] Penn-Lewis, for instance, wrote, "Let us note that not *all* expositors have been blinded. Dr. Adam Clarke writes. . . ."[43]

Irish biblical scholar Adam Clarke (1760–1832) was converted under Methodist preaching and wrote John Wesley to explain his 1782 sanctification experience. Wesley commissioned him as an itinerant preacher. Clarke published a six-volume Bible commentary based on his own translation of the entire Old and New Testaments.

Clarke's comments and critical notes reflected the Spirit-liberating approach to women's public ministry. His note on 1 Corinthians 11:5 linked women's prophecy and teaching to Joel's prediction mentioned by Peter in Acts. The silence of 1 Corinthians 14:34 referred to the Jewish law forbidding women from teaching or asking questions in the assembly. "This was their condition till the time of the Gospel, when, according to the prediction of Joel, the Spirit of God was to be poured out on the women as well as the men, that they might prophesy, i.e. teach."[44] Though maintaining the traditional view of the wife's subordination in marriage, Clarke emphasized that by no means should a woman gifted and enabled by God to teach disobey and remain silent.

Not only did the ten authors mentioned in this chapter generally find commentators to quote, but they frequently made reference to each other's writing or ministry. Booth and Willard both quoted Palmer, while Willard and Penn-Lewis both quoted Booth. Gordon argued from the example of the Salvation Army, whereas Roberts lifted up Willard's ministry as support for his thesis. Bushnell and Starr utilized Gordon's work, while Penn-Lewis and Starr extensively quoted Bushnell. All this is to say that rich literature circulated at the turn of the century, written from an Evangelical perspective (with its high view of Scripture), that exegeted texts and found the Bible to support, rather than forbid, women's public ministry.

To illustrate this phenomenon, I found two old copies of Starr's *Bible Status of Woman* currently in the stacks at the library of Moody Bible Institute. Interestingly, Fleming H. Revell—the Evangelical editor married to D. L. Moody's sister and associated with Moody's revivals—had published the book. Inside copy number one was stamped "Presented by the WCTU." The other copy had the stamp "Property of Frances C. Allison," the Moody Bible Institute Extension Department worker employed as a Bible teacher.

Elements of this tradition of feminist biblical exegesis even affected certain Presbyterians. In 1889, George P. Hays, pastor of the Second Presbyterian Church in Kansas City, Missouri, wrote *May Women Speak? A Bible Study By a Presbyterian Minister*.[45] Hays attributed his earlier prejudice against female preachers to women who attacked the Bible's inspiration. He also disliked unreasonably persistent Women's Christian Temperance Union representatives who foolishly demanded a hearing when unwanted. Hays proceeded to affirm his doctrine of plenary inspiration while insisting on women's right to speak publicly before a mixed audience. The last page of his book advertised Willard's *Woman in the Pulpit*.

Those who opposed women's public church ministry often claimed that supporters of women preachers made little or no attempt to defend their view from the Bible. The antifeminists labeled feminists "foes of the Bible and of Evangelical Christianity." In contrast, many Bible scholars and authors were pushed to their feminist conclusions while actively defending biblical authority.

This chapter has examined two general approaches to Evangelical feminist exegesis. Those authors who argued primarily for women's right to preach tended to focus on the Joel 2–Acts 2 prophecy–fulfillment passages regarding "your daughters shall prophesy." They viewed Pentecost as the pivotal experience in women's liberation. Other writers pushed for women's equality in all spheres of life, not just in the pulpit. Their theology tended to stress the broader issues of creation-redemption, especially the Genesis 3 promise of a Savior through the woman's seed. They saw the incarnation of Christ and his victory on the cross over Satan as the crucial event for women, since Christ's atonement reversed the effects of the Fall.

Indeed, the openness of many turn-of-the-century Evangelicals to women preachers and pastors cannot be explained on the basis of this biblical exegesis alone. But without these texts which grounded female ministry in Scripture, women's public church ministry would have been branded by them as unbiblical and therefore inconceivable in most Bible-believing circles.

7

CONCLUSION:
THE RISE AND FALL
OF EVANGELICAL WOMEN
IN PUBLIC MINISTRY

THE RISE

Female Evangelical preachers and pastors made up just one element in the surge of women entering Christian service at the turn of the century. With newly obtained lay rights, many women had begun in small ways to help govern church affairs.[1] Some chose the mission field or found new ministry opportunities within the church, in expanding programs such as the Sunday school. Others fulfilled their calling in interdenominational, parachurch agencies such as the Young Women's Christian Association or Women's Christian Temperance Union. In particular, the planting and blossoming of the American deaconess movement coincided with the founding of the earliest Bible institutes and clearly exemplifies women's increased interest in entering church ministry.

The American deaconess movement grew out of the German effort to establish a deaconess order at Kaiserworth, Germany, in 1883. Several American denominations, especially the Lutheran synods, introduced the practice in local settings. The Methodist Episcopal Church recognized the office of deaconess at the General Conference in 1888.[2] Since the General Conference that same year rescinded female preaching licenses and removed the vote from female delegates, the decision to grant deaconesses semiclerical status can be viewed as an attempt to restrict women. In addition, most churches granted male deacons authority and functions withheld from deaconesses.

Why did Protestant women of that era decide to form sisterhoods? Deaconesses, in primarily meeting the physical needs of the cities' poor, sick, widows, and orphans, represented a major Protestant response to the growing problems involved with urbanization, industrialization, and immigration.[3] Between 1888 and 1903, deaconesses founded 140 institutions—ninety controlled by the Methodist Episcopal Church, of which twenty were hospitals.[4]

Lucy Rider Meyer, considered the mother of the Methodist deaconess movement, opened the Chicago Training School for City, Home, and Foreign Missions in 1885 and the Deaconess Training School in 1887.[5] The Methodist order peaked in 1910 with 1,069 deaconesses. The 804 active deaconesses and probationers in the Methodist church in 1925 engaged in the following ministries: teaching (80), healing (87), welfare (139), general (183), and pastoral (315).[6]

In spite of its temporary growth and popularity, the deaconess movement never solved the "woman question" nor provided a sufficient outlet for Evangelical women gifted to minister. After the first decade of the twentieth century, the number of Protestant deaconesses declined. As nursing professionalized, the field of social work expanded, and public education secularized, people other than deaconesses began to meet the needs of the city poor.

The tremendous advance of women to the foreign mission field after the Civil War decisively affected attitudes and opportunities for women on the home front. Women organizing mission societies, raising funds, speaking while on deputation before departure, presenting field reports during furlough—these pioneers often constituted the first females to step behind an Evangelical church pulpit. Women prevented from overseas service by poor health became likely candidates to preach and pastor in American churches.

Women discovered leadership opportunities on the home

mission field as well. Whether on the frontier or in the inner city, women's public ministry was often born of necessity in an age of westward expansion and overcrowded urban centers. For example, as factories needed cheap labor, women's work in industry outside the home became increasingly acceptable. Likewise, women preachers and pastors often met the perceived need to evangelize an increasingly secular and expanding American population in desperate need of the gospel.

Apparently newer, smaller communities in the West, where few Christian men lived and public sentiment was unsettled, most rapidly received new practices such as women preachers.[7] Frances Willard's autobiography expressed the perception that "western women" were not afraid to preach. Baptist minister A. S. Hobart found it "incredible that any Baptist church, except some western one, where there are no men, would want a woman for a pastor."[8] These frontier female ministers set precedents, however, that could eventually affect the practice of more established churches.

Why did so many Evangelical women find pulpits and pastorates open to them for the first time at the turn of the century? Evangelical theology, social activism, and a charismatic style of church leadership provide the keys to understanding that phenomenon.

Evangelical Theology

Evangelical women entered the pulpit because significant elements of Evangelical theology supported such a practice. At interdenominational Bible institutes and conferences, many turn-of-the-century Evangelicals rubbed shoulders with groups like the Salvation Army, Evangelicals among the Quakers, and the United Brethren, whose theology promoted an egalitarian concept of women in ministry. In addition, the interaction of holiness churches and even some Pentecostal groups with other branches of Evangelicalism significantly influenced views toward women. For example, Moody Bible Institute opposed Aimee Semple McPherson's Pentecostal doctrine of healing but not her right to preach or pastor.

The emphasis of Evangelicals on the sanctifying, empowering work of the Holy Spirit usually corresponded with increasing openness to the exercise of women's gifts. Bishop Alma White, founder of the Pillar of Fire Church, declared that "so long as the Holy Spirit operates in the world, women must necessarily preach the Gospel."[9] Proponents of female preachers like Moody, Gordon, Simpson, and Franson also emphasized a second work of the Holy Spirit in the life of a Christian to provide power for witness and missions.

Fredrik Franson clearly tied his utilization of female evangelists to the urgent needs he sensed in world-wide missions.

> Brothers, the harvest is great and the laborers are few. If the ladies want to help out in the fields during the harvest time, then I think we should let them bind as many sheaves as they can. It is better that women bind the sheaves, than that the sheaves get lost. When one has been sent out on the field and heard the real cries for help from dozens of places, places to which one cannot possibly reach, then one cannot help but think, "It seems strange that only such a few verses of Scripture, about which there are so many disputes, should be made such obstacles to hinder those who otherwise would have responded to these calls for help."[10]

These pietistic Evangelicals sought personal holiness expressed concretely in terms of evangelistic witness and missionary concern. Given that context, who dares silence a sanctified woman who is Spirit-led to preach and testify? "It was the theology of the movement and the essential nature of the place of public testimony in the holiness experience which gave many an otherwise timid woman the authority and power to speak out 'as the Holy Spirit led her.'"[11]

The life and ministry of Uldine Utley partly illustrates this principle. Born in Oklahoma in 1912, Utley was converted as a child under Aimee Semple McPherson's ministry in California. Utley's subsequent experience of sanctification resulted in a deepened concern for the salvation of the lost. Her preaching ministry took her into Christian and Missionary Alliance, United Brethren, Methodist, Baptist, and Presbyterian churches. Eventually the Methodists licensed her as a preacher.

Utley described her clear call to ministry in *Why I Am a Preacher*. She asserted, "I am compelled to preach because of the love of Christ. He called me to preach and I cannot fail to do what He asks."[12]

Eschatology and prophetic interest as well as emphasis on the Holy Spirit contributed to new attitudes toward women's ministry. For many premillennialists, Joel's description of "prophesying daughters" in the last days took on vital significance. Franson concluded that "we seem to see Psalm 68:12 being fulfilled in our day, 'the Lord gives the command: the women who proclaim the good tidings are a great host.'"[13] Since Christ's second coming would be preceded by a special outpouring of the Holy Spirit, many interpreted the increase in women preachers as concrete evidence of the Spirit's outpouring.

Truly convinced the end was near and that the unconverted at Christ's return faced damnation in hell, turn-of-the-century premillennialists urgently pursued fervent evangelism and intensely promoted world-wide missions. Faced with what they considered an emergency situation with eternal souls at stake, these Evangelicals often enlisted male and female workers alike to preach the gospel to a dying world.

Bible institute founder Charles H. Pridgeon based his forceful appeal for women in ministry on the reality of hell and the imminent return of Christ in these "last days."

If it was "last days" on Pentecost, it certainly is now. Millions are perishing for the bread of life. If there is not only a present world that needs regeneration, but also a hereafter of heaven and hell, we who have the light can realize our awful responsibility. Our forces need to be mobilized and that not only of men but also women and children. The question of the ministry of women is more than just an academic question. The force of men who offer for His service is inadequate. Souls are perishing. There is no time to argue whether it be a man or woman that performs the service. The need must be met. The dying one that is saved will be saved just as well by whomsoever brings the Word of Life. We can split hairs, look wise, and hold up some possible meaning of a text or two of Scripture when the whole trend of God's Word is on the other side; millions are going to hell while we delay.[14]

It was said that God's obvious use of women preachers to convert sinners proved He was blessing their ministry. Surely God would not put such a seal of approval on women's disobedience, proponents argued. T. DeWitt Talmage viewed women as morally superior and consequently with the potential to be even more effective preachers than men. He praised women preachers who "have a pathos and a power in their religious utterances that men can never reach."[15]

Apart from the existence of Evangelical literature such as discussed in the previous chapter, the rise of women to positions of leadership in Evangelical, Bible-believing circles would be inexplicable. Evangelical women preached, pastored, and taught the Bible at the turn of the century, convinced that their ministry entailed obedience to God's Word, not rebellious disobedience.

When Christian Golder accused proponents of women's ordination of denying biblical inspiration and charged that "in order to emancipate woman, one must first divorce himself from the Word of God," he had not read the Evangelical feminist interpretations circulating.[16] When P. D. Stephenson blamed the women's movement on "free thinkers, Socialists, agnostics, evolutionists and other foes of the Bible and Evangelical Christianity," he failed to account for advocates of biblical inspiration who also fought for women's equality.[17]

The editor of the *Western Recorder,* who opposed women's public ministry, finally conceded that some faithful disciples do believe Scripture, yet do not silence women.[18] Obviously, one's commitment to biblical authority was not the deciding factor in whether to oppose or endorse women's ministry; inerrantists sat on both sides of the fence.

Evangelical belief in inerrancy and the practice of interpretation were two different matters.[19] These Protestants held that Spirit-led lay people with a teachable attitude could on their own understand the English Bible adequately. The "Bible reading" method simply utilized a concordance to string together a series of Bible texts on a particular subject. Moody Bible Institute's James M. Gray developed the synthetic method of reading the Bible or an individual book of the Bible in its totality before examining the parts.

Reading Scripture in totality meant, for some, examining the Bible through dispensational lenses. Yet even dispensational interpretation could assist in harmonizing various texts regarding women's ministry. A. J. Gordon, for example, did not bother justifying the role of women in Old Testament Israel, since believers today live in a new dispensation. Whatever the practice of interpretation, most Evangelicals at the turn of the century were forced to tolerate legitimate interdenominational differences of opinion on issues such as sacraments, church government, Calvinism, and even women's ministry.

Many Evangelicals advocated equality for women in the church as long as wives remained submissive to husbands. Even seeming opponents of women's ministry in that era often found biblical support at least for women preachers. After blasting women who seek ordination, pastorates, or authority over men, Mrs. George C. Needham encouraged women's prophecy.[20] She claimed Scripture prohibited the improper manner of women's speaking, not the act itself. Likewise, Oswald J. Smith advocated that halfway approach to women's ministry.

> What I am saying is that, ordinarily, woman's place is in the home, as a helper of man, that she ought not to be a pastor of a church, or lead. But that there are exceptional cases where she is called to preach and evangelize, even publicly—especially on the foreign field, that God's Word does not forbid, but rather encourages her.[21]

Along with Bible institutes, Bible conferences stood as key agencies in the promotion of premillennial and Fundamentalist theology among Evangelical laypeople. The earliest Bible conferences welcomed women preachers and Bible teachers, thus exposing thousands of conference participants to women in positions of authoritative leadership.

Presbyterian pastor James H. Brookes and his associates organized the Believers' Meeting for Bible Study in 1875, which

met at Niagara-on-the-Lake, Ontario, by 1883. Renamed the
Niagara Bible Conference in 1890, these annual meetings served
as an interdenominational rallying point for premillennialists
opposed to growing theological liberalism. Though Niagara
disbanded in 1901, other Bible conferences developed as a spin-
off, modeling Niagara's format and spirit. D. L. Moody, for
example, organized the Northfield Conference in 1880, which
frequently featured women such as Maria Gordon on its
schedule.

Winona Lake Bible Conference, founded in 1895 by Dr.
Solomon C. Dickey, stood foremost.[22] Dickey served as
superintendent of home missions for Indiana's Presbyterians
and promoted Bible conferences among both Northern Baptist
and Presbyterian clergy. In 1903 more than two thousand
ministers reportedly attended Winona's conference. During
Winona's "Golden Years" (1905–14) close to ten thousand
visitors came each summer to hear hundreds of nationally
prominent speakers.

Winona had close ties with Moody Bible Institute. Dickey
had consulted with D. L. Moody before establishing his Bible
Conference. MBI's radio station WMBI broadcast Winona
programs, and MBI directed the Winona Bible School. Interdenominational Winona emphasized fundamental beliefs and
evangelism. Doctrinally, it upheld biblical inspiration and
advertised "absolute, unswerving loyalty to the Word of God."

Winona Bible Conference widely publicized the public
ministry of women. Evangeline Booth-Clibborn, Salvation
Army evangelist and popular Winona preacher, lectured in
August 1913. That season both Angy Manning Taylor and E.
Stafford Millar represented MBI at Winona Bible School.
Taylor taught classes in New Testament and Christian funda-
mentals, while Millar presented "Christ and Modern Ques-
tions."

In 1914 suffragist and Women's Christian Temperance
Union representative Viola D. Romans lectured on equality
with men in home and church, basing her presentation on
Genesis.

I am a suffragist. . . . I understand most of you here are suffragists. . . . my grandmother was a Quaker preacher. I was brought up with the idea in the home and church that we had co-privileges along with our brothers. . . . "In our image,"—that gives, I believe, a feminine attribute to God that some of us may not have thought about before, and He blessed them and set them at much the same work, that of replenishing the earth and subduing it. He said not a word about subduing each other.[23]

Evangelist and Bible teacher Eva Ludgate lectured at Winona in 1924, Uldine Utley preached in 1927, and Grace Saxe spoke on Christ's second coming in 1925. Saxe, advertised by Winona as "a promoter of the Bible Class movement, having established Bible Study classes in every state in the Union and seventeen foreign countries," returned in 1931 to teach on Romans.

Dr. Henry Savage, a leading Fundamentalist and pastor of the First Baptist Church in Pontiac, Michigan, defended the right of Amy Stockton to serve as an evangelist.[24] He often included Stockton as one of the main speakers at Maranatha Bible Conference. John Roach Straton's first exposure to evangelist Uldine Utley occurred at Green Cove Springs Bible Conference in Florida.

Social Activism

The social activism of many Evangelical women at the turn of the century explains the context in which they often began their public church ministry. Bible conference speaker Viola D. Romans symbolized this relation between the temperance and suffrage crusades and Evangelical women in ministry. Temperance did then what the abolition movement did in antebellum America—provided an impetus for women's rights.

As socially concerned women spoke out on behalf of slaves or victims of alcohol abuse, they found the power and reason to speak out on their own behalf. Women trained through temperance and suffrage work to organize and speak publicly gained the confidence needed for local church leadership. In 1910 Stanton Coit called every suffrage platform a pulpit and each suffragist a preacher.[25] For many Evangelical churches, the first woman to preach from the pulpit was a temperance or suffrage worker.

Since many of the Evangelical women in church leadership were associated with the Women's Christian Temperance Union, understanding that organization is crucial to explaining why women stepped out into public ministry. Headquartered in Chicago, the WCTU grew out of the 1873–74 crusade of midwestern Protestant women to close saloons.[26] Annie Wittenmyer, WCTU president from 1874 until 1879, primarily advocated gospel temperance—the reliance on religious conversion to reform both the drunkard and liquor industry.

The WCTU identified with traditional morality in its defense of home values, similar to suffragists who urged women's vote to protect the purity of the family. The WCTU motto, "For God and Home and Native Land," typified the religious thrust of the movement which attracted many relatively conservative Protestant women. Church societies often provided functioning networks of women that could be organized as WCTU chapters; most local and national temperance meetings took place in churches.

Frances Willard, WCTU president from 1879 until 1898, developed the Union into the largest, most powerful and influential organization of women in the nineteenth century, enlisting more than two million members world-wide by 1897. Willard described the WCTU as the "largest army of women inside the realm of conservative theology." The WCTU enabled many women to develop a changing role for themselves and served as a base for other causes and reforms.[27] Though at first supportive of the gospel temperance approach, Willard later shifted focus to political means such as the ballot to achieve temperance goals.

Many Evangelical leaders openly promoted women's gospel temperance work. Moody utilized Willard herself in his campaigns, Maria Gordon led the Boston area WCTU, and Josephine Princell of the Free Church organized a Swedish WCTU. Riley, citing Willard as a convincing argument for women's right to preach, opened his church to suffrage meetings. MBI approvingly advertised the temperance work of several WCTU representatives such as national evangelist Helen L. Byrnes.

Not all Evangelical groups endorsed the movement and its methods, however. When Dr. Isaac See of the Presbytery of Newark, Synod of New Jersey, allowed two women to speak from his pulpit on temperance, the Presbyterian Church brought him to trial in 1876 and censured him.

Temperance involvement heightened a woman's social and political awareness, which in turn affected approaches to local church ministry. Even Catherine Booth at age twelve served as secretary of a small temperance society in England. Examining the gospel temperance activities of WCTU worker Sarepta M. Irish Henry reveals how temperance and local church ministries overlapped and fed each other.[28]

Henry's first daily temperance meetings were held at noon in a vacant factory and consisted of singing, prayer, Scripture, testimony, and sometimes a revival service. Her efforts resulted in numerous conversions. But when local ministers took control of the meetings, the work closed due to lack of interest. Henry explained how "working men had no use for ministers. If they wanted to hear ministers they could go to the churches."

At first Henry opposed women's ordination and even balked at the idea of a woman preaching. Once after being told to preach a good sermon, "the idea that anything she might say might be considered a 'sermon' never entered her mind, and so overwhelmed her with self-consciousness she almost fainted." Though preaching three times a day by 1877, Henry still had reservations about women in evangelistic work. Finally she prayed, "If I am called, and must go into public evangelistic work, let me know by the conversion of this man." The hardened sinner did repent, and Henry launched her public evangelistic ministry.

Henry soon obtained a year's leave of absence from the Rockford WCTU, claiming "if my work means anything at all, it means salvation through the Lord Jesus Christ." The WCTU helped transform Henry from a timid, unsure speaker to a well-known national evangelist. She faced occasional opposition such

as the Baptist who physically removed the church's Bible and
pulpit and hid them in his house to prevent their desecration
through Henry's preaching. Henry, however, overcame her
own initial misgivings and even helped organize a training
school to prepare other WCTU evangelists.

In 1924, Mrs. John H. Chapman, a Baptist, wrote
"Reflections of a Fundamentalist" in which she expressed deep
sympathy for temperance and suffrage advocates since "what
they fought for seemed the only right way."[29] Certain church
leaders, like Presbyterian minister S. G. Anderson, though anti-
women's rights, were pro-Willard.[30] Apparently Willard's
preaching alone did much to cause Evangelicals to reconsider
appropriate roles for women.

Charismatic Church Leadership

Evangelical women experienced increased freedom to preach
and pastor in those circles which emphasized Spirit-given gifts
of leadership as the essential qualification for ministry. In the
early charismatic stages of the revivalist, holiness, and Fundamentalist movements, Evangelicals often perceived women to
be as spiritually gifted as men.

Revivalism, for example, tended to loosen institutional
structure and fostered informal, spontaneous worship; women
experienced new opportunities to preach in such settings.[31] This
emphasis on charismatic authority and lay leadership resulted in
relaxed educational requirements for the clergy. Most early
Fundamentalists continued this concept of an unprofessional
ministry, sending workers with only Bible institute training or
less into gospel ministry and pastorates. Turn-of-the-century
women, barred from most Evangelical seminaries, could
prepare at Bible institutes equally with men for ministry in
revivalistic churches.

Spiritually gifted women received encouragement to
assume church leadership positions from their Evangelical
brothers. Granted, men supported the licensing or ordination of
women for a variety of reasons. Some may have pushed for
official church recognition because they feared the unaccounta-

bility of unlicensed women preachers. With the encouragement and public support of Evangelical leaders such as D. L. Moody, A. J. Gordon, A. B. Simpson, Fredrik Franson, W. B. Riley, and J. R. Straton, many Evangelical women stepped out into public ministry for the first time.

A. T. Pierson, for instance, agreed with his close friend A. J. Gordon on the need for wider opportunities for women in ministry.[32] A Presbyterian minister, missions organizer, and leader in the Niagara Bible Conferences, Pierson promoted premillennialism along with holiness. In 1895 Pierson fully supported his own daughter who served as a pastor and evangelist in Vermont. Using Scripture, Pierson argued for women's partnership with men and endorsed women preachers.

In 1898, Pierson wrote *Catherine of Siena, an Ancient Lay Preacher. A Story of Sanctified Womanhood and Power in Prayer.*[33] This biographical sketch was his attempt to defend women preachers by appealing to fourteenth-century church history. Pierson attributed Catherine's preaching power to the Holy Spirit and to her mastery of Scripture. His introduction declared that

> the elements of true testimony are independent of sex; and there is an especial fitness in bringing to the front such a woman preacher in the day when godly women are first coming into real prominence as workers in the mission field at home and abroad, and when the sisterhood of the race seems to be for the first time mounting to the true throne of woman's influence and kingdom.[34]

The wife-husband team ministry approach of women like Phoebe Palmer, Catherine Booth, and Hannah Whitall Smith paralleled this essential male support. At the turn of the century, women like Josephine Princell and Maria Gordon taught along with their husbands at newly opened Bible institutes. Gordon College's second president, Nathan R. Wood, married well-educated Isabel Warwich, a member of the first class of women to graduate from Brown University. She served as dean of faculty and professor of Bible, rhetoric, and literature.

On a smaller scale, Evangelical men who prepared for

ministry at coeducational Bible institutes increased their chances
of marrying women equally gifted and trained for preaching
and pastoring. Husbands who supported or shared a woman's
preaching ministry or pastorate enabled many Evangelical
women to enter church leadership. Women married to ministers occasionally received a call to pastor their husband's church
in the event of his illness or death.

Christabel Pankhurst

The life and ministry of Christabel Pankhurst tie together many
of the factors which led to the rise of turn-of-the-century
women to public church leadership.[35] A strategist of the
militant suffrage crusade in Britain before World War I,
Pankhurst developed her leadership and public speaking skills in
women's struggle to gain the vote. After her sudden conversion
to premillennial and Fundamentalist Christianity, a reporter
described how "she has been converted to Christianity of a
somewhat rigid type, which brings her into great demand as a
lecturer in churches on literal inspiration." Pankhurst combined
her prophetic message with the theme that laws and suffrage
could not cure original sin.

Pankhurst, like D. L. Moody, Catherine Booth, and
others, influenced Evangelicalism on both sides of the ocean.
She began her public ministry in 1921 and gained new fame in
America as a prominent preacher for the premillennial cause,
traveling nation-wide to speak at Bible conferences, including
Winona. A frequent visitor at Moody Bible Institute, Pankhurst
preached at Straton's Calvary Baptist Church in New York
City in 1924 and then at National Bible Institute. For more than
twenty years, she attracted immense audiences, rallied premillennialists, and claimed that thousands converted through her
evangelistic preaching. Books like *The Lord Cometh* and *Pressing
Problems of the Closing Age* also spread Pankhurst's prophetic
views.

In a sense, Christabel Pankhurst represented the end of an
era. Shortly after her ministry, other conservative Evangelical
women called to preach found the pulpits of revival tents,

Fundamentalist churches, Bible conferences, and Bible institutes off limits.

REASONS FOR THE FALL

What can account for the gradual decline of public ministry opportunities for Evangelical women between the World Wars? First, Fundamentalist separatist subcultures emerged which tended to harden on the women's issue. Second, as Fundamentalism increasingly institutionalized, women were squeezed out of leadership roles. Third, the conservative Protestant backlash against changing social values resulted in restrictions on women in ministry. Finally, a more literalist view of Scripture among Fundamentalists meant less flexibility in interpreting a topic like women in ministry.

Separatist Fundamentalist Subcultures

Between the World Wars, Fundamentalists lost the battle for control of the mainline denominations and schools; in regrouping, they created a host of separate institutions. Whereas the nineteenth-century Evangelical empire stood near the center of American culture, Fundamentalism of the 1930s withdrew and formed distinctive subcultures. Part of the movement veered in a militant separatist, extremist direction, often allied with far right-wing politics. In that process of narrowing, opportunities for women also tightened.

United briefly in the initial attack against Modernism, Fundamentalism began to splinter in defeat. While some Fundamentalist Baptists withdrew in the 1930s to form the General Association of Regular Baptist Churches, a decade later other conservatives organized the Conservative Baptist Association. These events reveal a basic inability of Fundamentalists to agree among themselves, much less with other Protestants.

This growing anti-ecumenical attitude among Fundamentalists eliminated earlier cooperative interdenominational undertakings such as Union meetings. The Pentecostal practices of tongues and healing and even Methodistic perfectionism increasingly antagonized Fundamentalists.

Donald Dayton suggests that even among the holiness churches, the feminist heritage was lost except where institutionalized, as in the Salvation Army. By World War II most Evangelicals could go a lifetime never having heard a woman preacher or pastor, and girls grew up with fewer and fewer role models of women in public ministry.

Significantly, Fundamentalism widened geographically during the same decades in which it narrowed denominationally. Whereas early Fundamentalist strength lay in the urban North, the welcoming of southern conservative cousins like the Southern Baptists into their fold produced a shift of strength to the southern Bible Belt. This change paralleled the establishment of Dallas Seminary, a Fundamentalist graduate school in the South. Southern conservative social values, which traditionally included the subordinate place of women in society and church, typified an increasingly larger segment of the Fundamentalist constituency.

The early Fundamentalist involvement in social action waned as the movement became more rigid. Historical distance from earlier temperance and suffrage crusades decreased one's chances of hearing Evangelical women speak publicly in church. The secular feminist movement certainly lost steam and direction after the passage of the Nineteenth Amendment granted women the vote in 1920. As Evangelicals turned from active social concern and reform to institution building and theological squabbles, women lost the momentum to speak out on behalf of others as they had in support of temperance and suffrage.

Institutionalization

Both Moody Bible Institute and the Evangelical Free Church picture for us in a vivid way the process of institutionalization and its effect on roles for women. Changes in educational programs furnish one barometer of this change in Evangelical schools and denominations. MBI, for instance, began as a practical training center for women and men in lay ministry. A century later, MBI's inauguration of a graduate school suggests an enormous transformation. Similarly, early Free churches supported itinerant lay evangelists but rarely settled, seminary-trained pastors. The recent establishment of doctoral programs at Trinity Evangelical Divinity School also indicates immense institutional transition.

With the rising social status of many churches came the demand for professional, seminary-trained clergy in place of charismatic lay ministry. As frontier churches previously viewed as home mission fields increased in numbers and wealth, congregations could afford to support a married man as minister. Some considered the presence of a female pastor a tacit acknowledgment of a church's poverty.

Educational attainment and credentials often replaced spiritual gifts as the essential leadership qualification. The establishment of interdenominational Dallas Theological Seminary in 1924—the nation's first strictly Fundamentalist seminary—symbolizes this shift.[36]

Women, at first excluded from even attending Dallas, are still prohibited from the Pastoral Ministries major.[37] Lewis Sperry Chafer, undoubtedly influenced by Scofield's view on women while teaching at Philadelphia College of the Bible, later founded influential Dallas, today the nation's fourth largest seminary.

Dallas arose from the Modernist-Fundamentalist debates of the 1920s. It opened as the Evangelical Theological College, admitting only born-again, male college graduates endowed with ministry gifts. Chafer clearly distinguished his school from Bible institutes, claiming "those Bible courses which have been designed for laymen and Christian workers generally are not adequate as a foundational Bible training for the preacher or teacher."[38]

If Bible institutes were the key educational structures to prepare turn-of-the-century Evangelical women for public ministry, Fundamentalist seminaries like Dallas were the pivotal schools which trained the new generation of male Fundamentalist leaders. In the first quarter of the twentieth century, Bible institutes furnished a large slice of local church leadership and influenced theology. Later Dallas and similar schools began to

train the men who administered and taught at Bible institutes.[39]
Consequently, a Fundamentalist seminary like Dallas could
affect local Evangelical church attitudes toward women's
ministry.

At the same time that many Evangelical churches were
clamoring for a seminary-trained pastor, Dallas sent out only
men to fill those posts. Other seminaries did train women but
discouraged them from preaching and pastoral roles. Even
today a school like Denver Seminary of the Conservative
Baptist Association admits women to all degree programs and
prepares them to preach and pastor, yet Conservative Baptist
churches do not call and ordain women professionally trained
for public ministry.

By mid-century, churches increasingly directed women
gifted to minister away from more controversial pulpit and
pastoral duties to safer spheres of service. Since World War I,
the rapidly rising field of religious or Christian education has
drawn trained women into its fold. A female Bible institute
graduate who in 1910 may have pastored a small church or
traveled as an itinerant revivalist would by 1940 more likely
serve as director of religious education.

Professionalization affected women's service on the mission field as well. Foreign missions continued as an acceptable
ministry option for women throughout the twentieth century.
But the shift to overseas specialties in medicine, education,
agriculture, and construction influenced perceptions of appropriate roles for women. Before specialization, churches sent
missionaries primarily as preachers, church planters, and Bible
teachers, with women filling those positions along with men.
As specialization increased, women more often than not filled
the supportive roles as men handled preaching and pastoring.
Female missionaries unused to preaching overseas felt less
comfortable in American pulpits on furlough.

In summary, women found declining opportunities for
leadership in Evangelical churches, schools, and agencies as
institutionalization squelched earlier charismatic forms.[40] In
worship as well as in education, this routinization set in. In this
shift toward regulated, more formalized church services,

prayers and speaking were no longer left to chance. Structured rather than spontaneous, Spirit-led worship tended to exclude women from public participation in worship. Concern for social propriety even dictated that only men take a service position like ushering in many congregations.

Fundamentalist Reaction to Social Change

Opposition to women's public ministry was part of a post–World-War-I reaction to vocal, radical feminism and a perceived decline in womanhood. Dress, appearance, and habits constituted the most conspicuous signs of American women's growing independence. Shorter skirts, bobbed hair, cosmetics, public smoking and drinking—these externals marked the "liberated" woman. More substantially, the expansion of women into the work force produced growing economic independence.

The onset of the Depression undoubtedly accelerated the reinforcement of traditional values. Evangelicals who watched alarming trends toward women's freedom in dress, habits, morals, and occupations, feared a fall from true femininity might destroy the family. As churches identified women preachers and pastors with the secular women's movement, opposition rose. Hoping to save the American home, many Evangelicals narrowed their view of appropriate women's roles. The attack by John R. Rice, a separatist Fundamentalist, against *Bobbed Hair, Bossy Wives, and Women Preachers* illustrates how these issues connected in this era.

This backlash in conservative Protestant circles against changing social mores can be traced in *Moody Monthly* magazines of the 1930s. Numerous articles appeared on the "new woman," exposing the ill effects of modern morality. The disturbing shifts in the roles and behavior of women in American society frightened conservative Christians. Convinced that the survival of the traditional family and of the entire social order was at stake, many Evangelicals tightened their approach to women in church ministry. Might not women's leadership there give encouragement to other destructive tendencies?

By World War II, *Moody Monthly* articles reflected the new image of God's ideal woman—no longer the Moody Bible Institute graduate who uses all her gifts for the kingdom, but the submissive, domesticated woman who knows her place. MBI and other Evangelical institutions began to push this more limiting role expectation for women in order to maintain traditional family and moral values. In the process, Evangelicals took away ministry opportunities from women in the effort to bolster slipping morality.

Fundamentalist Exegesis

This backlash against perceived threats to the family and society found ammunition in revised biblical exegesis. Fundamentalists no longer interpreted passages in 1 Timothy 2 or 1 Corinthians 14 as occasional advice for specific problems; instead, these passages gave transcultural principles for all times and places. In reaction to outside threats, many Fundamentalist institutions revised their earlier views about women.

In the early twentieth century, Fundamentalists tightened the lines around the concept of inerrancy; opposition to women ministers may have been formalized as a by-product. Just as the South needed extremely authoritative and literalistic views of Scripture to justify slavery, the North moved toward similar attitudes after the Modernist battles. As this type of literalism became entrenched, Fundamentalists interpreted passages about women more rigidly.

Consequently, opportunities for women to preach and pastor declined as Evangelical churches identified such service as contrary to Scripture. Support of such public ministry soon constituted a denial of biblical inerrancy. Straton's 1926 pamphlet was one of the last publications from the Fundamentalist camp arguing women's right to preach. Few Evangelical men followed in the steps of Moody, Gordon, Simpson, Franson, Riley, and Straton to publicly defend women preachers.

When the publications containing feminist exegesis from the Evangelical perspective went out of print, little appeared to replace them. Only in the past decade have reprints of those critical books, pamphlets, and articles been made available. Unable or unwilling to view women's public ministry as consistent with Scripture, Evangelical churches increasingly labeled their pulpits "For Men Only."

This shift in biblical exegesis produced theological reformulation. For example, the same premillennialism used by Gordon and Franson to advocate women preachers was utilized by later writers to restrict women. Certain dispensationalists began to interpret women's leadership as an *evil* sign of the end times, identifying such women with the whore of Babylon.

Turn-of-the-century Evangelicals committed to the imminent, premillennial return of Christ had put their intense convictions to action. The urgent need to mobilize workers to spread the gospel world-wide left no time for one sex to remain silent. Later premillennialists apparently retained the intellectual assent to Christ's soon return but relaxed considerably on the urgency of evangelizing the world at once. More concerned with opposing evolution than promoting evangelism, Evangelical recruitment of female preachers subsided.

AFTERWORD

It is amazing how one can get such a false idea as that not all God's children should use all their powers in all ways to save the lost world. There are, so to speak, many people in the water about to drown. A few men are trying to save them, and that is considered well and good. But look, over there a few women have untied a boat also to be of help in the rescue, and immediately a few men cry out; standing there idly looking on and therefore having plenty of time to cry out: "No, no, women must not help, rather let the people drown." What stupidity!

Fredrik Franson

Almost a century after Frances Willard published *Woman in the Pulpit,* many Evangelical and most Fundamentalist women find themselves excluded from the pulpit and prohibited or discouraged from entering the pastorate, ordained ministry, or other authoritative church offices. For example, the 1981 General Council of the Christian and Missionary Alliance adopted a new statement on women's role in ministry. Church elders must be male, since no biblical text conclusively proves a woman exercised authority as an elder. "We conclude that women may properly engage in any kind of ministry except that which involves elder authority."[1]

At the 1984 General Association of Regular Baptist Churches Annual Conference, delegates unanimously passed a resolution of "Women's Role in the Church and Home."

> Whereas the ordination of women to the Christian ministry is being advocated in both liberal and evangelical circles; and

Whereas women's subordination to male authority in the church and home has become a subject of controversy; and

Whereas there is outright rejection by a number of evangelicals of some of Paul's teaching in the New Testament regarding women, calling his instructions rabbinical and erroneous; and

Whereas some of the evangelical women's caucuses have both misinterpreted Scripture and also objected to the revealed names of God in the desire to eliminate gender-specific language;

Be it resolved that the messengers of the General Association of Regular Baptist Churches, meeting in Seattle, Washington, June 25–29, 1984, affirm their adherence to the New Testament teaching that women are not legitimate candidates for ordination and that God has committed to men the important responsibility of leadership and authority in the church and in the home (1 Cor. 11:3; Eph. 5:21–24; 1 Tim. 2:11–15; 3:1–7).

Be it further resolved that we recognize Christian women's spiritual equality with Christian men (Gal. 3:26–29), affirming that subordination is not equivalent to inferiority (was not Christ equal to and yet subordinate to the Father?), and that women's role in the church and home has its own unique function and dignity.

From the pulpit, press, and media, individuals as well as denominations are restricting Evangelical women's church ministry with renewed vigor. In the 1980 Radio Bible Class pamphlet "The Woman God Made—Her Creation, Submission, Equality, and Behavior," teacher Richard W. De Haan explained:

> If a woman is to honor God within the assembly of believers, she will not abdicate her divinely assigned role of subjection to the man. She won't strive for domination over men in the diaconate. Rather, she will submit to the order God Himself established to govern the relationship between the sexes.[2]

In 1983 *Moody Monthly* published the views of two well-known Evangelical leaders—pastor John F. MacArthur, Jr., and author Elisabeth Elliot.[3] MacArthur earlier caused a stir by firing several married church secretaries. The Bible, he explained, teaches that the husband should be the sole bread-winner; a married woman's church ministry "is not to be in leadership, except over other women and children . . . in the church's official assembly, men have the authority for leadership, preaching and teaching." Elliot likewise advocates a subordinate role for women.

> She is not to bear authority in the church or in the home. So women's ministries must be under the authority of the men God has put over them. . . . when women are unwilling to submit . . . they are disobedient to God. I'm hesitant to accept women who teach adult Bible classes on a regular basis.

Jerry Falwell, undoubtedly the foremost spokesperson for Baptist Fundamentalists in the 1980s, serves as executive editor of the *Fundamentalist Journal*, published by his Old-Time Gospel Hour. The January 1985 article "Women Preachers, Why Not?" typifies current attitudes toward women's public ministry in conservative Evangelical circles.[4] Author Susan T. Foh claims the Bible forbids women the pastoring, shepherding, and teaching functions of elder and, therefore, the office of elder. The New Testament also denies women the office of pastor-teacher, evangelist, and any authoritative teaching position. Biblical evidence even indicates women may not preach.

Evangelical churches enter the next turn of the century facing a secular American culture increasingly sensitized to demands for women's equality. For women now accustomed to equal rights and opportunities in the rest of society, sexist church practices do not seem to make sense. Katharine Bushnell explained that

> when the rule of males was universal, woman could accept membership in a Church without change of status. She cannot, today. An invitation to identify herself with any religious society which carries with it the inference that she will turn backward into servitude will be declined with increasing frequency, in days to come. . . . No mature human being has a right to yield unquestioning obedience to other than God Himself.[5]

As another consequence, gifted and trained women who sense a call to preaching or pastoral ministry will continue to be forced outside many Evangelical churches in order to serve freely. Lee Anna Starr described such a phenomenon decades ago.

> The church afforded these women of ten talents no tasks commensurate with their ability, so they lifted their eyes and looked on the fields outside, and lo! they were "white already unto harvest," and the laborers few. In the need, they read God's call to the larger service. The church lost, but the world gained when they responded: "Here am I: send me." Who can charge them with dereliction?
>
> A new term has been coined by the religious writers in these latter days—that of "detached service"—meaning Christian and humanitarian effort outside the pale of the church. The Woman's Christian Temperance Union; Salvation Army; Volunteers of America; Young Women's Christian Association and American Red Cross, all belong to this category.[6]

The undisputable fact that many Bible-believing Evangelicals approved of female preachers, pastors, and ordained ministers in the past does not necessarily make it right. The important question for Evangelicals is whether women's public ministry is biblical. As Jessie Penn-Lewis predicted, "the tide of liberation will not reach the *Christian woman,* those who are born of the Spirit and seek to conform their lives to the Word of God, unless they can be shown that their liberation is in harmony with that Word."[7]

Evangelicals believe God speaks through Scripture; they also claim God has spoken to the church through the Holy Spirit at work historically in the lives of believing women and men. While Evangelicals answer the biblical question, will they do so in the context of church history?

APPENDIXES

BIBLE INSTITUTES THAT ARE SOUND

No sane and intelligent person would think of unnecessarily exposing himself or others to infection from disease. Why should Christians be less careful of the spiritual health of themselves and of their children? If you or those dear to you are contemplating preparation for Christian service you will make no mistake in choosing from the sound Bible institutions listed below:

Anderson Bible Training School, Anderson, Ind.

Berean Bible Training School, 1538 Wylie Avenue, Pittsburgh, Pa.

Bethel Institute, 1480 North Snelling Avenue, St. Paul, Minn.

Bible Institute of Indianapolis, Lain College Building, Indianapolis, Ind.

Bible Institute of Los Angeles, 536 South Hope Street, Los Angeles, Cal.

Bible Institute of Washington, 1316 Vermont Avenue, N.W., Washington, D.C.

Bible Students League, Claremont, Cal.

Bible Training School of Fort Wayne, Fort Wayne, Ind.

Boston Bible Training School, 35 Kenilworth Street, Roxbury, Mass.

Boydton Institute, Boydton, Va.

Brookes Bible Institute of St. Louis, 2051 Park Avenue, St. Louis, Mo.

California College, 841 North Harvard Boulevard, Los Angeles, Cal.

Chicago Evangelistic Institute, 1754 Washington Boulevard, Chicago, Ill.

Cincinnati Bible Institute, 429 West Eighth Street, Cincinnati, Ohio.

Columbia Bible School, Columbia, S.C.

Cleveland Bible Institute, 3201–3231 Cedar Avenue, Cleveland, Ohio.

Denver Bible Institute, 2047 Glenarm Place, Denver, Col.

Dudley Bible Institute, Dudley, Mass.

Florida Bible Institute, Bradenton, Fla.

God's Bible School and Missionary Training Home, Ringgold, Young and Channing Streets, Cincinnati, Ohio.

Gordon Bible College, Clarendon and Montgomery Streets, Boston, Mass.

Hesston Academy and Bible School, Hesston, Kan.

Houston Bible Institute, Houston, Texas.

Midland Bible Institute, Shenandoah, Iowa.

Missionary Training Institute, Nyack, N.Y.

Moody Bible Institute, 153 Institute Place, Chicago, Ill.

National Bible Institute, 330 West Fifty-fifth Street, New York City.

North Pacific Evangelistic Institute, 1186 Borthwick Street, Portland, Ore.

Northwestern Bible and Missionary Training School, 6 South Eleventh Street, Minneapolis, Minn.

Omaha Bible Institute, 2224 Jones Street, Omaha, Neb.

Pennsylvania Bible Institute, 1418 North Sixteenth Street, Philadelphia, Pa.

Philadelphia School of the Bible, 1723 Spring Garden Street, Philadelphia, Pa.

Philadelphia School for Christian Workers, 1122 Spruce Street, Philadelphia, Pa.

Practical Bible Training School, Bible School Park, New York City.

San Antonio Bible Institute, 1720 South Presa Street, San Antonio, Texas.

Simpson Bible Institute, 101 West Fifty-eighth Street, Seattle, Wash.

St. Paul Bible Training School, 1635 Sherburne Avenue, St. Paul, Minn.

Toccoa Falls Institute, Toccoa, Ga.

Toronto Bible College, 110 College Street, Toronto, Ont., Can.

Union Bible Seminary, Westfield, Ind.

Vancouver Bible Training School, 356 Broadway West, Vancouver, B.C., Can.

Young Women's Bible Training Movement, 281 State Street, Albany, N.Y.

TURN-OF-THE-CENTURY AMERICAN BIBLE INSTITUTES*

*Schools listed by both the 1924 *Sunday School Times* ad and the 1930 *Christian Fundamentalist* ad will be marked by ● on the map.

SCHOOL (Current Name)	LOCATION	FOUNDED	AFFILIATION
*Missionary Training Institute	Nyack, N.Y.	1883	C&MA
Moody BI	Chicago	1886	
Gordon Bible College	Boston	1889	
*Cleveland BI (Malone)	Cleveland	1892	Quaker
*Boston Bible School (Berkshire Christian)	Boston	1897	Advent Christian
Practical	Binghamton	1900	
God's Bible School	Cincinnati	1900	Holiness
*Dudley BI (Barrington, now merged with Gordon)	Providence, R.I.	1900	
Bethel Institute	St. Paul	1902	Swedish Baptist
*Northwestern	Minneapolis	1902	
*Fort Wayne	Fort Wayne	1904	C&MA
*Hesston	Hesston, Kans.	1904	Mennonite
Toccoa Falls Institute	Toccoa Falls	1907	C&MA
National BI (Shelton)	New York	1907	
*BIOLA	Los Angeles	1908	
*Brookes BI	St. Louis	1909	
*Chicago Evangelistic Institute (Vennard)	Chicago	1910	Holiness
*BI of Indianapolis	Indianapolis	1911	
Union Bible Seminary	Westfield, Ind.	1911	Friends

SCHOOL (Current Name)	LOCATION	FOUNDED	AFFILIATION
*Young Women's Bible Training Movement	Albany	1912	
*BI of Pennsylvania (Philadelphia College of the Bible)	Philadelphia	1913	
Philadelphia School of the Bible	Philadelphia	1914	
*Denver BI (Rockmont)	Denver	1914	Berean Fundamental
St. Paul	St. Paul	1916	C&MA
*Anderson	Anderson, Ind.	1917	Church of God (Anderson, Ind.)
*North Pacific Evangelistic Institute (Cascade)	Portland	1918	Free Methodist
Midland BI	Shenandoah, Iowa	1918	C&MA
Houston BI	Houston	1919	

The following institutions, for which no information is available, are marked by ★ on the map.

Philadelphia School for Christian Workers	Philadelphia
Berean BI	Pittsburgh
California College	Los Angeles
Bible Students League	Claremont, CA
San Antonio BI	San Antonio
Florida BI	Bradenton, FL
Boydton Institute	Boydton, VA

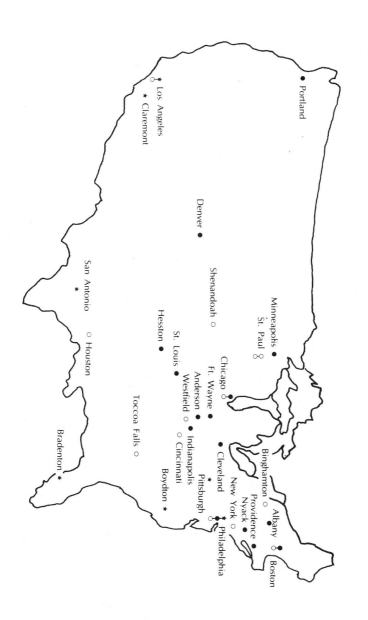

WOMEN AS EVANGELISTS*

By Mrs. A. J. Gordon of Boston

In the second chapter of Joel are these words: "And it shall come to pass, afterword, that I will pour out My spirit upon all flesh; your sons and your *daughters* shall prophesy. . . . And also upon the servants and upon the *handmaids* in those days will I pour out My spirit. . . . And whosoever shall call on the name of the Lord shall be delivered."

The first recorded fulfillment of this prophecy is in Acts, second chapter. In the little company in that upper room waiting for the promise of the Father, the eleven disciples, *with the women,* and *Mary, the mother of Jesus,* were gathered; and we read that the tongues of fire sat upon *each* of them; and they were *all* filled with Holy Ghost, and began to speak with tongues. This manifestation amazed the multitude who came together to hear them; but Peter explained that it was the fulfillment of the ancient prophecy. He referred to the two great characteristics of the New Dispensation just inaugurated, which were:

First—That sons and daughters were to prophesy; that spiritual gifts and qualifications were to be bestowed and exercised equally by servants and handmaidens, and,

Second—That whosoever should call upon the name of the Lord should be saved; that salvation was a universal gift to all who would claim and receive it.

This thought is developed by the apostle Paul in I. Cor. 12:13, where, in referring to this Pentecostal baptism, he says, "For by one Spirit we are all baptized into one body, whether we be Jews or Gentiles, whether we be bond or free," and the thought is still further amplified in Gal. 3:28, where the apostle declares that in this new body "there is neither Jew nor Greek, there is neither bond nor free, there is neither male nor female; for ye are all one in Christ Jesus."

*An address delivered Monday morning, June 25, 1894.

Yet so potent has been the sway of prejudice, united to false interpretation, that the two texts, "I suffer not a woman to teach," and, "Let your women keep silence in the churches," have been held over the heads of godly women sitting in the congregation of worshipers for hundreds of years.

The old minister, who, in reading the story of the interview of Abraham and the angels, came to the passage, "And they said unto him, 'Where is Sarah, thy wife?' and he said, 'Behold, she is in the tent';" commented, "And there let her stay; and the less she is seen outside the better;" and the other Connecticut preacher who learned that Abby Kelley Foster, that eloquent advocate of the slave, was in his morning congregation, and knowing that she was to speak for these oppressed ones in the afternoon, took for his text, Rev. 2:20: "Nevertheless I have somewhat against thee; because thou sufferest that women, Jezebel, which calleth herself a prophetess, to teach," are specimens of a class well-nigh extinct.

For a more correct exegesis of this passage, allow me to quote from Canon Garrett in his Commentary on Revelation, page 43:—

"The church of Thyatira was probably founded by Lydia, converted at Philippi under Paul's teaching, and certain to carry the good news back to her own city. It was not unnatural that a church founded by a woman should have been especially inclined to listen to female teaching. The angel is not blamed for allowing a woman to prophesy, *for in the early days of the church there were many prophetesses.*"

Wendell Phillips said that "a nation is judged by the men whom it crowns"; and the sentiment which has prevailed in the Christian church concerning the appropriate sphere of Christian women may be judged by the women of the Bible who have been most universally selected for imitation.

The memory of Dorcas has been kept fragrant by the thousands of Dorcas Societies, before whose members the coats and garments which Dorcas made have been held as a perpetual object lesson.

But who ever heard of a "Society of Daughters of Philip the Evangelist" to commemorate the virtues of these excellent women, and incite others to emulate them? These four unmarried daughters of this devout deacon of the church, himself a successful evangelist, kept their father's house, and exercised the grace of hospitality; for we read that in his last journey to Jerusalem, Paul tarried there many days. But the occupation of housekeeping was subordinate to the real business of their lives, which was prophesying. This prophesying is defined in I. Cor. 14:3, to be "to speak to men to edification and exhortation and comfort." These "daughters" seem to be notable examples of what women may be to-day: faithful home makers, keeping the machinery of their households wound up so that it will run without continuous watching; and then consecrating the spiritual experience of their mature years to leading others into the same truth which has saved and sanctified them.

Of the number of sermons which have been preached on the care-taking housewife Martha and her spiritually minded sister Mary, we might almost say that if "they should be written every one . . . even the world itself could not contain" them.

But in the ordinary ministrations of the pulpit, how much attention is called to Anna the prophetess, that venerable dweller in the temple, who could say with David, "I have loved the habitation of Thine house and the place where Thine honor dwelleth"? Here is one of the most glowing pictures of New Testament history! This venerable saint, with the halo of the glory into which she was about to enter irradiating her countenance, was led into the temple by the Spirit, as was Simeon, just in time to hear the "Now lettest Thou Thy servant depart in peace" while he held the infant Redeemer in his arms, and pronounced the blessing and the prophecy upon the virgin mother. Then the spirit of prophecy came upon her, and "she spake of Him to all them who looked for redemption in Israel."

We have been accustomed to read in Psalms 68:11, "The Lord gave the word; great was the company of those that published it." It is very interesting to observe, that at the present day, when the demand for heralds of the Word, both at home and in foreign lands, is so urgent, that in revision we read, "The Lord giveth the word; the women who publish the tidings are a great host;" showing that the Holy Spirit had anticipated this emergency, and sanctioned and provided for this women's ministry.

These passages have been quoted to show that the weight of Scripture testimony and example is in favor of women doing the work and exercising the gifts of evangelists. And in these "last days" it would seem as if the Master were saying to every woman, "Behold, I have set before *you* an open door." Doors which have long been shut through a misapprehension of Scripture are now flung wide open, and Phebe and Priscilla, Lydia and Junia, Tryphena and Tryphosa, and the beloved Persis have full liberty to perform any ministry to which the Holy Ghost may call them; and the majority of the Christian church will bid them "God speed."

There have been occasional examples of women evangelists in all stages of church history. One of the most eminent was Catherine of Sienna, who was so moved with distress at the seething corruption in church and state that, in spite of prevailing custom, she began to speak against them and to plead in public as well as in private for a reform in morals. She was counted to be out of her sphere by those who felt the keenness of her rebukes. She was so much in earnest that she had the audacity to press herself into the presence of the Pope and his Cardinals, and plead with them to repent and change their lives. So true was she to conscience, and so evidently sent of God, that even from the reluctant lips of the Pope was the confession extorted, "Never man spake like this woman."

Probably the most eminent woman evangelist of this century was Mrs. General Booth, the mother of the Salvation Army. Her first public address was before a Band of Hope in their temperance meeting. Her sense of personal responsibility to every one with whom she came in contact was the dominating principle of her life, and God honored her faithfulness to individuals by giving her opportunity to address the multitudes, and bring them to surrender to the Lord Jesus.

Scattered all over our land and in foreign lands are women evangelists who are acceptably helping pastors in series of meetings, restoring scattered flocks, holding revival services in destitute places, and the seal of blessing which the Spirit of God sets upon their labors is the best credential of their call to the work.

A missionary from India wrote that while conferences in America were debating the propriety of allowing women to preach the gospel, the women stationed among the heathen, who realized the appalling famine of the bread of life, were settling the question under the pressure of the "Woe is me, if I preach not this gospel."

Miss Fielde, one of our most eminent missionaries in China, while detailing the experience of work among that people, was interrupted by one of the committee with the query, "What! you preach without having been ordained?" and she quietly replied, "But I was fore-ordained."

There has sprung in response to the demand for trained workers, a number of schools where women as well as men are being taught the Scriptures, that they may be prepared to answer any call of the Spirit through the church. And from our own Training School in Boston about twenty young women have been sent out by two and two into the rural districts of New England, to visit from house to house, to gather the people into schoolhouses and churches, and give out the message of eternal life. One pastor has proved his confidence in the young women sent to his parish, by taking his summer vacation during their visit to his town, and leaving them in full possession of parsonage and church. Another lady, who undertook to supply a little church in New Hampshire, has sent for her former pastor to come and baptize twelve converts who are awaiting the ordinance.

The first requisite for this work is the anointing of the Spirit. It is useless to attempt work for God without this qualification. "Upon My handmaidens . . . I will pour out of My Spirit." With this preparation for service, God will certainly provide a field for work. Whether it is to lead individuals to Christ as members of the "Win-One" Society, or as called to address large congregations, the commission is the same, "Let him that heareth say, Come."

Woman's gift of tongues has been the theme of many satirical jokes. Let us acknowledge the gift as from God, and let us take the sting from the satire, by consecrating that gift to the proclamation of His truth. Let us say with that saintly singer, Frances Ridley Havergal,

> "Take my lips and let them be
> Filled with messages from Thee,"

and let us hold ourselves ever in that attitude of heart and life expressed in the words in II. Samuel 15:15, "Ready to do whatsoever my Lord the King may appoint."

Sample of Alumni News of

Northwestern Bible and Missionary Training School

Miss Hauser, who was graduated last year has been engaged since that time in evangelistic work at Deer River where her service has been greatly blessed of God. She writes as follows:

Deer River has a population of 1500 and until Uncle Sam closed the saloons two years ago, it was considered one of the toughest lumber towns in the northwest. There is one Protestant church there but it has been spiritually dead for years. It had no prayer-meeting, no young people's society and had not seen a revival for more than a decade.

With Isa. 55:10–11 as God's promise, our work was begun. Knowing that much prayer was needed, I asked the pastor if I might come to his home that we might unitedly lift our voices to God in intercession for souls. He told me also of a little Swedish woman who knew God and I went to her. The Lord heard both the Swedish and the English prayers and we received assurance of success in our work. A prayer-meeting was started in the church, a young people's society organized and Sunday School work revived.

About a mile from the business section of the town, where the lumber mills are located, is a little village of foreigners. These people are very poor and did not feel free to attend church "up town", so services were begun in a dance hall for them. I visited each home and invited them to attend. Some asked who the preacher was. I said, "Come and find out" and they did. (Miss Hauser was, herself the preacher). Praise God, souls were won and His Name honored!

On Tuesday evening a cottage prayer-meeting was held. The homes were filled every week and in these meetings young people were saved, backsliders reclaimed and God glorified.

Twice a month social evenings were enjoyed. A short musical program was given and games were played. A number of the young people gave up dancing and these social hours helped them to realize that a Christian might have a good time without indulging in the pleasures of the world.

Opportunities to help destitute families, care for the sick, comfort those robbed by death were constantly presented and to these we went in His Name.

One remarkable conversion I must speak of. A young woman from Michigan with whom I played during the "mud pie" age, divorced from her husband, was living a life far from pure. To my surprise she made a visit to Deer River and after much prayer for her the blessed Lord made her see what a wreck her life was. She became such a sweet Christian and has given her life to the Lord Jesus for service to save others.

In connection with the town work, a service was held at a country school house every Sunday afternoon, the pastor and myself speaking alternately.

An evangelistic campaign is to be opened this spring and we need the prayers of our friends for this field.

Praise God for what has been and will be accomplished in His Name!

LIGHT ON PUZZLING PASSAGES
AND PROBLEMS

By R. A. Torrey

How do you explain I Tim. 2:12: "But I suffer not a woman to teach nor to usurp authority over the man, but to be in silence?"

The Revised Version gives the meaning more plainly: "But I permit not a woman to teach, nor to have dominion over a man, but to be in quietness." The meaning of the passage is determined by the words used and by the context. Paul is giving instructions for the conduct of different classes of individuals in the Church. He first gives instructions as to what the men should do (v. 8), then what the women should do (vs. 9–15), and then what a bishop should do (v. 3:1), and so on. He has evidently in mind, from the context, married women (note vs. 13–15). Paul's thought for women generally was that they should marry, though he sets forth elsewhere the excellence of an unmarried life for some of them. And the general teaching is that a woman's position is that of subjection or subordination to the husband (see vs. 11, 13 and 14). He elsewhere teaches along the same line that the husband is the head of the wife, even as Christ is the head of the Church (Eph. 5:22, 23), and this verse also sets forth the thought that the man should be the one in authority in the home and not the woman; that the man should teach and not the woman, and that the man should have dominion over the woman, and not the woman over the man. However, the passage does at least imply that the woman should not have the place of authority in the Church, though it does not forbid her teaching the truth, or giving her testimony for Christ. Paul, himself, elsewhere gives instructions just how the woman should prophesy, if she has the gift of prophecy (1 Cor. 11:4, 5), and the Holy Spirit records with approval that Priscilla, a woman, as well as Aquila, her husband, being better instructed in the things of the Lord than Apollos, who was a man, took him aside and expounded unto him the way of God more perfectly (Acts 18:24–26). And Paul in another place speaks approvingly of two women, Euodias and Syntyche, who labored with him in the Gospel (Phil. 4:3).

How do you explain I Corinthians 14:34: "Let your women keep silence in the churches?"

What is said in answer to the first question largely answers this question, but the context here is different. It has been suggested that the word translated "women" here should be translated "wives." This would be a legitimate translation, but the Greek word here used does mean "women" more commonly than "wives." However the next verse shows that Paul had primarily the married women in mind. The full meaning of this verse is determined by the context as in the previous instance. There was confusion in the church in Corinth (v. 33) arising from several people trying to talk at once, and often times to talk in an unknown tongue (vs. 26, 27). There also seems to have been a tendency for the women to *just talk* in meeting, asking questions of one another and talking to one another while others were prophesying or interpreting. Paul sent word that this thing should end; that the women should keep silence during the meeting and not be talking and interrupting and asking questions; that there should be order in the churches, and that everything should be done decently and in order (v. 40), that if the women didn't understand what was said, let them quietly and modestly wait until they got home and ask their husbands there (v. 35); that it was a disgraceful thing for a woman to talk in Church. He also gives instructions, to the same end of maintaining order in the Church, that the men also, even if they had a revelation, or a tongue, or an interpretation, should observe order and only one talk at a time (v. 27). That Paul did not intend to forbid any woman who had the gift of prophesy, or who was led by the Spirit of God to say something, doing it, seems clear from the instructions that he gives in the eleventh chapter as to how a woman should pray, if she were led to pray, and how she should prophesy, if she were led to prophesy (ch. 11:5). Furthermore, we are plainly told that when Paul was in Caesarea that the four daughters of Philip, the evangelist, prophesied (Acts 21:8, 9). Of course, Paul had no use for the noisy, self-assertive woman who always wanted to be seen and heard, and who wished to take the leadership to herself, and Paul in this matter, as in all other matters that he taught, was the mouthpiece of the Holy Spirit.

SERVING AND WAITING QUESTION BOX

By the Editor*

Woman's Ministry

Will you let me know through your question box to what extent to your understanding is the exhortation in 1 Cor. 14:34, 35 applicable to our present time. Am I correct in believing that Paul says in the opening, "To those who at all times and at all places call upon the name of the Lord Jesus?" This I believe to include myself as well as the saints at the church at Corinth. There seems to be considerable controversy on this subject.

In reply to this question we pass on to our readers the following from Dr. Scofield, written in response to the question, "Is it unscriptural for a woman to preach?" It is included in *Dr. C. I. Scofield's Question Box* ($1.25, plus postage; this office). He says: "There is no verse which says a woman must not preach. Three things are forbidden to women: (1) They must not interrupt meetings where the Holy Spirit is at work, by asking questions (1 Cor. 14:23–35); (2) A woman must not 'teach.' The word *didaskein* here means, as defined by Thayer, 'to deliver didactic discourses,'—i.e., to teach doctrinally by authority,—as we would say, dogmatically. It is the same word used by the apostle of himself [in] 1 Timothy 2:7. A woman must not set herself up as an authority in matters of doctrine, like an apostle (1 Tim. 2:12); (3) A woman must not be put in a place of authority in the church, such as the office of elder would be (1 Tim. 2:12, 13). The ordination of women is an abomination. It should be remembered that two great principles govern the relation of subordination in marriage (Gen. 3:16; 1 Tim. 2:13). The second is like, but has special reference to marriage as a type. The wife is to be in subjection to her husband as the church is unto Christ. It is obvious that 1 Corinthians 14:34, 35 relates to married women, as also do 1 Timothy 2:12 and Ephesians 5:24. The prohibition to 'teach' is, however, general. 'I

---

*William L. Pettingill, ed., *Serving and Waiting*.

suffer not a woman to teach (authoritatively).' So far all is negative. What a woman clearly may do is (1) to 'prophesy' (1 Cor. 11:5; Acts 21:9). The gift of prophecy is not exclusively, nor even chiefly, foretelling, but forth-telling—speaking to edification, and exhortation and comfort (1 Cor. 14:3). Such speaking, therefore, is permissible to women. A word as to covering the head in 1 Corinthians 11:5: Nothing could be more contrary to the whole spirit of this dispensation than to use the casual mention of an ancient custom in a Greek city as fastening a legal and, so to speak, Levitical ceremonial upon Christians in all ages. The point is that 'the head of the woman is the man.' It is the divine order. The angels know this. To them any inversion of that order would be disorder. In Corinth a shorn or 'uncovered' head in the presence of men was a badge of harlotry, and a harlot is not only a woman who sells her body, but she is a woman who has thrown off the restraints of the subordination—of the divine order. In a mixed assembly, therefore, a spiritually-minded and biblically-taught Christian woman who speaks or prays would do so in a modest and womanly manner, keeping her place in the divine order. It will be obvious, therefore, that, within the limits expressly fixed, and with the spirit of modesty and subordination, a Christian woman may exercise a wide and varied ministry. (2) She may teach, in any sense not involving dogmatic declaration of doctrine; (3) she may speak 'to edification and comfort;' (4) she may also pray (1 Cor. 11:5); and, (5) since 'him that heareth' is commanded to say 'Come,' she may evangelize.''

FEMALE EVANGELISTS PUBLICIZED BY
MOODY BIBLE INSTITUTE

CWM = *The Christian Workers Magazine*
MBIM = *Moody Bible Institute Monthly*
MM = *Moody Monthly*

Assorted Evangelists

1. "Mrs. M. F. Bryner, June 2–4, Tulsa, Oklahoma." *CWM* 8 (June 1908): 792.
2. Evangelistic Future Engagements—"Mary Foster Bryner, Sept. 24–26, Douglas, Wyoming." *CWM* 10 (Sept. 1909): 79.
3. "Mrs. Moody and I assisted the pastor of the First Baptist Church, Galesburg, Ill., in a series of meetings. . . . The pastor did most of the preaching though Mrs. Moody accepted the pulpit several times." *CWM* 16 (June 1916): 794.
4. "Rev. Dr. and Mrs. James B. Ely, Presbyterian evangelists." *MBIM* 25 (Jan. 1925): 245.
5. "The College Hill Baptist Church of Lynchburg, Va., has just closed a very successful meeting of two weeks. . . . Mrs. C. L. Steidley of Gastonis, N.C., brought the gospel messages." *MBIM* 25 (Jan. 1925): 246.
6. "The Bonney Workers report sixteen campaigns in 1929. . . . Mr. and Mrs. Bonney formerly worked as pastor's helpers but this year are working as evangelists with Mrs. Bonney as the preacher." *MBIM* 30 (Jan. 1930): 263.

Lydia E. Brown

1. "Mrs. Lydia E. Brown closed her work with the Free Baptist Church at Plainfield, Mich., and has some open dates." *CWM* 15 (Jan. 1915): 318.
2. "Mrs. L. E. Brown closed evangelistic meetings at Broadview, Ill., with 100 conversions." *CWM* 15 (Aug. 1915): 576.
3. "Lydia E. Brown . . . held several meetings in Belvidere, and at Epworth Camp Grounds." *CWM* 15 (Aug. 1915): 791.
4. "Lydia E. Brown has been holding meetings in the M.E. and Baptist churches Leavenworth, Kans." *CWM* 16 (Sept. 1915): 48.

5. "Mrs. Lydia E. Brown, who for some time was doing evangelistic work, has taken a pastorate of two country charges at McCook, Neb." *CWM* 17 (Nov. 1916): 214.

Emma Paige

1. "Miss Emma Paige and Miss Alpharette Smith are engaged in evangelistic work." *CWM* 11 (Aug. 1911): 1058.
2. "Miss Emma Paige and Miss Madeline James have organized an evangelistic party for denominational and union meetings. . . . Miss Paige will do the preaching." *CWM* 16 (Nov. 1915): 217.
3. "The Lord is giving us a blessed meeting at Postville, Ia. . . . the people are responding more readily to the gospel than in any place I ever preached." *CWM* 16 (Jan. 1916): 400.

Sara C. Palmer

1. "The evangelistic campaigns conducted by Miss Sara C. Palmer at Mount Carmel, Pa., resulted in 155 conversions and reconsecrations. The First M.E. Church, where the meetings were held, received great blessings." *CWM* 16 (Jan. 1916): 399.
2. "Report from John E. Beard, pastor of the M.E. Church, Freeland, Pa.: The Palmer Party concluded an evangelistic campaign. . . . Freeland is a better community because of the work of Miss Palmer, and her helpers." *CWM* 16 (March 1916): 561.
3. "Sara C. Palmer and Party closed a four week campaign in the First M.E. Church, Milton, Pa." *CWM* (April 1916): 635.
4. " . . . evangelistic meetings from May 16 to 18, with Miss Sara C. Palmer and Miss Florence H. Saxman in charge of the meetings, which were held in the First Baptist Church. . . . The pastor cooperated heartily in the work." *CWM* 17 (July 1917): 904.
5. "Miss Sara C. Palmer . . . closed a campaign in Grace M.E. Church Patterson, N.J." *MBIM* 21 (Jan. 1921): 240.
6. "Miss Sara C. Palmer has just closed an evangelistic campaign at Johnsonburg, Pa." *MBIM* (25 July 1925): 518.
7. "Miss Sara C. Palmer has just closed a most blessed revival in the North Berwich (Pa.) Evangelical Church." *MBIM* 29 (Jan. 1929): 259.
8. "Sara C. Palmer conducted what has been reported as the greatest revival that has ever been held in Tunkhannock, Pa., and vicinity since the tabernacle meetings of seventeen years ago. . . . More than 200 responded. . . . The remarkable success of the campaign was a fine tribute to Miss Palmer in her home community." *MBIM* 32 (Jan. 1932): 268.
9. "Sara C. Palmer conducted two weeks of meetings. . . . Thirty-seven accepted Christ. . . . the evangelist's Bible temperance work was highly commendable." *MM* 43 (Jan. 1943): 315.

Violet Heefner

1. "Violet Heefner and Anna Sudenga held a campaign in Hudson, Iowa, . . . twenty-two decisions." *MBIM* 33 (July 1933): 515.

2. "Violet Heefner and Anna Sudenga report 25 decisions for Christ in the eight day campaign . . . Marne, Iowa, Methodist Protestant Church." *MBIM* 34 (July 1934): 526.

3. "Will you join us in prayer for them?" (editors). "Violet and Ruby Heefner, and Anna Sudenga, held an eight day campaign . . . nearly a hundred conversions." *MBIM* 36 (Jan. 1936): 276.

4. "Violet Heefner assisted by Anna Sudenga, musician, and Ruby Heefner, song leader, held an evangelistic campaign." *MBIM* 36 (July 1936): 575.

5. "During the month of May, Violet Heefner and Anna Sudenga were busy in meetings in the northwest." *MBIM* 37 (July 1937): 593.

6. "Violet Heefner . . . held an eight-day campaign in Miss Heefner's home church, the Galilee Baptist Church, Des Moines, Iowa. . . . Two days after the close of the meeting, Violet Heefner was ordained as a Baptist preacher-evangelist." *MBIM* 38 (Jan. 1938): 283.

7. "The week of services held by Violet Heefner and Anna Sudenga in the Northern Baptist Church, West Frankfort, Ill., resulted in 35 conversions." *MM* 41 (Jan. 1941): 314.

8. "Violet Heefner and Ida Vogel held a week's meeting in the Barr United Brethren Church near Drummand, Okla." *MM* 42 (July 1942): 673.

9. "An eight-day series of meetings was conducted by Violet Heefner and Ida Vogel." *MM* 44 (Jan. 1944): 344.

10. "Violet Heefner and Ida Vogel held a week's meeting in the Congregational Church, Grandin, Mo." *MM* 45 (Jan. 1945): 304.

FEMALE STUDENTS AND ALUMNAE PUBLICIZED BY MOODY BIBLE INSTITUTE

CWM = *The Christian Workers Magazine*
IT = *The Institute Tie*
MAN = *Moody Alumni News*
MBIM = *Moody Bible Institute Monthly*
MM = *Moody Monthly*

Ordained Ministers

1. "Miss Rosa Lizenby is now in charge of a church in Wheaton, Kansas." *CWM* 9 (March 1909): 621.
2. "Miss Rosa A. Lizenby ('01–'03) was ordained in the Congregational Church of Wheaton, Kansas, October 18th. She has accepted a call to serve this church another year." *CWM* 10 (Dec. 1909): 339.
3. Rosa A. Lizenby, Wheaton, Kansas—"Spiritual blessing is our continual portion in the pastoral work here. Since Jan. 1, 1910, there have been 22 additions to our church membership." *CWM* 10 (April 1910): 646.
4. Rosa B. Lizenby writes from Wheaton, Kansas—"Three months of my third year's pastoral work in this place are already gone. God has been good to me. Am earnestly looking forward to better things." *CWM* 11 (April 1911): 738.
5. "Rosa A. Lizenby will soon begin her fourth year as pastor of the Congregational Church at Wheaton, Kansas. There are many evidences of God's blessing on her work." *CWM* 13 (Sept. 1912): 58.
6. "Rosa A. Lizenby, '01, Rodedale, Kansas, is pastor of a Congregational mission church. This is her second year in this field, and the church has already doubled its membership." *CWM* 15 (May 1915): 583.
7. 1903—Rev. Rosa A. Lizenby Robb. "Oct. 9, 1926, I finished 18 years in the gospel ministry. Have just finished three months of my fifth year in the Butler Ave. Congregational Church." *MAN*, March 1927, 11.
8. "Bertha Fogelberg, '05, Solomon, Kan., is pastor of the United Brethren Church of the North Kansas Conference. She was ordained three years ago." *CWM* 15 (May 1915): 583.
9. "Mrs. Ellery Aldridge, '20, who was ordained to the Christian ministry some months ago in the First Baptist Church, Gloversville, NY, preached her first sermon in that church May 27." *MBIM* 29 (Nov. 1928): 145.

10. 1925—"Rev. and Mrs. Emiel J. Schott were ordained to the gospel ministry on Jan. 17, 1931. They have been doing evangelistic work in the past six years and have been used in the salvation of many souls." *MAN*, Sept. 1931, 15.

11. Elizabeth A. Warner, '97—"She makes her home with the first woman ordained by a Congregational Council, the pastor of a local church." *CWM* 14 (June 1914): 698.

Pastors and Preachers

1. 1891—(Rev.) Miss Hattie E. Alvord, pastor of the M.E. Church, Ontario, N.Y.—"All can see that God is working here. A changed place, thank God." *MAN*, March 1927, 7.

2. 1891—Rev. Hattie E. Alvord, Ontario, N.Y., pastor of the M.E. Church. "God is blessing. The whole community has and is changing its attitude towards the church." *MAN* 1938, 9.

3. 1891—"Rev. Hattie E. Alvord has been assisting in evangelistic meetings." *MAN*, Dec. 1930, 10.

4. Miss Sarah N. Cobb—leads a large adult Bible class, works among Germans of Louisville, Ky. In Nebraska and Iowa—"Miss Emma K. Henry has been conducting special meetings in various places;" 2 1/2 weeks in Avoca, Iowa (town of 1,600 people and nine saloons); "some of the saloon men came out and heard the gospel;" Fontanelle, Iowa—"As the Congregational church there had no pastor, I accepted an invitation to serve that church as supply through the summer. My effort has been to develop the church along two lines where it, or rather they, for I was supplying two churches, were noticeably deficient," one in the exercise of Christian charity and the other in the grace of Christian giving; "The Word of God was the means for the accomplishment of both these ends and proved an efficient weapon." *IT*, 24 Nov. 1891, 14–15.

5. Miss Grace Bilger, Tacoma, Washington—"he desires me to take a Sunday night service regularly at another mission"—she consented. *IT*, 15 July 1892, 134.

6. Miss Mary Moore in Kentucky—"My efforts have been in many directions; First, a revival, thence to the country to organize a Sunday School and to help build a church." *IT*, 30 July 1892, 142.

7. "Martha, '95, is pastor of the Congregational Church, Arcadia, Neb." *CWM* 15 (June 1915): 647.

8. "Martha Nichol, '95, pastor of the Congregational churches of Madrid and Venango, Neb." *CWM* 17 (Dec. 1916): 311.

9. 1898—"Rev. Harry F. Bohn and Mrs. (NEE Anna L. Adams '97) have charge of a Methodist church at Webster Grove, near St. Louis, Mo." *MAN*, Dec. 1926, 5.

10. "Mrs. L. B. Mayos has taken charge of the Congregational church at Stafford, Kansas." *IT* 4 (May 1904): 292.

11. "Mrs. Lydia Brock Mayos, '97, after leaving the Institute received a call to become pastor of a Congregational church, Clay Center, Kansas, where she served five years. Soon after, she married the Rev. J. C. Mayos, and together they have been working as pastors." *CWM* 16 (Sept, 1915): 56.

12. 1899—Rev. Lydia Brock Mayos. "In work in Kansas as a pastor for the past 28 years. My husband is also a minister, Rev. J. C. Mayos, and we work together." *MAN*, June 1927, 6.

13. 1899—"Mrs. Lydia B. Mayos, pastor Congregational Church, Ford, Kan." *MAN*, March 1928, 10.

14. 1900—"Mrs. Lina Zook Ressler, Scottdale, Pa. Preacher." *MAN*, March 1927, 10.

15. "Mrs. Minnie J. Dickinson, '01, has resigned the pastorate of the Central Park Congregational Church, Boise, Ida." *CWM* 17 (Feb. 1917): 494.

16. "Miss Leo Noah Harris, '00–'01, is assistant to Rev. Mrs. I. E. Taylor, pastor of the Congregational church at Littleton, Colo." *IT* 3 (Nov. 1902): 104.

17. 1901—"Mary F. Turnbull . . . she supplied the pulpit of the LaSalle Street Methodist Church, in Beatrice, Neb." *MAN*, Dec. 1932, 8.

18. Mrs. Ada Andress Heyse—"In September, 1902, I married to another M.B.I. student, Henry E. Heyse, then pastor in Leadville, Colo. Mr. Heyse died after 16 years and at his death, I was called as regular pastor, remaining in my husband's pulpit five years, at Melvin, Ill." *MAN*, March 1927, 11.

19. "Mrs. H. E. Heyse, '01–'02, has been called to the pastorate of the Congregational church at Leadville, Colorado. Mr. Heyse becomes pastor of the Congregational church at Meredith, Colo." *IT* 4 (June 1904): 364.

20. "Miss Emma Fiel is doing pastoral work in a Baptist church in Biddeford, Maine." *CWM* 9 (March 1909): 621.

21. "Miss Mabel J. Dustin, '01–'02 is engaged in pastoral work in Eden, Vermont." *IT* 2 (May 1902): 418.

22. Miss Maggie Grimes, '03–'05—"each town having two or three churches and almost every Sunday since I have had the privilege of telling the Gospel story in one of these churches. Our methodist pastor has gone to conference, and yesterday I held two services at different towns, . . . both churches were filled with people." *IT* 6 (Dec. 1905): 139.

23. "Mary E. Murrell, '04, is now serving her eighth year as pastor of the United Brethren Church at Henderson, Ill." *CWM* 17 (Sept. 1916): 66.

24. "Miss Iona Brosius, '04, is acting as pastor of a Congregational Church in Galt, Ia.." *CWM* 17 (March 1917): 590.

25. "Miss Cora Tester has had a successful winter in evangelistic work." *CWM* 9 (May 1909): 785.

26. "Cora Tester, '05 of Wapakoneta, Ohio, reports that her present pastorate is a good one." *CWM* 16 (April 1916): 642.

27. 1907—"Ella Montgomery . . . was for five years in charge of a little mission church in West Mansfield, Ohio." *MAN*, Dec. 1929, 7.

28. 1909—"Miss M. W. Rouzee . . . conducting extension Bible classes of an interdenominational character . . . hundreds of young men and women of college age are attracted by plain straightforward Bible teaching." *MAN,* Sept. 1938, 6.

29. "Miss Mabel Rouzee went to Colorado some months ago for a needed rest and found a section where religious services had never been held. Work was thrust upon her. People drive from 6–10 miles to attend the services. God is blessing the work, which included rough cowboys, farmers, and their wives." *CWM* 11 (Feb. 1911): 548.

30. "Miss Mollie McMillan is pastor's assistant of the First Baptist Church in Springfield, Mo." *CWM* 11 (Nov. 1910): 221.

31. "Miss Florence M. Price . . . will this summer have charge of two small churches, one a Methodist and one a Congregational church. She is the only minister in the entire township." *CWM* 11 (Aug. 1911): 1058.

32. Clara G. Richmond, '11—"I have been traveling in evangelistic work for three years, but at present I have charge of a country church." *CWM* 17 (Oct. 1916): 147.

33. "Mrs. Winnifred G. Rhoads, '11, is pastor of the Second Baptist Church, Oshkosh, Wisc." *CWM* 17 (Dec. 1916): 311.

34. "Lillian D. Jones, '11, who was acting as missionary pastor in a small church in Ontario, Wisc., is now located on Washington Island, Wisc." *CWM* 15 (Jan. 1915): 323.

35. "Mrs. Wickman is pastor of the Baptist Church at Washington Island, Wisc., and was formerly Miss Lillian Jones, '13. . . . Mrs. Winnifred G. Rhoads, '14, pastor of Second Baptist Church, Oshkosh, Wisc." *CWM* 16 (July 1916): 877.

36. "Mrs. William Wickman, '13 (Lillian D. Jones), has again accepted the pastorate of the Baptist Church on Washington Island, Wisc." *CWM* 18 (Feb. 1918): 516.

37. 1913—Mrs. Mabel C. Thomas. "Served 10 years in field with husband, L. H. Thomas, now deceased, as singing evangelists. Called to pastorate at Phillipsburg, Kansas, Christian Church two years ago. Besides the preaching taught a week night class in Outline Studies in Old Testament . . . baptized about 30 . . . expect to continue pastoral work, if Lord so leads. Could not have met the many and varied opportunities for service without training of M.B.I." *MAN,* June 1927, 12.

38. Mrs. S. L. Brown, '14—"is a Baptist pastor at Bellingham, Wash." *MBIM* 21 (Jan. 1921): 246.

39. 1914—"Harriet H. Albee, West Stewartstown, N.H. Pastor, Congregational Church." *MAN,* March 1927, 13.

40. 1914—"Harriet H. Albee . . . in charge of the Congregational Church." *MAN,* Dec. 1927, 9.

41. "Mrs. M. H. Wakefield . . . writes that her husband is pastor of the Windsor Baptist Church . . . also supplying for two other churches. . . . This gives her an opportunity to supply for him when he is serving the other churches." *CWM* 16 (Dec. 1915): 323.

42. 1916—N. Grace Cooledge, Greenfield, Mass. Teaching and preaching . . . "supply the pulpit in a tiny church Sundays." *MAN,* March 1927, 15.

43. 1917—Mary Isabella Bradley, New York City, Methodist Episcopal Deaconess. "Was granted local preacher's license last July." *MAN,* March 1927, 15.

44. "Mrs. M. S. Patterson, '17, is pastor of the Central M. E. Church, Bay City, Mich., and her husband is pastor of a church on the west side of the city." *MBIM* 27 (March 1927): 362.

45. Mrs. H. K. W. Patterson, Aug. '17, at M. E. Church in Lincoln, Mich., where husband was severely injured in a car accident—"Mrs. Patterson was obliged to assume the duties of the pastorate. She occupied the pulpit and preached sometimes three times on a Sunday." *CWM* 19 (Feb. 1919): 428.

46. "Florence Merle Elmer, '18, has been licensed to preach by the Methodist church and pastor of a church at Tupper Lake, N.Y." *MBIM* 22 (Dec. 1921).

47. 1919—"Ruth Haake is assistant pastor of two churches, Lansing, Mich. . . . she has been granted a local preacher's license." *MBIM* 22 (July 1922): 1126.

48. "Mrs. G. A. Eakins (Pattie Mather '20), is occupying the pulpit of the Presbyterian church at Saratoga, Wyo., in place of her husband . . . who lost his life." *MBIM* 27 (Jan. 1927): 269.

49. Aug. 1920—"Mabel E. Shultz has been appointed pastor of her home church, Sutton, Neb." *MBIM* 23 (March 1923): 321.

50. "Myrtle Rayburn, '20, is preaching in a small church in Champaign, Ill." *MBIM* 21 (April 1921): 382.

51. 1922—Rev. Margaret Flanigan, student Pittsburgh Theological Seminary. "I had a very unique experience—preaching before the faculty and student body and of being only the second woman preacher who has done so in the history of the school, which is in its 102nd year. I have been a licensed minister of the Methodist Episcopal Church for four years, spending most of that time as a missionary pastor of some of the churches of the Coke Mission, Pittsburgh Conference." *MAN,* Dec. 1927, 12.

52. 1922—Miss Margaret Flanigan. "Assumed the pastorate of the M. E. Church. . . . There are four churches in the town. I am the first woman pastor. They considered me quite a novelty at first; also, there was some prejudice among the men. Two have changed their attitude and I believe are among my best friends. . . . God has surely proved this is my appointment." *MAN,* March 1928, 14.

53. 1922—Rev. Margaret Flanigan, New Alexandria, Pa. "I am returning for my second year's work . . . the Lord very definitely led me to get Miss Edna P. Wright, Dec. '25, to assist me in a four weeks campaign in our church . . . she also ably filled the pulpit several times." *MAN,* Dec. 1928, 6.

54. 1922—"Margaret Flanigan . . . is pastor of the New Alexandria, Pa., Methodist Episcopal Church." *MAN*, Dec. 1929, 10.

55. 1922—"Mary E. Washington, . . . New Albany, Ind., pastoring a church." *MAN*, March 1927, 19.

56. 1922—Mary E. Washington, New Albany, Ind. "I have been engaged in evangelistic work, and for the past three years I have been pastor of a small church." *MAN*, Dec. 1929, 9.

57. 1923—Mrs. Violet J. G. Bagley, Franklin, Maine. "Have spent three years as a rural pastor, going to remote places where the churches are too poor to pay a man." *MAN*, Dec. 1927, 13.

58. 1923—C. Regina Cash. "This is my first full-time Christian work—coming here to Searsmont, Maine, as supply pastor." *MAN*, Sept. 1928, 8.

59. 1923—Edna M. Dexter, Pine Ridge, Ky. ". . . hold S.S. and preaching services in four places, riding horseback from one station to another." *MAN*, June 1928, 6.

60. "Anna Nelson, '23, is serving her fourth year as pastor of the M. E. Church, Emmet, Neb. She expects to be ordained a deacon next September." *MBIM* 30 (April 1930): 415.

61. "Fanny B. Mills is serving as pastor in the Presbyterian Church at Wayland, S.D." *MAN*, Dec. 1926, 6.

Evangelists

1. "Miss Ellis, the Evangelist, rejoices the hearts of her many friends here by the good news of her work in Sioux Rapids, Iowa. . . . 'God has graciously poured out his Spirit upon the people . . . last night every inch was taken up.' " *IT*, 30 Dec. 1892, 29.

2. "Miss Preston writes encouragingly of the evangelistic services in which she is assisting Miss Emma K. Henry in Iowa . . . 'nearly forty have taken a stand in the meeting.' " *IT*, 30 Dec. 1892, 29.

3. "Since her return to the States, Miss Jameson has been conducting revival services for four weeks in N. Tonawanda, N.Y. She says, 'I am so thankful for the privilege of service. I have had the great joy of seeing seventy persons accept Christ, these last few weeks.' " *IT* 2 (March 1902): 266.

4. Miss Mary Jameson, '96–'97, spending the winter in Brooklyn in city mission work—"about 250 decisions for Christ in meetings she conducted." *IT* 3 (May 1903): 334.

5. "Miss Mary Jameson, '96–'97, held meetings in Chautauqua Co. In the six evangelistic meetings she held there were 66 decisions for Christ. . . . This fall and winter she is engaged for meetings for the grape pickers in Western N.Y." *IT* 5 (Oct. 1904): 106.

6. Miss Mary Jameson, located at Irving, N.Y. "I am holding meetings in villages around here and there have been many decisions for Christ." *IT* 5 (Nov, 1904): 144.

7. Mary Jameson—"During my last four weeks of meetings held in villages in Chautauqua County, I received 108 names of those who publicly confessed Christ." *IT* 5 (Jan. 1905): 238.

8. Mary Jameson—recent evangelistic meetings in Grace M. E. Church, Corning, N.Y. "I have been here ten days, and there has already been 56 decisions for Christ among the adults, besides more than 100 children." *IT* 2 (March 1902): 236.

9. Mary Jameson in Rochester, N.Y.—75 decisions for Christ in Brockport; Begin in Niagara Falls, March 19th. *IT* 4 (April 1904): 368.

10. Mary Jameson—"recently completed a three weeks itinerary in Orleans Co., N.Y., where she spoke afternoons and evenings in Gospel temperance work for the W.C.T.U., gaining forty new members and 25 decisions for Christ, and about fifty Christians surrendering for the 'more abundant life'. Then she went to Slater Island for similar work until Christmas." *IT* 6 (Dec. 1905): 138.

11. Mary Jameson—has been holding revival services at Smithtown Branch, Greenport, and Islip, Long Island during April. 300–400 conversions. *CWM* 7 (May 1907): 452.

12. "Miss Mary Jameson began evangelistic meetings at Owen Sound, Canada, on Oct. 14." *CWM* 8 (May 1908): 240.

13. The Evangelistic Field—recent meetings of Miss Mary Jameson at Brigden, Ontario. *CWM* 10 (Nov. 1909): 241.

14. 1897—"Mrs. William (Virginia) Asher is doing evangelistic work with the William A. Sunday party." *MAN,* Dec. 1926, 5.

15. "Miss Anna E. Smith, '99–'01, has accepted a call to engage in evangelistic work under the Duluth Bethel Association. Miss Smith is now preaching in a tent on the corner of one of the leading business streets in Duluth. The pastors seem to be cooperating in the work and souls are being saved." *IT* 3 (Sept. 1902): 22.

16. "Miss Anna E. Smith and Miss Josephine Millard, '99–'01, who is accompanying her as singer, are holding meetings at Bemidji, Minn. The people are supporting the meetings well and souls are being saved." *IT* 3 (Nov. 1902): 173.

17. Miss Anna E. Smith, Crookston, Minn., writes of revival—"We have been here almost a month for every night, and the interest is at its very height. Three towns are waiting, but the people here will not let us go." *IT* 3 (April 1903): 296.

18. Miss Anna E. Smith, '99–'01, writing recently about her evangelistic work—"I closed the meeting at Glenwood Springs, Colo., after holding it for three weeks. I count it the best and most successful meeting ever held. There were eighty conversions. . . . Some were business men of the town. . . . crowds so large that the ushers could hardly seat all who came in." *IT* 4 (Feb. 1904): 253.

19. Anna E. Smith—at her last meeting in Crookstone, 85 conversions. *IT* 3 (May 1903): 334.

20. Miss M. Theodora Auman, '00–'02, at St. Albans, Vt.—"My work at present is evangelistic, staying from ten days to two weeks in a place, singing, speaking, personal work and visiting in homes." *IT* 3 (May 1903): 334.

21. Miss M. Theodora Auman, '00–'02—from Alburg Springs, Vt.—"The idea of open air meetings was a new one here. . . . I had to do all the singing (four or five solos an evening) and the speaking, for the minister who came to help me confessed he was scared to death" when I called on him to lead in prayer. *IT* 3 (Jan. 1903): 152.

22. 1903—"Martha Elnora Mann, . . . Muncie, Ind., Evangelist." *MAN*, June 1927, 6.

23. "Miss Eva Ludgate conducted a successful campaign at Washington, Michigan last month." *CWM* 8 (Jan. 1908): 386.

24. "Miss Eva Ludgate recently conducted successful meetings in Lee Center, Joliet, Geneseo, and Platteville, Ill. While at Joliet, Miss Ludgate spoke and sang to the prisoners at the penitentiary. . . . Miss Ludgate has been asked to conduct a service for them at an early date." *CWM* 10 (April 1910): 647.

25. "Miss Eva Ludgate, '07, of Wheaton, Ill., was ordained a Congregational minister, May 29, by members of the Denmark Association at the Congregational Church, Danville, Iowa. She will supply this church for the summer." *CWM* 13 (June 1913): 735.

26. "Eva Ludgate and her chorister, Miss Florence Ories, have had a successful season. They conducted nine evangelistic campaigns." *CWM* (July 1916): 867.

27. Emma V. Paige, '07, writes of rich blessing in the evangelistic field—"I know the Institute was the instrument most largely used of God to prepare me for this work." *CWM* 18 (Oct. 1917): 147.

28. "Miss Goldia Whitsell, '08, is doing evangelistic work in Kansas." *CWM* 12 (Jan. 1912): 379.

29. "Miss Josephine Nance Kivell is very much encouraged by her work as an evangelist in Canada." *CWM* 9 (April 1909): 705.

30. "Miss Florence Heagle, as Gospel singer, is associated with Mrs. A. H. Stetson, evangelist. They are open to engagements in churches." *CWM* 11 (Nov. 1910): 221.

31. "Miss Bessie Lane, '11, has been assisting Mrs. Muirhead in evangelistic meetings in Ellwood City, Pa. . . . during the month." *CWM* 12 (Jan. 1912): 442.

32. "Helen Byrnes, '12, has become associated with Mrs. Bertha J. Harris, Cleveland, Ohio, in evangelistic work." *CWM* 13 (May 1913): 608.

33. "Bertha J. Harris and Mrs. Helen Byrnes will be in Florida for evangelistic meetings." *CWM* 15 (Jan. 1915): 319.

34. 1912—"Helen L. Byrnes . . . was elected national evangelist for the W.C.T.U." *MAN* Dec. 1926, 6.

35. "Ethel and Mary Closson have returned to Pennsylvania for evangelistic work and have good prospects for a successful season." *CWM* 15 (Nov. 1914): 187.

Bible Teachers

1. "Miss Grace Saxe, '95–'97, the Bible teacher following Evangelist Williams' meetings, has recently closed a most helpful course of Bible study with the converts and others at Fremont, Nebraska." *IT* 3 (Nov. 1902): 107.

2. "Miss Grace Saxe has been retained by the Torrey Mission Committee of Buffalo, NY, for a second series of interdenominational Bible lectures, covering twelve weeks, beginning Jan. 15; over 1,500 persons attended the first series." *CWM* 8 (Feb. 1908): 495.

3. Miss Grace Saxe—Gave Bible lessons in Buffalo, growing out of interest in Dr. Torrey's meetings last year. "She has nine classes weekly and much interest in the work by pastors . . . and their people." *CWM* 8 (March 1908): 576.

4. "Miss Grace Saxe expects to supply the pulpit of Plymouth M.E. Church, Buffalo, in August during the pastor's vacation, and will conduct another six-months' course of Bible readings beginning Oct. 1, under the auspices of the Torrey Mission committee." *CWM* 8 (July 1908): 855.

5. Miss Grace Saxe—Bible Study classes in Buffalo, Oct. 1–17; classes open to both men and women. *CWM* 9 (Oct. 1908): 159.

6. Miss Grace Saxe in Egypt—"I have been in Assiut where the big American Mission College is situated (600 young men in attendance) and have been teaching Bible in the college. . . . The college boys are enthusiastic over Synthetic Bible Study and also Chapter Summary study. They themselves requested, no just insisted, on having more, so I am going back there for two weeks also." *CWM* 10 (May 1910): 751.

7. Grace Saxe—"I had two weeks Bible work with the theological students in Cairo last month. . . . You should have seen the great meeting of Egyptian men and women last evening. I spoke through an interpreter." *CWM* 10 (May 1910): 752.

8. 1897—"Miss Grace Saxe is doing independent Bible teaching." *MAN,* Dec. 1926, 5.

9. Grace Saxe, '97—"She began her work in and around Waterloo, Iowa, as an organizer and teacher of Bible study classes, following a series of evangelistic services . . . member of the Billy Sunday Party . . . member of the Biederwolf-Rodeheaver Evangelistic Party." *MAN,* Dec. 1930, 5.

10. 1890—Emily S. Strong. "Have a number of Bible classes." *MAN,* March 1927, 7.

11. 1895—"Miss Martha Spencer . . . is doing volunteer service by teaching a Bible class nightly to converts at the Gospel Mission, Washington, D.C." *MAN,* Dec. 1926, 5.

12. 1899—"May N. Blodgett, Bible teacher." *MAN,* Dec. 1926, 5.

13. Miss Eliza N. Finn—"on her way west, where she will take up Bible teaching in a Bible institute to be opened this fall under the management of Rev. A. B. Pritchard at Los Angeles, CA." *IT* 2 (Sept. 1901): 22.

14. 1906—"Miss Eugenia L. Aunspaugh . . . Lynchburg, Va. Bible teacher . . . weekly Bible classes and gospel meetings at the noon hour in certain factories, also, weekday Bible classes in church . . . and the Bible course for high school and college boys and girls." *MAN,* March 1927, 11.
15. 1911—"Miss Margaret E. Tarrant . . . Extension teacher, Brooks Bible Institute." *MAN,* March 1927, 12.
16. 1921—Esther Sabel. "I am at present teaching Bible and Greek in the Bible and Missionary Training Dept. of Bethel Institute, of St. Paul." *MAN,* Dec. 1927, 12.

Assorted

1. Miss Sarah Dennison—Bible Reader in the Norfolk Mission College, work in pastoral visiting. *IT,* 22 Dec. 1891, 38.
2. Miss Gurney—does work among police in England. *IT,* 19 Jan. 1892, 50.
3. 1915—"Anna B. MacKenzie . . . Salvation Army Officer." *MAN,* March 1927, 14.
4. 1926—Rev. Florence Randolph. "I finished the Synthetic Course in 1926 and entered Drew Theological Seminary to specialize in three subjects." *MAN,* Dec. 1929, 11.

THE INSTITUTE TIE

"WORK FOR WOMEN"

Mrs. J. Ellen Foster

I have first a complaint to make to you, brethren, who are teachers and preachers. In your public leadership you are inclined as a rule to emphasize that which is petty and small in woman's life and duties, and not to emphasize as much as you should that which is broad, wide and inspiring. By this I mean that you forget, or rather you overbalance, in your teaching the effeminacy of woman rather than her humanity. You ought to try more to lift woman to a comprehensive thought in Jesus Christ. There is neither male nor female, bond nor free, but we are all one in Christ Jesus; and it is eminently appropriate that I should say this from this platform, for if there was any thing for which D. L. Moody stood it was for this.

You need not exhort women to be true to their homes, — they are going to be anyhow, but they will be true just in proportion as you lead them to the higher planes of fellowship with Christ. A great deal that men say about women's duties, and all that, is perfect bosh! Do not emphasize the things which are small and petty; emphasize the things which are great and wide. What are they? That we all of us do the thing to which God puts us. If you had not emphasized so much the duty of woman to the home, men would not have shirked their duty to the home as they have. There are certain responsibilities which do fall to women, and which never can be passed to the father, but the responsibility of the father cannot be assumed by the mother.

What would I have you do with woman? I would have you enforce her responsibility to God for whatever He puts in her way to do. Sisters, what would I have you do? I would have you study, of all things, the higher Christian life. I would have you get away from the things which are small and transitory. Oh, I am so weary in my soul of associating with women who talk only of small things! They talk about the color of their children's eyes. I know how sweet that is. I know the blue eyes that have looked up to me as mother. I know the joys of womanhood and motherhood. But blue eyes are nothing as compared with white souls. I hear women talk by the hour about recipes for cooking, but the thing is to furnish such food as will keep the body in a normal condition, so that the soul may have a chance. Women, do not spend your time over the inconsequential things, over the things that perish with the using!

The woman who is in the home needs more help than the man on the street does. Out in the street he touches other men; he gets aid, somehow, by the touch. The touch that comes in the family relation is so beautiful; the touch of the woman by the man who is out there in the big world, his view of passing events does her so much good; and her view of passing events, touched by her relation to the home, does him good. If I speak to any woman who walks alone today, as I do, she knows what the absence of that touch means to her.

Now do not forget this, that the woman in your audience, the woman in the school, the woman you meet everywhere,—even the poor woman of the street who falls into sin—the woman in the home who is so compassed about with duties that she scarcely thinks of the higher things, each has a human soul, and the thing she needs most is soul nurture.

MINISTRY OF WOMEN IN THE SOCIETY OF FRIENDS*

By Miss Mildred B. Allen, Fairmount, Ind.

While in some denominations preaching by women is forbidden, the Friends denomination has for over two hundred years had women ministers.

Beginning with the Old Testament, there are found numerous examples of women who were impelled to speak to others on matters of religion by direct and immediate visitations of the Holy Ghost. It was under such influences that Miriam responded to the song of Moses, that Deborah uttered her song of thanksgiving, that Hannah spake her acceptable thanksgiving and praise, that Huldah prophesied to King Josiah and his officers, that Anna spake of Christ to all them that looked for the redemption of Israel, that Elizabeth addressed the mother of her Lord, and Mary sang praises to God her Saviour. Of the individuals here mentioned, Miriam, Deborah and Huldah are expressly called prophetesses. The wife of Isaiah was also a prophetess (Isa. 8:3).

Among the early ministers of the gospel dispensation, particular mention is made of the four daughters of Philip, who preached. Priscilla, the wife of Aquilla whom Paul called his helper or "fellow-laborer in Christ," was also a preacher.

See the definition of the word preach in 1 Corinthians 14:3: "But he that prophesieth speaketh unto men to edification, and exhortation, and comfort." So we see that lip service rendered for the Lord means to preach.

---

*We publish this article because of our regard for the writer and for the Society of Friends which she so well represents. Also with a good part of it we are in hearty accord, especially that part in which man and woman are said to be on equality in Christ. But we raise a question as to whether Miss Allen has said the last word on 1 Timothy 2:12. However, it is re-assuring to note that the inspiration of Paul in that Scripture is not challenged, but that it is a question of interpretation merely. — Editors.

It is recorded in Acts, that when the men and women were gathered together to the number of one hundred twenty, "they were all filled with the Holy Ghost, and spake as the Spirit gave them utterance." This is an indisputable fact, and is the more important because of the prophecy of Joel. It was prophesied that in the last days the Spirit would be poured out upon all flesh; that the daughters as well as sons would prophesy.

Women spake publicly at Corinth, for Paul here tells them to wear something on their heads and in so doing avoid unnecessary criticism. When we remember that men and women dressed alike, we can see the propriety of a woman wearing something on her head to designate her from a man.

Women Disturbers

1 Corinthians 11:5 tells how a woman should dress when she speaks, and 1 Corinthians 14:34 says it is a shame for a woman to speak in public. Here again we are guilty of reading only a part of the Scripture and that part only which justifies our views. This would seem like a contradiction if conditions of time and place are not considered. It is a well-known fact in rhetoric that every antithesis has two co-equal arms. One is prohibitory as in verse 34, and the other permissive as in verse 35. The permissive is that of finding out at home, and the prohibitory is that of talking in church. The Greeks were the most educated people at this time, but education was confined to the men. The Greek word for speak is "lalein" meaning an articulate sound or speaking in an undertone. Verses 31 and 33 of chapter 14 plainly teach that Paul's only motive was to quiet these uneducated women, who were disturbing the meeting.

In 1 Timothy 2:12 Paul says: "But I suffer not a woman to teach, nor to usurp authority over the man, but to be in silence." That women are teaching, whether ordained or not, in every denomination, is an indisputable fact. Especially is this true on the foreign field.

We believe that Paul is here expounding domestic government of which man is the constituted head. The church and state are blighted if the home is not a success. While man is the constituted head, Paul says, "Nevertheless neither is the man without the woman, neither the woman without the man, in the Lord. For as the woman is of the man, even so is the man also by the woman; but "all things of God" (1 Cor. 11:11, 12). Thus Paul puts the Christian man and woman on an equal basis in the Lord. The Christian man will not want to usurp authority over the woman and the Christian woman will not want to usurp authority over the man.

Unfair Criticisms

One of the most unfair criticisms against women ministers is, that women have been the propagators of most false doctrines, such as Christian Science and Russellism. In making a careful study of the kings and queens of England, we find more wicked kings than queens according to their number. Would it be right to brand all the kings of England on account of a few wicked kings? Have we a right to say that women are weaker mentally and morally, on account of a few false women such as Mrs. Eddy, Anne Lee and Johanna and Dr. Julia Sears, as one opponent has recently done? A recent survey shows that Protestant Christian women outnumber the men.

The Friends' interpretation of Paul's writings does not change the fact that they are divinely inspired, but the influence of time, place, occasion and conditions have much meaning when interpreting any Scripture.

To believe that Christ has bestowed a special power upon men, is to believe that God is a respector of persons, and contradicts Paul's statement in Galatians 3:28: "There is neither Jew nor Greek, there is neither bond nor free, there is neither male nor female: for ye are all one in Christ Jesus."

DOES THE BIBLE FORBID WOMEN TO PREACH AND PRAY IN PUBLIC?

With an Estimate of Uldine Utley, the Wonderful Fourteen-Year-Old Girl Evangelist— the Joan of Arc of the Modern Religious World

By Rev. John Roach Straton, D.D.,
Pastor of Calvary Baptist Church, New York

My dear friend the editor of the Western Recorder, "Senex," and other friends among the Southern Baptist Fundamentalists have taken me severely to task because I have tried to help Uldine Utley, the wonderful child evangelist, in her work, and because I invited her to deliver messages in the Calvary Church, New York. Senex says:

> "Dr. Straton has made a good fight against modernism in the past, but in his endorsement of this girl evangelist he denies the authority of the Scriptures, discredits Paul, and in doing so deals a heavy blow against Genesis for which he has fought against the liberals."

The editor of the Western Recorder takes the same grounds, and makes it even more personal by saying:

> "We admire Dr. Straton for his brave defense of fundamental truth. We wonder why on earth he has given the modernist group a club to beat him over the head with by putting a young girl evangelist in his pulpit. We sincerely regret that Dr. Straton should weaken his position as a Baptist voice of Fundamental truth by putting a woman preacher into his pulpit. We beg pardon—not a woman, a girl child."

Another one of our Southern Baptist editors refers to my acts in these matters as "queer capers", and declares that what I have done is a flagrant violation of the clear teaching of the Scriptures. But is it?

As one Bible teacher and preacher I declare my own honest and sincere conviction that it is neither unbiblical nor upbaptistic to help a true prophetess in her testimony and work for God, and I ask an open minded attitude on the part of all who are interested, and a frank and unprejudiced consideration of the whole trend of Scripture teaching, instead of taking one or two isolated verses, that are usually quoted without their context, and apart from the historical and social conditions which called them forth and which made the admonitions they contain obviously applicable only in the localities to which they were addressed. And as this is a matter of general interest, and as the opposition to women preachers is not limited to Southern Baptists, but is found in some measure among all denominations, I beg leave to submit this article about it.

To begin with, I feel that I do not need to defend myself personally from any insinuation of lack of fidelity to Scripture teaching and Bible authority. I have suffered misunderstanding, loss of friends, and opposition in my ministry, even up to the point of vicious persecution itself, because of the fact that I believe without any qualification that the Bible—all of it—is the inspired Word of God and that its teachings are not to be twisted or altered by any consideration of expediency, human fellowship, or influence from those who set themselves up as ecclesiastical overlords and dictators to others. After 24 years of Christian work in Texas, Chicago, Baltimore, Norfolk and New York, (where I have served and suffered now for eight years), I thank God that, with all humility, I have the serene consciousness that I have "contended earnestly for the faith once for all delivered to the saints", and that I can say with Paul, "I have fought a good fight, I have kept the faith."

The Whole Bible on Women Preachers

What, then, does the Word of God teach concerning the relationship of women to the Gospel testimony? Years of faithful study on my part have convinced me absolutely that, seen in the large and taken as a whole, the teaching of Scripture is clear that woman has her rightful place both in the ministry of prayer and in the proclamation of the saving truths of the Gospel. Who can really give the whole Bible, — which we Baptists claim as our sole rule of faith and practice—careful and prayerful study without seeing this truth, and without being driven to the conclusion that one or two texts, which may seem upon the surface to be contrary to the general teaching of Scripture, must be interpreted in harmony with the whole, in accordance with the accepted principles of sound Bible exegesis?

From the very beginning God himself has called and commissioned women and children to have their share in the great work of human salvation. The first prophecy and promise of redemption, coming directly from God Himself, was that "the seed" of "the woman" would bruise the serpent's head. Thus as sin entered the world through woman's thoughtlessness in heeding the adversary and disobeying God, so our heavenly Father seems to have purposed that woman shall also have a chance to redeem this unfortunate record by participating with man in the blessed work of overcoming sin and finally defeating the devil who deceived her. And surely it would have been a strange thing if a God of wisdom, mercy and love had deliberately shut out one half of the human race from any participation in His wise and loving plan of human redemption. It manifestly could not have been so, and the Bible makes this clear.

I will not take space to trace out the large place that the prophetess had among God's people from the very beginning. I merely mention the fact in passing that Miriam and the women of Israel were inspired of God to celebrate publicly the deliverance of Israel, equally with the men. I would call attention to the great work of Deborah and other God inspired women. I would remark upon the striking fact that it was Hulda, a prophetess in the reign of Josiah, who gave the people the truth of God in connection with the finding of the lost Scripture, and who thus was one of the main factors in the great revival of spiritual religion which swept over all Israel, for the glory of God and the redemption of the people.

Woman in the Organization of Christ's Church

And so far as the church dispensation is concerned, the same fact of woman's prominence and blessed influence in prayer, prophecy, and soul saving proclamation of the truths of God, stands out from beginning to end with startling and glorious clearness.

To begin with, it was prophesied that the Saviour would be born of "a Virgin." And Mary, the mother of our Lord, under the direct inspiration of the Holy Spirit, poured out her soul to "magnify the Lord," as her spirit rejoiced in God her Saviour. In what has been called "The Magnificat", she uttered prophecies of world wide significance and application, and expressed for God His determination to scatter "the proud in the imagination of their hearts", to show forth the divine mercy "from generation to generation", to "put down the mighty from their seats", to "exalt them of low degree", to "fill the hungry with good things", and to send the rich "empty away", and she declared for God that He had spoken to His own people with an everlasting message. So, likewise, Elizabeth, her cousin, heard the salutation of Mary, and it is recorded that her own babe—who was to be John the Baptist—leaped in her womb, and Elizabeth was filled with the Holy Ghost, and spoke out with a loud voice and prophesied that there should be "a performance of those things" which were told from the Lord. (See Luke 1)

When the infant Saviour was presented in the Temple, not only did Simeon, the prophet, speak concerning Jesus Christ and His future, but Anna also, the prophetess, "gave thanks likewise unto the Lord and spake of Him to all them that looked for redemption in Jerusalem." (Luke 2:38)

Remember, now, that this prophecy of Anna was uttered in the Temple of God and was spoken publicly to those there gathered—"all them that looked for redemption in Jerusalem."

I will not comment here upon the large space given to descent of Mary the mother of our Lord in connection with the genealogy of Jesus, but will pass on rapidly that I may point out how women were directly connected with the public exercises of religion, not only at the time of the coming of our Saviour in fulfillment of prophecy, but in connection with the divinely ordained organization of the Christian church.

Following the ascension of our Lord, it is recorded that His followers

> "went up into an upper room, where abode both Peter and James and John, and Andrew, Philip and Thomas, Bartholomew, and Matthew, James the son of Alphaeus, and Simon Zelotes, and Judas the brother of James. These all continued with one accord in prayer and supplication, with the women, and Mary the mother of Jesus, and with his brethren." (Acts 1:13–14).

It is to be observed here that not only Mary the mother of Jesus but the other women, who were active already in Christian brotherhood, were accustomed to meet with the male followers of Jesus on terms of absolute equality. They were evidently leading in prayer and outspoken utterances—"supplications"—and "continued with one accord" with the men.

Power for All at Pentecost

Furthermore, on the day of Pentecost "they were all with one accord in one place",—the same group ("all") who had before been in the upper room, and who in obedience to the direct commandment of our Lord were tarrying in Jerusalem until they were "endued with power from on high." (Luke 24:49) While the whole company of them were there—men and women gathered together—

> "suddenly there came a sound from heaven as of a rushing mighty wind, and it filled all the house where they were sitting. And there appeared unto them cloven tongues like as of fire, and it sat upon each of them. And they were all filled with the Holy Ghost, and began to speak with other tongues, as the Spirit gave them utterance." (Acts 2:2–4).

Observe that they were "all filled with the Holy Ghost and began to speak as the Spirit gave them utterance." Following this manifestation and this speaking (the women—"all"—being included in the speaking), when some mocked and said that they were drunk, Peter stood up and corrected this false idea of those who had gathered, and then told them that these manifestations of the Spirit's power were in direct fulfillment of the prophesies uttered by Joel when he said:

> "And it shall come to pass in the last days, saith God, I will pour out of my Spirit upon all flesh; and your sons and your daughters shall prophesy, and your young men shall see visions, and your old men shall dream dreams; and on my servants and on my handmaidens I will pour out in those days of my Spirit; and they shall prophesy". (Acts 2:17–18)

What Joel and Peter Meant

This utterance from Peter at the very organization of the Christian church, and this quotation which he gave from Joel, thereby explicitly applying it, under direct inspiration of the Holy Spirit, to the Christian dispensation, is without question worthy of most profound study and most earnest consideration, because it is absolutely determinative in connection with the question of women speaking in public.

It is to be observed here that Joel in his ancient prophecy had declared that in the "last days, God would pour out His Spirit upon all flesh"—not the male part of the race only—and that both "sons and daughters" shall prophesy, and then he repeated, seemingly for reemphasis, that on both the "servants" (or "bondmen") of God, and on God's "handmaidens" the Father promises that He will pour out in those days—that is "the last days"—of His Spirit, and "they shall prophesy." (Acts 2:18)

Now, Peter, as before remarked, under the immediate guidance of the Holy Spirit of God, took over this ancient prophecy and declared that it applied directly to the new dispensation, and that what the people had seen and heard—of the speaking of both men and women through the Spirit's power—was the fulfillment of that prophecy.

Thus it was proclaimed afresh that in the last days the Spirit of God would be poured out on all flesh, and that both our sons and daughters—God's "handmaidens"—shall prophesy.

I will not take the time to point out in detail that the term "last days", used in this connection, applies to the Christian dispensation. As they are related to the church of Christ, "the last days" began with the coming of Christ. So we read in Hebrews 1:1-2:

> "God, who at sundry times and in divers manners spake in times past unto the fathers by the prophets, hath in these last days spoken unto us by His Son, whom He hath appointed heir of all things, by whom also He made the worlds." (Hebrews 1:1-2).

If, then, God inspired His ancient prophet Joel to see that "in the last days", not only our sons, but our daughters,—God's "handmaidens"—should have the Spirit poured out upon them, leading them to prophesy, and if the Apostle Peter at the very beginning of Christian church, and, as observed, under the direct inspiration and guidance of the Holy Spirit, took over and repeated that prophecy and declared that the manifestations of the Spirit's power poured out on both men and women were from God and therefore that "they shall prophesy", who will dare to say that women shall not prophesy when the Holy Spirit of God has been poured out upon them, and they are commanded of the Lord thus to utter their testimony, thus to prophesy?

Are we not driven by such considerations to the conclusion that the few texts which seem to teach the contrary,—which I will take up a little later for specific consideration—must not really so teach but, properly understood, and given their due setting, that they must be in harmony with this general teaching of scripture? Unless this is true, then Scripture is to be broken and one part of it is to contradict another, which is contrary to all the rules of Bible exposition that I learned in my training days at Southern Baptist Theological Seminary, and elsewhere.

And that women, equally with men, "preached" at the time that the Gospel message was first sent out from Jerusalem is perfectly clear. It is written in Acts 8 that at the time of the martyrdom of Stephen,

> "there was a great persecution against the church which was at Jerusalem; and they were all scattered abroad throughout the regions of Judaea and Samaria, except the Apostles," and that "they that were scattered abroad ("all" the Jerusalem church, "except the Apostles") went everywhere preaching the Word" (Acts 8:1 and 4).

Then, it tells us how Phillip went down to the City of Samaria and "preached Christ unto them". Then later, after "preaching" to the crowds at Samaria, where "the people with one accord" (the assembly) gave heed, etc. the Holy Spirit called Phillip to leave the "big meeting" at Samaria and go down "unto Gaza which is desert", where he found the Ethiopian Eunuck, to whom (one man) it is said he "preached unto him Jesus" (Acts 8:35). The sort of "preaching", therefore, that both men and women did when they were "all" scattered abroad and "went everywhere preaching the Word", was the proclamation of the Gospel both to crowds and to individuals alone, as opportunity offered.

The Meaning of "Prophesy"

But let us return for a moment to a further consideration of this general line of Scripture teaching concerning women speaking and praying, before we come to a definite consideration of the texts which are quoted from Paul upon the subject, which my critics seem to stand upon, to the neglect and exclusion of all the remainder of Scripture teaching.

What does it mean when God declares that in "the last days" He will pour out His Spirit upon all flesh, and that our "sons and daughters" "shall prophesy?" That it does not mean that they are to prophesy privately and only in the sense of foretelling future events is perfectly evident from the immediate text here, and the Scripture teaching throughout. It is evident that when those who were filled with the Holy Spirit—men and women alike—on the day of Pentecost spoke "with other tongues as the Spirit gave them utterance", this was done in order that representative people who heard—"the devout men of every nation under heaven"—might hear the good news about Jesus, each in his own tongue, in order that all might understand and thus be saved. So those who heard the speaking with tongues expressed their amazement and said:

"We do hear them speak in our tongue the wonderful works of God."

What were these "wonderful works of God", by the proclamation of which multitudes were saved? What could they be except the works of God in offering up, and then raising up in newness of life, His own Son, the Saviour of the world?

The "prophesying" that was done, then,—by both men and women—at the beginning of the Christian church, openly and before the whole assembly there gathered, was the proclamation of the saving truths of the Gospel of Jesus.

This is made abundantly clear elsewhere in Scripture, as, for example, in the fourteenth chapter of First Corinthians. Here Paul himself speaks of prophecy and sets it over against speaking in "unknown tongues" as more profitable and advantageous. In Paul's age evidently there was no longer any necessity for the speaking in tongues, since the speaking in Paul's day was not to representatives of "all nations" as on the day of Pentecost, but to people in local communities who mainly had but one language. Paul, therefore, admonishes the church people against emphasizing too much the speaking with the unknown tongues, and tells them that it is not to edification, unless there is interpretation to give the meaning. Then over against this speaking with tongues he sets the far more useful custom of testifying and prophesying. So he says:

> "He that prophesieth speaketh unto men to edification, and exhortation, and comfort." (I Cor. 14:3).

And that he meant by prophesying the proclamation of the Christian message in such ways that the lost would be saved, is made clear where he says:

> "Yet in the church I had rather speak five words with my understanding, that by my voice I might teach others also, than ten thousand words in an unknown tongue. If therefore the whole church be come together into one place, and all speak with tongues, and there come in those that are unlearned, or unbelievers, will they not say that ye are mad? But if all prophesy, and there come in one that believeth not, or one unlearned, he is convinced of all, he is judged of all: And thus are the secrets of his heart made manifest: and so falling down on his face he will worship God, and report that God is in you of a truth." (I Cor. 14:19, 23–25)

Here, then, is the plain declaration from Paul himself that when the whole church (including of necessity females as well as males) come together, "all prophesy"—that is speak with such "edification", "exhortation", and "comfort" that an unlearned man or an unbeliever will be "convinced" (that is convicted of sin), "the secrets of his heart made manifest"—(that is he will confess his sins), and so "falling down on his face he will worship God" (that is be converted), "and report that God is in you of a truth", (that is he will go forth to bear his own testimony to the reality and power of the Gospel of Christ thus presented to him) (I Cor. 14:23).

Paul's Prohibition

But it is urged by those who oppose the teaching, speaking and praying of women in public, that Paul himself, in this very connection, says:

> "Let your women keep silence in the churches; for it is not permitted unto them to speak; but they are commanded to be under obedience, as also saith the law. And if they will learn any thing, let them ask their husbands at home; for it is a shame for women to speak in the church." (I Cor. 14:34–35).

Yes, Paul did say that, and he meant precisely what he said.

I will not seek to evade the issue, as some do, by saying that Paul was here not speaking by inspiration, as he sometimes confessed was the case with him. I gladly admit that he was speaking by inspiration here, because in this very connection he declared that what he wrote to the church at Corinth was the "commandments of the Lord" (I Cor. 14:37). Paul then meant exactly what he said.

But we can only know what he did mean when we get the setting of his words and read them in the light as I have before observed, of the other God-inspired Scripture teaching. Paul himself in this very chapter has evidently recognized the right and duty of "all",—both men and women—to prophesy and to speak the saving truths of the Gospel. And that he did recognize the general right of women, as well as of men, so to speak is made clear further by what he says in I Corinthians 11:5:

> "But every woman that prayeth or prophesieth with her head uncovered dishonoreth her head."

He here clearly admits the right of women to pray and prophesy and to participate otherwise in religious work, merely remarking that they should not violate a well known social usage, and thus lay themselves liable to harmful misunderstanding, by uncovering their heads as they preached or prayed. And he certainly would not in another place, if there were not some specific reason for the local rule, nullify his own injunction and set at naught his own teaching.

Let me hasten to say, therefore, that if Paul, under evident guidance of the Holy Spirit, had declared that women should not pray or preach, then whether I understood it or not, I would stand on that teaching as the inspired Word and will of God, and despite all of my natural desires and predilections would say that no woman or girl anywhere ought ever to raise her voice in prayer, testimony, or the proclamation of the Gospel message in any public assembly.

But it must be perfectly evident from the Scripture teachings which I have already presented that such cannot be the case. The Holy Spirit cannot deny Himself, and when He has directed women to speak equally with men in one place He certainly cannot reverse Himself and forbid their so doing in another place!

What, then, did Paul mean when he says here in the Epistle to the Corinthians that women were "to keep silence in the churches", and that "it is a shame for women to speak in the church?" Well many sound Bible expositors have held that he could have meant only that there were local conditions in Corinth which made it inexpedient and even shameful for women so to speak. Those who know the record of the appalling immorality and the open vice of Corinth will readily understand this. So deep was this moral degradation and so brazen the vice in Corinth that there was a public term current for expressing the thought of the utmost limits of degradation and shame, namely, he speaks or acts "like a Corinthian." The public women, —the defiers of all morality, —were given to speaking in public assemblies in Corinth, thereby exploiting their unholy and vicious means of livelihood. Paul very naturally, therefore, may have felt that any woman who thus rose in a public assembly in Corinth to speak, even though she might be in the church, would immediately lay herself liable to misunderstanding as to her morals, and also create the impression that there had been an abandonment by Christians of the truth of the headship of man in the religious and domestic relationships of life, and that thereby disrepute and dishonor would be brought upon the young Christian Church.

I am well aware, too, that some claim that this could not be the case, because this Epistle was addressed not only to the church at Corinth but to "all that in every place call on the name of Jesus our Lord."

Yes, that is in the first Epistle to the Corinthians, but it by no means declares that every specific utterance in that particular Epistle was for "all in every place." Indeed, there is not an epistle that Paul wrote that does not give certain things of local and immediate application to the particular church or group addressed, even while the general teaching of the epistle was applicable to "all" the saints of God.

"Neither Male nor Female in Christ"

But there is a further and deeper consideration which may throw light on Paul's attitude toward women speaking in the church at Corinth. Paul himself established a vital distinction which may be determinative upon this question and which helps to show us the real mind of Paul. In Galatians 3:28 Paul himself says:

"For as many of you as have been baptized into Christ have put on Christ. There is neither Jew nor Greek, there is neither bond nor free, there is neither male nor female; for ye are all one in Christ Jesus."

Here, then, Paul himself explicitly declares that when we are born again, —that is when we become children of God by faith in Christ Jesus, —there is no longer any distinction of sex but we all become "one in Christ." Thus we are made what Paul calls "saints". In other words we enter into a new status, and a new relationship founded upon a new condition, namely, our regenerated hearts and our changed lives. There is in this spiritual relationship no recognition of race or condition or sex. Through regeneration, we become partakers of the divine nature and begin our preparation for the heavenly joys in which there will be no sex, but, as Jesus Himself said, we shall all be like the angels of God. Just as in secular courts there is no distinction of sex among witnesses—a witness, whether male or female, being acceptable if only the facts are properly testified to, so Jesus said to all—both men and women—"ye shall be my witnesses."

But, it is further asked, what did Paul mean, then, when he said in writing to Timothy, the young preacher, "I suffer not a woman to teach"? (I Timothy 2:12). Well we will certainly not get at what Paul meant if we quote just that part of that verse, as is usually done by those who are opposed to women praying and speaking in public. The entire quotation here is as follows:

"But I suffer not a woman to teach, nor to usurp authority over the man, but to be in silence" (I Timothy 2:12).

Paul's declaration here that he does not "suffer a woman to teach" is explained by what follows after, namely, that she is not to "usurp authority over the man", and that the headship of man is grounded in the teaching of Genesis. All of this is absolutely true and proper, and I do not know any spiritually minded women who are seeking to "usurp authority" over men, or who turn away from that modesty and reserve which have been characteristic of Christian womanhood down all the ages. The women preachers with whom I have had anything to do have uniformly declared that they recognize the necessary headship of man, and do not desire, or purpose—even, trying to usurp authority. Some I have known have declined ordination specifically on that ground, and have preferred to follow simply the guidance of the Holy Spirit, without any dependence upon ecclesiastical power or authority.

In this connection, I would further emphasize that Paul seems to have had in mind the distinction between truly Christian women—"Saints"—and those, even though they might be in the churches, who had not experienced a real rebirth; and doubtless it was those "women"—not "Saints"—to whom Paul referred when he declared that they were not to speak nor to teach. Paul no where says that "saints" whether men or women—are not to pray or preach in the open assemblies.

When he says, therefore, in the Epistle to the Corinthians, "let your women keep silence in the churches, he meant just that, and he said it by commandment of the Lord. Their "women"—any unregenerate who had gotten into the churches,—not "saints", were to keep silence, because their speaking would obviously be out of place, would cause confusion in other minds about Christian truth, and would indeed be a "shame". But that Paul intended that truly regenerated women—"saints"—all "one in Christ", should not be permitted to pray and preach is impossible and even absurd! And this very passage, that is often quoted so oracularly, indicates that these women whom he forbad to speak were of the unregenerated class, and therefore lacking in knowledge of Christian truth, because he tells them to learn of their "husbands at home."

Unless we are to fall into confusion worse confounded, and have Paul contradict in one place what he has taught in another, we must recognize the local application of his teaching to the Corinthians concerning their "women" participating in the public services of the church.

Paul and Women in Joint Service

Furthermore, there is a very practical line of evidence that makes this plain. That Paul was not antagonistic to the activity of women in the churches generally, becomes clear in the light of every known fact about his life. It is recorded, for example, that Paul accepted hospitality in the house of Philip the evangelist, and "abode with him", and it is specifically declared that this "same man had four daughters, Virgins, which did prophesy" (Acts 21:9). There is not the slightest hint or suggestion that Paul thought that this was wrong. On the other hand, if he had so thought he certainly would not have entered in and made that house his home! And the fact that the Holy Spirit puts into this inspired record that this home, in which Paul abode, contained four young women who preached the message of Christ, is rather an indication of approval and fellowship than anything to the contrary.

Again, in the 16th chapter of Romans, that glorious chapter in which Paul calls the roll of some of his devoted friends and fellow workers in the Christian church, we have indications that women were among the brethren who thus labored with Paul in his public ministry among the churches. He says here, for example:

> "I commend unto you Phebe our sister, which is a servant of the church which is at Cenchrea; that ye receive her in the Lord, as becometh saints, and that ye assist her in whatsoever business she hath need of you; for she hath been a succourer of many, and of myself also. Greet Priscilla and Aquila my helpers in Christ Jesus; Who have for my life laid down their own necks; unto whom not only I give thanks, but also all the churches of the Gentiles. Likewise greet the church that is in their house. Salute my well beloved Epaenetus, who is the first fruits of Achaia unto Christ. Greet Mary who bestowed much labor on us." (Romans 16:1–6).

Here, then, we have a revealing glimpse of the activities of Paul, in full fellowship with women workers in the early church. Phebe was a "servant of the church which is at Cenchrea," and as such it is inconceivable that she should not have participated in the public services. In fact Paul here specifically admonishes the church (not just certain individuals) at Rome "to receive her in the Lord as becometh saints", and "to assist her in whatever business she has need of you." She went to them on church "business", then, and that that included public activities in the church is indicated by Paul's statement concerning her past record, where he said "she hath been a succourer of many".

And what shall we think of Priscilla and Aquila? This man and his wife, who are referred to in the 18th chapter of the Acts, verse 2, and elsewhere, are termed by Paul himself; "My helpers in Christ Jesus." Must it not mean that they helped Paul in the ministry of Christ Jesus? Evidently they were so completely identified with the public activity of the churches in proclaiming the truths of God in connection with Paul that they endangered their own lives when he was persecuted. So he says of them, "who hath for my life laid down their own necks." And they were not only known in one place but Paul tells us here that "all the churches of the Gentiles" give thanks for them, doubtless because of their activity in Christian service. For example, it is recorded of Apollos, the eloquent man, who was also "mighty in the Scriptures", but who knew "only the Baptism of John", that both Aquila and Priscilla "took him unto them, and expounded unto him the way of God more perfectly" (Acts 18:24–26). And that these activities were of a soul winning nature is further made evident by the fact that Aquila and Priscilla had established a church in their own home, and so Paul says "likewise greet the church that is in their house." (Romans 16:5). Now I ask is it conceivable that a man and his wife would be so active in Christian work as to start a church in their own house without both of them participating in the services of that church?

After this, Paul refers feelingly to other women who had helped him in the work of the ministry.

Male Inconsistency

In the light of all this, I would lovingly recommend to the editor of the Western Recorder, and others who have criticized me for inconsistency and lack of common sense, and even lack of orthodoxy at this point, that these dear brethren, and any others who may have shared their prejudices against Christian women speaking in public, give themselves anew to the study of God's Word—not in spots, but as a whole—in order that they may know what is in the mind of God in this connection, and what are the wishes of the Holy Spirit.

As for the suggestion of these dear brethren that my success in the north has been due in part to the prayerful and loving support that I have received from Southern Baptists, I will say that I am grateful for all such cooperation, but when the editor of the Recorder declares in connection with my effort to help the noble little disciple of the Lord Jesus, Uldine Utley:

> "Dr. Straton knows very well that Southern Baptists do not stand for that sort of performance",

I will only say that I do not believe he voices the sentiments of a majority of Southern Baptists in this regard. The truth of the matter is that most Southern Baptists have given little thought or investigation to this particular question, because it has never presented itself very actively to them as an issue, and I am serenely confident that when they do turn their minds and hearts to an open-minded consideration of the teaching of the whole Bible on the subject, they will gladly accept the teaching of the Word and no longer seek to hold back any servants of the Lord from praying or proclaiming the message that the Holy Spirit of God may lay upon their hearts.

I will not touch either upon the inconsistency of some brethren who cry out against women participating in public services, and yet seize upon every woman available to teach in their Sunday Schools, and who enthuse over sending an army of women to foreign fields to proclaim the saving message of Jesus Christ to the lost souls of heathendom.

With all good humour and a heart full of gratitude to and love for the Southern brethren who have so nobly helped me with their prayers and support in my arduous battle in the Northland for the faith once for all delivered to the saints, I, nevertheless, must call upon them to open their minds and hearts to the full rounded teaching of God's Word as it applies especially to these "last days".

It is a profound conviction of my own soul that we are to witness in the near future a great revival of real religion in America. The Master commanded us, in connection with "the last days", to "strengthen the things that remain." (Rev. 3:2) And the promise that he made through Joel and Peter "to pour out His Spirit on all flesh", and that our sons and daughters alike should prophesy, must and will be fulfilled. The revival that is coming, therefore, will doubtless center around the glorious truth of the return of our Lord, in "the last days", and we should be as diligent as the Bereans in searching the Scripture to see whether or not these things be so, and not allow ourselves to be stopped on one or two passages, when the whole great stream of Christian teaching shows what these passages really mean.

How God Uses Little Children

That there will be unusual and miraculous events in "the last days", the Bible makes very plain. Charles Spurgeon declared it as his own conviction, that in the end time of this dispensation, God would raise up unusual people and do unusual things to warn the disobedient and turn them to God.

God has again and again used children to proclaim His truth and do His work. He revealed Himself directly to little Samuel in the Temple. He enabled the shepherd boy David to slay Goliath, when all grown Israel were afraid. He used the little maid of Israel to redeem the great Naaman, "the captain of the Kings host". Jesus used the little lad with his few loaves and fishes to feed a great multitude; and when He Himself was only twelve years old He disputed with the learned doctors in the Temple and amazed them with his questions and answers. We have the declaration:

> "God hath chosen the foolish things of the world to confound the wise; and God hath chosen the weak things of the world to confound the things which are mighty; and base things of the world, and things which are despised, hath God chosen, yea, and things which are not, to bring to nought things that are; that no flesh should glory in his presence" (I Cor. 1:27–29).

We have also the Master's word that "out of the mouth of babes and sucklings thou hast perfected praise" (Matt. 21:16); and His prayer when He said "I thank thee, O Father, Lord of heaven and earth because thou hast hid these things from the wise and prudent; and hast revealed them unto babes" (Matt. 11:25). And again Jesus said:

> "except ye be converted, and become as little children, ye shall not enter into the Kingdom of God" (Matt. 18:3).

Uldine Utley told me that when she was shrinking away from God's call to preach, because she felt her unworthiness and incapacity as a little child, her Bible opened to that passage in Jeremiah where it is written:

> "Then said I, Ah, Lord God! behold, I cannot speak: for I am a child. But the Lord said unto me, say not, I am a child: for thou shalt go to all that I shall send thee, and whatsoever I command thee thou shalt speak. Be not afraid of their faces: for I am with thee to deliver thee, saith the Lord. Then the Lord put forth his hand, and touched my mouth, and the Lord said unto me, Behold, I have put my words in thy mouth" (Jeremiah 1:5-9).

And surely he has! I believe that God has raised up this little child, with her great faith and her marvelous powers, as a rebuke to our vanity over "scholarship", our deference to "science falsely so-called", and our dependence upon man-made forces and methods of work; and, as in the case of Peter and the other preachers of the early church, God is showing us through her what He can do in making real preachers.

In any event, if the record of the activity of women and children—including girls—were taken out of the history of God's people it would be indeed and in truth a sadly dimmed history. As I once heard Uldine herself say in a sermon, it was a woman who brought the first resurrection message of New Testament times, and a woman was the first Christian convert in Europe. The gratitude of women to Jesus for transforming their lives, and the impulses which He puts into their hearts to proclaim to others the saving truths of His Gospel, are imperative, for the Holy Spirit has said they "shall prophesy." These are the Holy impulses, and no man has the right to deny opportunity for a proper expression of them, under the guidance of the Holy Spirit of God. In the case of Uldine Utley, she had after her conversion such an impulse to preach that she would round up the children at play time in the school yard and try to preach to them. And her father told me how, when they were all still tied down on his ranch in California, Uldine would come to him almost in tears and say, "Oh, Daddy, I do so much want to preach. Can't you get me some place to preach in?" She seemed even as a child of ten, to feel with Peter "woe is me if I preach not this gospel". Who will say that a child with such holy impulses in her heart, and one who shows forth the very power of God when she is given opportunity to preach, and who wins souls in large numbers, should be choked off, discriminated against, and not allowed to exercise the gifts that God Himself seems to have bestowed upon her? So far as I am concerned, I cannot find it in my heart to oppose such an one, but my desire is rather to help her forward in every possible way!

For myself, I will say that I do not think there is a man upon this planet who abhors more deeply than I do the brazen, pushing, unspiritual, self-assertive type of so-called "modern woman". With the memories of my own devoted mother and the little daughter whom we lost, and with the influence of my own dear wife in my heart, I say, that I glory in the old-fashioned type of Christian woman, and I know nothing sweeter or more beautiful than to see such women offering their prayers to God in assemblies of the saints, or modestly and lovingly presenting their testimony and preaching His truths for the saving of the people.

Who Uldine Utley Is

And so far as this precious little child, Uldine Utley, is concerned, I will just say that no man or woman can really know her, as we know her in our family, or hear her pray and preach, and see the witness of God's power in her ministry, and then deny that she is being led by the Holy Ghost.

I had heard of this child's meetings in the west and south before I ever met her personally, and I admit that I was rather prejudiced against her. I classed her with other boy and girl evangelists, some of whom I had seen and heard who could be justly classed as freaks. I had expected, when I did meet her to see a bright little girl who had written out and memorized some short catchy messages, and who could declaim or "speak" them to the people in a striking way. Instead of that, when I heard her for the first time speaking along with Dr. T. T. Shields, of Toronto, Dr. B. D. Gray, of the Southern Baptist Home Mission Board, Dr. Davidson, of India, myself, and others in the great Bible Conference at Green Cove Springs, Florida, I had one of the surprises of my life. To my amazement I heard her, though she was then only thirteen years old, as a great extemporaneous Bible preacher.

She held the crowds that assembled there with as much ease, and she led them into the deep things of God's Word, just as successfully as did those men of national and international reputation who were with her at the Bible Conference. She also showed a modesty and a tact in adapting herself to the messages of preceding speakers on the programs, and she showed such power in holding the attention and swaying the minds and hearts of the people that it was all manifestly from the Spirit of God, and could not have been otherwise.

When she was converted at the age of nine, under circumstances that were clearly and directly ordained of God, she was training for a career in the movies and upon the stage. She had become already an expert dancer, and was taking dramatic lessons, when the Spirit of God laid His hand upon her and turned her young heart to Jesus; and immediately God laid upon her a burden for lost souls which led her to give up her ambitions and plans for a stage career, and to accept invitations from the young people's societies and churches to bear her testimony and to witness for her Lord. Thus, step by step she was led into the preaching of the Gospel.

She has had very limited technical education, having gone only for a few years to the public schools. And yet she has the vocabulary of a grown woman and modesty and refinement of speech and manner, which are at once the wonder and delight of all who hear her. She knows but one book and that is the Bible. She has simply saturated herself with the Word of God. She uses very few illustrations in her sermons, but preaches the Bible with faith and fervour, and with such winning winsomeness that the hardest hearts are touched and opened. She can quote so much scripture from memory, and she has such skill in her sermons in turning rapidly from passage to passage with unerring accuracy, and she interprets even the "deep things of God" so strikingly, that I honestly regard her in many respects as already one of the greatest Bible preachers to whom I have ever listened.

After hearing her for a week in the Green Cove Springs Bible Conference I was led to invite her to come to the Bible Conference which we had planned at Palm Beach, Florida, and she made such an impression there upon both the church and the community, and there was such a striking manifestation of the Spirit's power even during the Bible conference that the church unanimously invited her to stay longer with us, and to conduct a revival service. Throngs of people waited upon her ministry in that great Southern Tabernacle, and though she was then only thirteen years old her wonderful voice—also I believe, a direct and miraculous gift of God—filled the Tabernacle with its sweetness and its power, and she was instrumental in winning, in that brief meeting, many souls. The secret of this child's power is her utter devotion to Christ and the Bible, her unquestioning faith and her wonderful prayer life. She spends more time in her prayer closet and has more freedom and power in her prayers in public and at the family altar than any one I have ever known. She comes near to the Bible injunction to "pray without ceasing".

There is more of the direct manifestation of God's presence and power in her meeting than I have ever seen before. I have seen not only boys and girls but strong men broken all to pieces and coming, in response to the invitation, to confess their sins and accept Christ as their Saviour. I have seen mature women, some of the highest culture, profoundly moved and influenced to nobler and higher living.

She speaks during her meetings often three and four times and sometimes even five and six times a day. She preaches not only to the great crowds that come to hear her in the meetings, but in shops and to schools and other groups wherever she can have an open door to say a word for Jesus.

We are planning for a great city-wide campaign in Calvary Church this fall. In preparation for that, and by way of introduction, on a recent Sunday, Uldine appeared for messages afternoon and evening. The greatest throngs of people that have ever tried to get into that historic building came to hear her, and there were such manifestations of the power of the living God, in response to her eloquent and beautiful Bible messages, that even the New York Times gave a front page story to the messages, and the other leading papers of the city spoke of those services in terms of wonder and, I am glad to say, with respect and sympathy.

A Modest and Humble Child

I have seen this young girl put to the test in every way. In addition to our work together in Florida last winter, I went over to help her for a few days in her great city-wide campaign in the famous Cadle Tabernacle of Indianapolis, where she spoke to 15,000 people each Sunday, and to large crowds afternoons and nights daily for five weeks. We have had her and other members of her family for weeks at a time as guests in our home, and her presence at our family altar and her influence in our daily lives have been always sources of joy and blessedness to us all. Mrs. Straton and our four boys feel toward her, therefore, just as I do, and we all thank God for her and are set upon giving her all the help that, under God, we can give.

We have found, too, in our social and domestic contacts with her that despite her deep consecration—or, perhaps, I should say because of it, she is a perfectly normal child. There is not one morbid touch in her character. She has a quaint and delightful sense of humor, which leads at times to the merriest of laughter. There have naturally been occasions for the play of humor in her relationships with a doctor of divinity, a ministerial student (my eldest son) and the other members of our happy family. She called up on the telephone at Palm Beach one day last winter, and when I answered I did not immediately recognize her voice. I asked "Who is this?" The reply came back, with a chuckle of suppressed merriment, "This is the Reverend Doctor Uldine!" "Oh," I said, "You haven't got nearly all of it in! From the way you can beat us preaching, it ought really to be 'the Very Reverend and Most Worshipful Doctor Uldine, Bishop Plenipotentiary and Preacher Extraordinary'." Then she replied in awe and wonder, "Doctor, what does that Plenipo—what-ever-it-is-thing mean?" I answered, "Well, young lady, that is for you to find out!" But ever since, during lighter moments in the family we have addressed her as "Your Riverence".

But the deep things of God are Uldine Utley's real joy and delight. As a further proof that her life and ministry are under the guidance of God stands the fact that, despite her successes in her preaching, and as editor of the bright and beautiful little monthly magazine which she publishes, and despite the adulation and praise that are everywhere showered upon her, she has remained just a sunny-hearted, noble-souled, modest little girl.

It has been a source of almost merriment with us to hear her preach a glorious message from God's Word, that has simply swept the people with power, and then see her come to our home, immediately after, and enter into a romp on the floor with our ten year old lad! Yes, she is beautifully humble, natural and unspoiled, and yet there is about her a certain detachment, a reserve power, and a spiritual atmosphere that command the respect and confidence of all who come into contact with her—young and old alike.

During the campaign at Palm Beach, knowing the danger of so much praise and adulation for one so young, I one day tactfully sought to put Uldine on her guard by saying half-laughingly; "Well, Uldine, you do not believe all of these extravagant things that the people say about you, do you?" And she looked at me, in her frank and honest way, and said: "Dr. Straton, I don't take a bit of that to myself. I know that I am only an ignorant little girl, and that the Lord simply uses me to speak His message and do His work. Therefore I give Him all the glory." And another day, when I expressed my great pleasure and delight that she stuck so close to the Bible in her messages, she looked up brightly and said: "Well, Dr. Straton, that's all I have. I do not know anything except a little about the Bible, and if I did not preach that I wouldn't have anything to preach to the people."

At the opening of the campaign in Indianapolis she was met at the train and escorted to the Tabernacle for the first services by quite a delegation. The presiding officer of the meeting, who was chairman of the general Cadle Tabernacle committee, then introduced the Mayor of Indianapolis, who in turn, and with glowing and enthusiastic words, introduced Uldine. When it came her time to speak her first message she bowed to the great throng of people and said modestly: "And now I want to introduce you to One Who is nobler and better than us all." Then she presented Jesus, and challenged them all to accept Him as Saviour and truly follow Him as Lord. It was a master stroke of platform management, though entirely unstudied and impromptu, and it was also such a heart felt expression of devotion to Jesus that it melted every one and made her place in the confidence and esteem of the people secure from that moment.

A Consecrated Family

I cannot here tell of the deep consecration that has come to Uldine's mother and father and her little sister because of her life and example. Nor can I tell of their sacrifices, even up to the point almost of hunger itself at times, through their efforts to help her forward with her work. These friends have literally given up all to follow Jesus, for His Gospel's sake. Her father and mother gave up their ranch in California—sacrificing all their business interests—and went forth with their little daughter to witness and work for Jesus. I know of nothing more touching and beautiful than their consecration to these tasks, and than the devotion of Mrs. Mosely, who has so wisely counselled and led Uldine in all human ways. Nor can I tell how, from these simple and humble beginnings, she has gone on and up into mighty achievements for her adored Saviour. To me, it has all been like a little touch of Apostolic times in the midst of the worldiness, unbelief, and barren powerlessness of today.

Despite the criticisms, therefore, of those who do not understand, and the distress even of some whose good opinion I cherish, and whom I truly love, I cannot do otherwise than go forward with the purpose and plan to help Uldine Utley get God's message to the largest possible number of people, for the saving of souls and the glory of the living God.

She has been with us in the suburbs of New York in a series of tent meetings this summer, where God mightily used her, and now this fall she will be with us in a great city-wide campaign, that will continue as long as the Holy Spirit directs, in Calvary Church, at the heart of New York City. I ask that those who have not understood will forbear in judgment until they have seen and heard this modern prophetess. I also most earnestly ask the prayers of God's people everywhere for the success of the meetings in New York. The people of Calvary Church, having heard her, are fixed in their attitude of enthusiasm and loving support. Our noble officers, —experienced men of God, and our great body of consecrated women and young people are of one mind in feeling that God's set time has come for a true spiritual quickening in the world's greatest city. My own hope is that the meeting this fall will bring to New York the widest and deepest spiritual blessing that the city has ever known; and I will repeat here what I said in the statement in the New York papers announcing the coming of Uldine Utley that, in my judgment, she is today the most extraordinary person in America. She is the Joan of Arc of the modern religious world.

ORDAINED AMERICAN BAPTIST WOMEN

NAME	ORDINATION DATE	LOCATION
1. Susana Arieta	26 March 1902	Carlsbad, N.Mex.
2. Mary E. Frey	30 Oct. 1905	Brocton, N.Y.
3. Fannie Pemble	24 Aug. 1910	Scranton, Iowa
4. Ina G. Stout	13 Jan. 1913	Champlin, Minn.
5. Mrs. A. L. Miller	10 June 1913	Farlin, Iowa
6. Florence M. Carver	14 June 1917	Linneus, Maine
7. Mrs. W. G. Rhoads	25 Feb. 1918	Greenleaf, Wis.
8. Christine MacKenzie	30 Oct. 1918	Linden, N.H.
9. Frances MacNeill	18 Feb. 1919	South Lyndeboro, N.H.
10. Emma J. C. Park	5 Sept. 1919	Bellingham, Mass.
11. Ada M. Hills[1]	27 Sept. 1920	Glenwood, Iowa
12. Helen H. Carlson	1 Dec. 1920	Paris, Maine
13. Margaret M. Joshua	1 Dec. 1920	Bethlehem, Pa.
14. Emmet Russell	12 July 1921	Charleston, Maine
15. Gertrude E. Teele	21 July 1921	Hudson, Mass.
16. Elizabeth M. Campbell	29 July 1921	Bolton, Mass.
17. Lennie A. Rhodes	2 Aug. 1921	Pontiac, Ill.
18. Martha P. Filson	23 Sept 1921	Hartsville, N.Y.
19. Linnie B. Treadwell	28 Dec. 1921	Carroll, N.H.
20. Mary Witter	8 June 1922	Des Moines, Iowa

[1] Hills, married to Rev. C. E. Hills of Glenwood Baptist Church, preached twelve years before ordination.

NAME	ORDINATION DATE	LOCATION
21. LaVerne Minniss[2]	24 July 1922	Bradford, Pa.
22. Edith V. Amsler	12 Oct. 1922	Grove City, Pa.
23. Mrs. F. A. Childs	27 Oct. 1922	Aldenville, Pa.
24. Grace M. Brooks	3 Nov. 1922	Georgia Plain, Vt.
25. Mrs. L. Edwin Fineout	24 Nov. 1922	Mountaindale, Pa.
26. Mrs. J. R. Roycroft	12 June 1923	Chillicothe, Ill.
27. Elizabeth B. LaFlash[3]	25 July 1923	Forestdale, Mass.
28. Bessie M. Deemer	28 Sept. 1923	Bells Landing, Pa.
29. Ruth Walsh	Nov. 1923	Waterboro, Maine
30. Alma Broadhead	27 Dec. 1923	New Castle, Pa.
31. Mildred T. Palmer	27 Aug. 1924	Dexter, Maine
32. Mrs. U. M. Over	28 Nov. 1924	Caldwell, Idaho
33. Katherine M. Leonard	1925	Lynn, Mass.
34. Ethel M. Knapp[4]	29 Jan. 1925	Fulton, N.Y.
35. Ruth K. Hill	16 Feb. 1925	McKeesport, Pa.
36. Mrs. J. H. Vatcher	20 March 1925	Port Huron, Mich.
37. Edith Grace Craig[5]	19 Nov. 1925	Hoosick, N.Y.

[2] After long service as a missionary in China and then as a local home missions worker, Minniss's friends initiated her ordination, aware of her gifts and desire to serve in broader fields. At the ceremony in the First Baptist Church, Rev. Margaret Joshua gave the charge to the church.

[3] LaFlash pastored the Forestdale Baptist Church while her husband Rev. George LaFlash served the Mashpee Baptist Church on an Indian reservation. The Pocasset Baptist Church ordained LaFlash's friend Eva M. Tedford on 11 Sept. 1923.

[4] Knapp graduated with honors from the Chicago Baptist School. A member of the First Baptist Church, she did educational and religious work at the State Tonawanda Indian Reservation near Akron, New York, as acting pastor/teacher. She eventually was installed as pastor of the Baptist church on the reservation.

[5] Born in England in 1875 and educated at Edinburgh University, Craig married Rev. Reynolds of the Established Church of Scotland. The Northern

NAME	ORDINATION DATE	LOCATION
38. Alice W. Linsley	29 Dec. 1925	Whittier, Calif.
39. Mrs. Harry A. Smith[6]	20 June 1926	Winchester, Mass.
40. Mrs. John J. Sherman	29 Aug. 1926	Olyphant, Pa.
41. Mrs. Ralph W. Lisher	17 Oct. 1926	Lapeer, Mich.
42. Elizabeth M. Finn	14 Dec. 1926	Mullica Hill, N.J.
43. Bessie W. Winchester[7]	31 Dec. 1926	Urbana, Ill.
44. Margaret S. Holley[8]	30 June 1927	Bristol, Conn.
45. Mrs. E. G. Aldridge	1928	Gloversville, N.Y.
46. Freda M. Ehrlich[9]	24 April 1928	Macedon, N.Y.
47. Mary C. Vining	12 June 1928	Averill Park, N.Y.
48. Violet G. Bagley	30 July 1928	Eastbrook, Maine
49. Cora Mae Brown	Aug. 1928	Lincoln Center, Maine
50. Mabel S. Burton[10]	11 Sept. 1928	Moscow, Idaho

Baptist Convention invited her in 1924 to the United States to lead evangelistic meetings. She was pastor of the First Baptist Church in Hoosick and the first female chaplain to the New York State Legislature, House of Assembly.

[6] Smith graduated from Bangor Theological Seminary along with her husband. The New Hope Baptist Church ordained them both before Mr. Smith's start of a college chaplaincy position in the South.

[7] Winchester graduated with an M.A. and B.D. from Garrett Biblical Institute of Northwestern University (Evanston) in 1925. The First Baptist Church of Urbana ordained her, and she expected to complete her Ph.D. at the University of Chicago in 1927.

[8] Holley earned an A.B. from Vassar (1921), attended Newton Theological Institution (1921–22), earned a B.D. from Union Theological Seminary (1925), and Master of Sacred Theology degree from Hartford Theological Seminary (1927) before her ordination in Bristol Baptist Church.

[9] Ehrlich was trained in the Salvation Army and worked with them for seven years in New York.

[10] After the sudden death of Burton's minister husband, the First Baptist Church asked her to assume the pastorate. She ministered from 1927 until 1931.

ORDAINED CONGREGATIONAL WOMEN

NAME	ORDINATION DATE	LOCATION
1. Annis (Ford) Eastman	1889	Brookton, N.Y.
2. Mary Leona Moreland[1]	19 July 1889	Wyanet, Ill.
3. Mary E. Drake	18 Dec. 1890	Iroquois, S.Dak.
4. Elvira Cobleigh	2 April 1891	Colfax, Wis.
5. Juanita Breckenridge	19 July 1892	Gaylord, Mich.
6. Abi Townsend Huntley[2]	1892	Emery, S.Dak.
7. Esther Smith	1893	
8. Emily C. Woodruff	9 Feb. 1893	Little Valley, N.Y.
9. Clarissa L. Buell Harbridge	19 July 1893	Gaylord, Mich.
10. Dora Read Barber	30 Aug. 1893	Oreg.
11. Eliza Burson Perkins	21 Sept. 1893	Clarks, Nebr.
12. Margaret J. Smith	24 Sept. 1893	Ala.
13. Mrs. J. H. B. Smith	20 Nov. 1893	Overbrook, Kans.
14. Elizabeth Miller Todd Howland	1894	Napoli, N.Y.
15. Amelia A. Frost	14 Feb. 1894	Littleton, Mass.
16. Ella F. Leonard	1 April 1894	Rice, Colo.
17. Ella Gurney	14 June 1894	Clayton, N.Y.

---

[1] Moreland (1866–1918) left Massachusetts to attend MBI. After her church in Wyanet, Illinois, she held Illinois pastorates in McLean, Normal, Chebanese, Mazon, and Belvidere. She earned a Ph.D. in 1905 and authored numerous books and pamphlets.

[2] Huntley (1842–1914), born to a Quaker family in Philadelphia, married a Friends minister in 1872. She co-pastored and pastored several congregations. Her work in Emery "was so fruitful and acceptable to the people that they made urgent request for her ordination."

NAME	ORDINATION DATE	LOCATION
18. Mrs. M. J. Borden	8 Nov. 1894	Albuquerque, N.Mex.
19. Abi Lucette Nutting[3]	3 Oct. 1895	Osage, Iowa
20. Harriet Eddy Williams[4]	1896	Lone Rock, Wis.
21. Henrietta Crane Lyman	29 Jan. 1896	Ft. Pierre, S.Dak.
22. Eva R. Kinney Miller	2 April 1896	Eldon, Iowa
23. Mrs. J. H. Heald	8 April 1896	Tempe, Ariz.
24. Alice May (Coombs) Robinson	28 April 1896	Palermo, Calif.
25. Alice Ruth Palmer	28 May 1896	Wayzata, Minn.
26. Alice S. Barnes	12 Sept. 1896	Castle, Mont.
27. Salva Tompkins[5]	1897	Elkhart, Ind.
28. Sarah A. Dixon	16 June 1897	Tyngsboro, Mass.
29. Bertha Juengling Harris[6]	22 June 1897	Orient, Iowa
30. Rosine M. Edwards	1898	Hillyard, Wash.
31. Anna O. Nichols	1898	Sioux City, Iowa
32. Eliza Remington	1898	
33. Emma Keats Henry[7]	24 May 1898	Huron, S.Dak.
34. Lillie D. Stewart	18 Oct. 1899	Douglas, Wyo.
35. Bertha Bowers	31 Oct. 1899	Orient, Iowa
36. Lydia I. James	12 Nov. 1900	Lloyd, Ohio
37. Grace Ellen Stanley	1901	Temple, Maine

[3] Nutting (1853–1927) co-pastored with her husband. After her ordination, she pastored the Ledyard, Iowa, Congregational Church. "As her husband is pastor at Buffalo Center, they can lighten their labors by exchanging pulpits or sermons once in a while" (*Osage News,* 3 Oct. 1895).

[4] Williams (1842–1916) studied at Rockford College in Illinois before attending MBI. She pastored the Brown Church in Bear Valley, Wisconsin, as well as churches in Footville, Lone Rock, and Black Earth.

[5] Tompkins (1833–1915) taught until her marriage in 1858. After her ordination, she served as pulpit supply in Oberon, North Dakota. She was a prominent Women's Christian Temperance Union worker.

[6] Harris (1867–1945) worked in association with 1912 MBI graduate, Helen Byrnes.

[7] Henry (1851–1919) taught school for four years before studying at MBI. She engaged in mission and evangelistic work in South Dakota, Iowa, and Nebraska.

NAME	ORDINATION DATE	LOCATION
38. Laura Hulda Wild[8]	25 June 1901	Lincoln, Nebr.
39. Marion Darling	10 Sept. 1901	Detroit, Mich.
40. Lydia M. Whitlock Allen[9]	2 Oct. 1902	Hornby, N.Y.
41. Lydia S. Brock[10]	5 Nov. 1902	Clay Center, Kans.
42. Ella Anna Evans	1903	
43. Mary A. Helser	17 Sept. 1903	Wescott, Nebr.
44. Minnie J. Dickinson	2 March 1904	Linwood, Nebr.
45. Ella White Brown	26 April 1905	Powhattan Kans.
46. Katherine Walker Radford Powell[11]	24 May 1905	Custer, S.Dak.
47. S. Abbie Chapin Guyton	1906	Worthington, S.Dak.
48. Mrs. J. J. Luce	2 June 1906	Etna, Calif.
49. Lucy Whittier Carter Woodford	1907	Gettysburg, S.Dak.
50. Annie E. Switzer	1907	Dayton, N.Y.
51. Isabelle Phelps	25 Oct. 1907	Pittston, Maine
52. Kate H. Haus	1908	Hayden, Colo.
53. May Abbie Andrews Williams	1909	Wayland, Ohio
54. Hettie Francis Douglass[12]	23 June 1909	Little Shasta, Calif.

[8] Wild (1870–1959) attended Hartford Theological Seminary and pastored the Butler Avenue Church in Lincoln, Nebraska.

[9] Allen (1842–1919) ministered as a Methodist Episcopal evangelist from 1889 to 1902 before her ordination as a Congregational minister. Rev. Annis Ford Eastman, another ordained woman, delivered her ordination sermon. Allen received an annual salary of $250 her first year.

[10] Brock attended MBI.

[11] Jessie Y. Sundstrom, a historical researcher in Custer County, is in the process of studying Powell (1860–1938). Contact Sundstrom at P.O. Box 528, Custer, SD 57730.

[12] Douglass married a minister in 1866 who died in 1906. After the Little Shasta Congregational Church ordained her, she pastored three years there for thirty dollars per month. In 1909, Douglass organized women's missionary and young people's societies. She died in 1919 after pastorates in Santa Cruz and Santa Rosa. See Mrs. Helen Haight Rohrer and Rev. K. E. Linton, "Little

NAME	ORDINATION DATE	LOCATION
55. Barbara Slavinski	1910	Shenandoah, Pa.
56. Grace Edwards Kellogg	1911	Nepaug, Conn.
57. Mary P. Wright	1911	Emmetsburg, Iowa
58. Ada Stone Anderson	24 Sept. 1912	Annawan, Ill.
59. Mary F. Macomber	22 May 1913	Stoughton, Mass.
60. Mabel T. Winch[13]	30 Sept. 1913	East Arlington, Vt.
61. Eunice C. Haley	28 July 1914	Forman, N.Dak.
62. Jessie Heath	1915	Exira, Iowa
63. Emma Kautsky	14 Nov. 1915	East Joplin, Mo.
64. Rachel Luch Rogers	1916	Ingle Chaple, Oreg.
65. Grace Mayer-Oakes[14]	7 May 1916	East Hadley, Mass.
66. Mabel Q. Stevens[15]	18 May 1916	Interlachen, Fla.
67. K. June Pollard	24 May 1916	Farnam, Nebr.
68. Mary B. M. Briggs	13 Nov. 1917	Indian Orchard, Mass.
69. Elizabeth Carlyon	15 Nov. 1917	Seward, Okla.
70. Alice Mae Handsaker[16]	10 June 1918	Portland, Oreg.

Shasta Congregational Church," *The Siskiyou Pioneer* (Siskiyou County Historical Society, 1950), 5–6.

[13] Winch (1875–1967) studied religious education and Bible at Northfield Seminary in Massachusetts, the school opened by D. L. Moody in 1879. From 1910 until 1935 she was pastor of the Olivet Congregational Church in East Arlington, simultaneously serving other southern Vermont churches via stagecoach.

[14] Grace Mayer-Oakes attended Bible Teacher's Training School in New York and the religious education department at Yale. She graduated from Hartford Seminary and assisted her husband Rev. S. R. Mayer-Oakes at the First Congregational Church, Hadley, Mass. The church ordained her to serve as pastor during the absence of her husband during World War I. Liberal in theology, Mayer-Oakes stated she ignored Paul's teaching on women.

[15] Together with her husband, Dr. E. L. Stevens, and Rev. Lillian Fulton, Mabel Stevens worked as a strong temperance advocate in Florida.

[16] Alice Mae Handsaker (1875–1951) attended Northwest Christian College before doing missionary work with her husband Rev. J. J. Handsaker in Jamaica and the British West Indies. After her ordination she served pastorates in two

NAME	ORDINATION DATE	LOCATION
71. Helen F. Lanham	19 Oct. 1918	Wessington Springs, S.Dak.
72. Ada Andress Heyse[17]	1919	Melvin, Ill.
73. Lillian B. Fulton	1919	
74. Miriam L. Woodberry	19 April 1919	Albuquerque, N.Mex.
75. Miriam Crumley Bartholomew[18]	26 Sept. 1919	
76. Charlotte Brown	5 Oct. 1919	New Boston, Mass.
77. Bessie F. Crowell	20 Oct. 1919	Monmouth, Maine
78. Miriam Louise Woodberry	1920	Albuquerque, N.Mex.

districts in Portland, at Russellville and Clackamas. See "Services Set For Woman Pastor Here," *Oregon Journal,* 31 May 1951, 19.

[17] Heyse (1876–1931) attended MBI.

[18] Bartholomew (1864–1920) was born into a Quaker home in Iowa. After graduating from Penn College (Oskaloosa, Iowa) in 1891, she spent ten years teaching and another ten in hospital work. She married a doctor in 1897. After attending Chicago Theological Seminary in 1919, the Congregational church ordained her. She had pastorates in South Dakota from 1914 until her death.

NOTES

Preface

1. *Moody Alumni News* (June 1927), 12.
2. See Nancy A. Hardesty, *Women Called to Witness: Evangelical Feminism in the 19th Century* (Nashville: Abingdon, 1984); and Donald W. Dayton, *Discovering an Evangelical Heritage* (New York: Harper and Row, 1976).
3. George M. Marsden, *Fundamentalism and American Culture: The Shaping of Twentieth-Century Evangelicalism 1870–1925* (New York: Oxford University Press, 1980), 80, 249–50, n. 40.
4. Donald W. Dayton, "Evangelical Roots of Feminism" (unpublished paper, Chicago), 14. Candace Waldron-Stains also equated early Fundamentalist biblical literalism with silencing women in "Evangelical Women: From Feminist Reform to Silent Femininity," *debarim* 3 (1978–79): 65, 72.
5. See R. Pierce Beaver, *All Loves Excelling* (Grand Rapids: Eerdmans, 1968, rev. as *American Protestant Women in World Mission: A History of the First Feminist Movement in North America,* 1980); Ruth A. Tucker's chapter on "Single Women Missionaries" in *From Jerusalem to Irian Jaya: A Biographical History of Christian Missions* (Grand Rapids: Zondervan, 1983); Jane Hunter, *The Gospel of Gentility: American Women Missionaries in Turn of the Century China* (New Haven: Yale University Press, 1984).
6. For a recent anthology, see Dale A. Johnson, *Women in English Religion, 1700–1925* (New York: Edwin Mellen, 1983). Note bibliographic entries by British authors. Anglican A. Maude Royden, popular turn-of-the-century British preacher, theologian, suffrage worker, and author represented the liberal Protestant camp overseas.
7. Clarence E. Walker, in *A Rock in a Weary Land: The African Methodist Episcopal Church during the Civil War and Reconstruction* (Baton Rouge: Louisiana State University Press, 1982), briefly remarks on the 1848 General Conference vote to license women preachers. See Jualynne Dodson, "Nineteenth-Century A.M.E. Preaching Women" in *Women in New Worlds,* ed. Rosemary Skinner Keller and Hilah F. Thomas (Nashville: Abingdon, 1982), vol. 1; Sylvia M. Jacobs illumines black women's role overseas in "Three Afro-American Women: Missionaries in Africa, 1882–1904," *Women in New Worlds,* vol. 2.

Chapter 1

1. William Bell Riley, "Women's Rights and Political Righteousness" (sermon preached at First Baptist Church, Minneapolis, 2 June 1901), W. B. Riley Archives, Northwestern College Library.

2. *Moody Bible Institute Monthly* 30 (Sept. 1929): 49.

3. James O. Henry, *For Such a Time As This: A History of the Independent Fundamental Churches of America* (Westchester, Ill.: Independent Fundamental Churches of America, 1983), 127.

4. Ferenc M. Szasz, "Three Fundamentalist Leaders: The Roles of William Bell Riley, John Roach Straton, and William Jennings Bryan in the Fundamentalist-Modernist Controversy" (Ph.D. diss., University of Rochester, 1969), 300.

5. Frederic May Holland, "Our Clergywomen," *Open Court* 6 (28 Jan. 1892): 3123.

6. J. T. Sunderland, *The Liberal Christian Ministry* (Boston: G. H. Ellis, 1889), 78, 92.

7. A. Maude Royden, *The Church and Woman* (London: James Clarke and Co., 1924), 116.

8. Victor I. Masters, "Does the Bible Place Special Limitations on Women?" *Western Recorder,* 28 Dec. 1922, 11.

9. See Robert H. Wiebe, *The Search for Order 1877–1920* (New York: Hill and Wang, 1967), for an in-depth account.

10. See Sydney E. Ahlstrom, *A Religious History of the American People* (Garden City, N.Y.: Image Books, 1975), vol. 2, pt. 7, "The Ordeals of Transition," for an evaluation of religion in turn-of-the-century America.

11. Bill J. Leonard, "The Origin and Character of Fundamentalism," *Review and Expositor* 79 (Winter 1982), discusses Fundamentalist historiography. That volume touches the debate as to its essentially conservative or radical nature in "Fundamentalism as a Social Phenomenon" by Martin E. Marty.

12. Marsden, in *Fundamentalism and American Culture,* provides the most comprehensive analysis of Fundamentalist roots. See also Timothy P. Weber, *Living in the Shadow of the Second Coming: American Premillennialism 1875–1925* (New York: Oxford University Press, 1979); Bruce Shelley, "Sources of Pietistic Fundamentalism," *Fides et Historia* 5 (Fall 1972 and Spring 1973), examines the relationship of pietistic Fundamentalists to rationalistic militant ones.

13. Timothy L. Smith, *Called Unto Holiness: The Story of the Nazarenes—The Formative Years* (Kansas City: Nazarene Publishing House, 1962), 79, 319; Paul Merritt Bassett, "The Fundamentalist Leavening of the Holiness Movement: 1914–1940. The Church of the Nazarene: A Case Study," *Wesleyan Theological Journal* 13 (Spring 1978): 69, 74–75.

14. *Moody Bible Institute Monthly* 24 (April 1924): 402. Even the World's Christian Fundamentals Association list of "Fundamental Schools" in 1930 does not include MBI or Gordon Bible College.

15. The first women's rights convention at Seneca Falls, New York, in 1848 drafted resolutions on these issues. See Eleanor Flexnor's standard account, *Century of Struggle: The Woman's Rights Movement in the United States* (Cambridge, Mass.: Harvard University Press, 1959).

16. Carl N. Degler develops this thesis in *At Odds: Women and the Family in America from the Revolution to the Present* (New York: Oxford University Press, 1980).

17. Earl Kent Brown, "Women of the Word" in *Women in New Worlds,* ed. Rosemary Skinner Keller and Hilah F. Thomas (Nashville: Abingdon, 1982), vol. 1.

18. P. D. Stephenson, *The Woman Question* (Charlotte, N.C.: Presbyterian Publishing Co., 1899), 208.

19. Christian Golder, *History of the Deaconess Movement in the Christian Church* (Cincinnati: Jennings and Pye, 1903), 526; Peter Zaccheus Easton, *Does Woman Represent God?* (New York: Revell, 1895), 3.

20. I am defining public ministry as the church work of female clergy and laywomen who preached, pastored, evangelized, and taught the Bible, as distinct from the service of benevolent workers and deaconesses in the church. However, the two spheres sometimes overlap, as in the case of Methodist deaconess Iva Durham Vennard, who was assigned in 1895 as a field representative in conference evangelism and preached regularly. These public ministers include licensed and ordained women, as well as the many who served without any formal credentials.

21. U.S. Department of Commerce, Bureau of the Census, *Tenth Census of the United States, 1880,* vol. 1; *Fourteenth Census of the United States, 1920,* vol. 4; *Thirteenth Census of the United States, 1910,* 4:54, 93.

22. U.S. Department of Commerce, Bureau of the Census, *Eleventh Census of the United States, 1890,* vol. 1, pt. 2, table 91, p. 414.

Chapter 2

1. Virginia Lieson Brereton, "Protestant Fundamentalist Bible Schools 1882–1940" (Ph.D. diss., Columbia University, 1981), 12. Brereton investigates four schools in-depth: MBI, Gordon, Nyack, and Boston Bible School (Advent Christian).

2. Morgan Dix, *Lectures on the Calling of a Christian Woman and Her Training to Fulfill It* (New York: D. Appleton, 1883), 71.

3. Leon McBeth, *Women in Baptist Life* (Nashville: Broadman, 1979), 107.

4. William C. King, *Woman—Her Position, Influence, and Achievement Throughout the Civilized World. Her Biography, Her History from the Garden of Eden to the Twentieth Century* (Springfield, Mass.: King-Richardson, 1900), 524. The Divinity School reference occurs in Willard E. Waterbury's article "Woman in the Professions."

5. Warren Palmer Behan, president of the Baptist Missionary Training School in Chicago, wrote "An Introductory Survey of the Lay Training School Field," *Religious Education* 11 (Feb. 1916–Dec. 1916). Omitting any reference to Nyack under the "Home and Foreign Missionary Training Schools" category while mistakenly classifying Northwestern as a Baptist deaconess training school, Behan represents the confusion in categorizing turn-of-the-century religious institutions.

6. Virginia Lieson Brereton and Christa Ressmeyer Klein, "American Women in Ministry," in *Women in American Religion,* ed. Janet Wilson James (University of Pennsylvania Press, 1980), 178. Brereton's "Preparing Women for the Lord's Work" in *Women in New Worlds,* ed. Rosemary Skinner Keller and Hilah F. Thomas (Nashville: Abingdon, 1982), vol. 1, explores three Methodist deaconess training schools (Chicago Training School, New England Training School, and Scarritt Bible and Training School) founded between 1885 and 1892. Comparing women's training for ministry in the coed Bible institutes to the all-female settings might prove enlightening.

7. William C. Ringenberg, *The Christian College—A History of Protestant Higher Education in America* (Grand Rapids: Eerdmans, 1984), 174. See also Paul M. Bechtel, *Wheaton College—A Heritage Remembered 1860–1984* (Wheaton, Ill.: Harold Shaw, 1984), 92–94.

8. "Information Concerning the Baptist Bible Union of North America with By-Laws and Aims and Confession of Faith" (issued by the BBU of North America, December 1925), 12, American Baptist Historical Society Archives, Colgate Rochester Divinity School.

9. "Bible Institutes That Are Sound," *The Sunday School Times* 66 (2 Aug. 1924): 464. This popular conservative weekly, edited by Keswick proponent Charles G. Trumbull, reached over 100,000 readers in the 1920s. See appendix 1.

10. "Fundamental Schools," *The Christian Fundamentalist* 3 (July 1930): 26–28. Edited by W. B. Riley, this monthly magazine promoted the interests of the WCFA.

11. S. A. Witmer, *The Bible College Story: Education with Dimension* (Manhasset, N.Y.: Channel, 1962).

12. See appendix 2. Exceptions include Toccoa Falls, Houston, San Antonio, and Florida Bible Institutes. Robert C. McQuilkin founded Columbia Bible College in South Carolina in 1923, the institutional heir of Keswick teaching along with Nyack.

13. John H. Cable, *A History of the Missionary Training Institute 1883–1933,* 20, A. B. Simpson Historical Library, C&MA headquarters building, Nyack, New York.

14. George P. Pardington, *Twenty-Five Wonderful Years* (New York: Christian Alliance Publishing Co., 1914), 206, Simpson Historical Library.

15. Wendell W. Price, "The Role of Women in Ministry of the Christian and Missionary Alliance" (D.Min. diss., San Francisco Theological Seminary, 1977), Simpson Historical Library.

16. *Christian Alliance* 1 (June 1888): 96.

17. "The Work at Home," *The Christian Alliance and Foreign Missionary Weekly* 14, no. 2 (1895): 28, Simpson Historical Library.

18. Revivalistic Mennonites formed the Defenseless Mennonite Conference, known today as the Evangelical Mennonite Church. Such scant pre-1920 data remains at Fort Wayne that few conclusions regarding women's ministry can be drawn.

19. Lorene Moothart, *Achieving the Impossible . . . with God—The Life Story of Dr. R. A. Forrest* (Harrisburg, Pa.: Christian Publications, 1956), 31.

20. Troy Damron, *A Tree God Planted* (Toccoa, Ga.: Cross Reference Books, 1982), 177–78. The statement prepared by the official Alliance conference in May 1906 included three sections: (1) The Fundamentals (the Apostles' and Nicene Creeds), (2) Open Questions, and (3) Our Distinctive Testimony (the fourfold gospel). Desiring that individual convictions on other matters not cause controversy, Alliance leaders listed five open questions: (1) church government; (2) subjects and mode of baptism (though believers' immersion was almost universal); (3) Calvinism and Arminianism; (4) foot washing, open or closed communion, dedication of children; and (5) the ministry of women.

21. Ruth A. Jones, *The St. Paul Bible College, 1916 . . . Decades of Training* (Aug. 1962), 21, St. Paul Bible College Library.

22. Otto A. Simon, *The Rock That Followed Me*, n.d., 48, St. Paul Bible College Library. Simon later left the C&MA to join the Independent Fundamental Churches of America.

23. *The Full Gospel Messenger*, Sept. 1925, 3, C&MA Northwest District Headquarters, St. Paul.

24. Ibid., March 1922, 2.

25. *The Bible Banner* 1, no. 1 (1919): 1, Augsburg College Library. A bimonthly bulletin published by Lutheran Bible Institute.

26. A. J. Gordon, "The Ministry of Women," *Missionary Review of the World* 7 (Dec. 1894): 910–21, discussed in detail in chapter 6. Compare to Gordon's "Should Women Prophesy?" *The Watchword* 8 (1886–87): 248–50; and "May A Woman Prophesy?" *Christian Herald and Signs of the Times*, n.d.

27. B. F. Austin, ed., *The Prohibition Leaders of America* (St. Thomas, Ontario, 1895), 119. Gordon served as a leader of the Prohibition Party.

28. Mrs. A. J. Gordon, "Women as Evangelists," *Northfield Echoes* 1 (1894): 151. See appendix 3.

29. "Miss Macomber To Be Ordained," *Stoughton News Sentinel*, 6 Feb. 1914, 1, 6.

30. 1934 Gordon Yearbook, 104. By this time, Gordon's school had become a hybrid—part Bible school, part liberal arts college, part theological seminary.

31. "Woman Ordained to the Ministry" (article from local Munnsville newspaper, 11 Dec. 1931). See also 1944 necrology information on Olive Eaton in the Congregational Yearbook.

32. Maria Hale Gordon, "Women and the Temperance Movement," n.d., Gordon College Library.

33. C. Allyn Russell, "William Bell Riley: Architect of Fundamentalism," *Foundations* 18, no. 1 (Jan.–March 1975).

34. Mrs. W. B. Riley, "From the Beginning," *Northwestern Scroll,* 1952, W. B. Riley Archives, Northwestern College Library.

35. W. B. Riley sermon file, W. B. Riley Archives, Northwestern College Library.

36. *Northwestern Pilot,* 1926, Riley Archives.

37. *Northwestern Pilot,* 8 Feb. 1923, 38. The Reiber-Murray team later led revival in a Danish Norwegian Baptist Church in Howard Lake, Minnesota; Reiber was listed as an alumni pastor in November 1930.

38. "Our Alumni," *School and Church* 1, no. 9 (May 1917): 92–93, Riley Archives. This journal, edited by Riley and published in the interest of Northwestern, was devoted to the cause of "evangelical Christianity and orthodox theology." See appendix 4.

39. *Northwestern Pilot,* 11 Jan. 1923, 28.

40. *Northwestern Pilot,* Feb. 1931, 147; and March 1930, 183.

41. "Perplexing Questions," *Northwestern Pilot,* Aug. 1930, 319.

42. "A Short Story of Los Angeles Bible Institute," *The King's Business* 1 (Nov. 1910): 171, Biola University Library.

43. Robert Williams and Marilyn Miller, "Chartered For His Glory—Biola University 1908–1983," *Biolan* 2 (1983), 16, Biola University Library.

44. *The King's Business* 31 (Jan. 1940): 21.

45. "The Purpose and Methods of the Bible Institute," *The King's Business* 3 (May 1912): 101–2.

46. R. A. Torrey, "Light on Puzzling Passages and Problems," *The King's Business* 6 (Jan. 1915): 71. See appendix 5.

47. Philadelphia School of the Bible merged in 1951 with the Pennsylvania Bible Institute to form today's Philadelphia College of the Bible. Founded by Charles E. Hurlburt in 1894 and closed in 1904, PBI was reopened by former student W. W. Rugh in 1913 under the auspices of National Bible Institute of New York City (called the Philadelphia branch of NBI). In 1923, PBI separated from NBI.

48. The Scofield Reference Bible, C. I. Scofield, ed. (New York, 1909), 9.

49. Ibid., 1224.

50. William L. Pettingill, "Question Box," *Serving and Waiting* 10 (Nov. 1920): 406.

51. Ibid., 11 (Aug. 1921): 227.

52. Ibid., 12 (Aug. 1922): 165.

53. Ibid., 12 (July 1922): 110. See appendix 6.

54. James H. Brookes, "Woman in the Church," n.d. This article was later published as a pamphlet by Brookes Bible Institute in St. Louis.

55. Denominational schools will be examined in chapter 4, in connection with each particular church.

56. "Alumni," *The Brookes Bible Institute—An Historical Sketch* (St. Louis: Brookes Bible Institute, 1984), 34.

57. Rev. Virgil P. Endsley, current director of Alumni Affairs at Practical, wrote in a letter dated 22 May 1984: "Several women graduated and assumed pastorates and were ordained as well as others who conducted Bible classes. This policy remained virtually unchanged until only in recent years."

58. *Indianapolis Bible Institute,* 25 Sept. 1917, 2.

59. "Indianapolis Bible Institute to Open Thirteenth Year Monday," *Indianapolis News,* 27 Sept. 1923, 8.

60. *The Bible To-Day,* Feb. 1908, 48; "Who's Where in the Institute's Alumni," *The Bible To-Day,* Aug. 1926, 411, Shelton College Library, Cape May, New Jersey.

61. Jessee Roy Jones, "The Founder of Denver Bible Institute," *Grace and Truth,* Sept. 1924, 334. Denver Bible Institute (now Rockmont College) was listed in both the 1924 *Sunday School Times* ad and the 1930 World's Christian Fundamentals Association ad.

Chapter 3

NOTE: *Moody Monthly* (*MM*), the official publication of MBI, was first entitled *The Institute Tie* (*IT*). The title changed to *The Christian Workers Magazine* (*CWM*) in February 1907, to *Moody Bible Institute Monthly* (*MBIM*) in September 1920, and to *Moody Monthly* in September 1938. Hereafter, references to *Moody Monthly* will be designated by the appropriate initials.

1. *MBIM* 30 (Sept. 1929): 49.

2. See Virginia Lieson Brereton, "Protestant Fundamentalist Bible Schools, 1882–1940" (Ph.D. diss., Columbia University, 1981), ch. 4, "Marketing the Gospel: Moody Bible Institute," for an in-depth description of early MBI life. Mary McLeod Bethune, one of MBI's first black students, studied there from 1895–96 and experienced sanctification under D. L. Moody's ministry. See Clarence G. Newsome, "Mary McLeod Bethune as Religionist" in *Women in New Worlds,* ed. Rosemary Skinner Keller and Hilah F. Thomas (Nashville: Abingdon, 1982), vol. 1.

3. MBI Bulletin of January 1916, Moodyana Historical Room, Moody Bible Institute Library.

4. Norman H. Camp, "M.B.I.—A Brief Historical Sketch," 1915, 4, Moodyana Historical Room.

5. Statistics provided by Moody Alumni Association, letter dated 25 January 1985.

6. Dr. John L. Patten, *For the Truth's Sake—A History of Faith Baptist Bible College* (Ankeny, Iowa: Faith Baptist Bible College, 1979), 7.

7. *The Bible Training School Recorder,* Dec. 1911, 2, Ontario Bible College Library. Baptist minister Elmore Harris established the school in 1894 as the first of many Bible institutes in Canada.

8. "Historical Sketch," *Providence Bible Institute Catalogue 1931–1932,* 3–4. Founded originally as Bethel Bible Institute by John and Susan Marble and Rev. Essek W. Kenyon in 1900, the school moved from Spencer to Dudley, Massachusetts, in 1923. Called Providence Bible Institute in 1929 and eventually Barrington College, the school recently merged with Gordon College.

9. Donald W. and Lucille Sider Dayton, "Women in the Holiness Movement" (unpublished paper), 11.

10. Nancy A. Hardesty, *Women Called to Witness: Evangelical Feminism in the 19th Century* (Nashville: Abingdon, 1984), 20.

11. Frances E. Willard, *Woman in the Pulpit* (Chicago: Women's Temperance Publication Association, 1889; reprint, Washington, D.C.: Zenger, 1978), 58.

12. George M. Marsden, *Fundamentalism and American Culture: The Shaping of Twentieth-Century Evangelicalism 1870–1925* (New York: Oxford University Press, 1980), 31.

13. Bernard R. DeRemer, *Moody Bible Institute: A Pictorial History* (Chicago: Moody Press, 1960), 21.

14. Gene A. Getz, *MBI—The Story of Moody Bible Institute* (Chicago: Moody Press, 1969), 39.

15. Bible Work pamphlet, 1885, Moodyana Historical Room.

16. "Autobiographical Notes of Ellen Louise Haines 1936–1939" (published by E. H. K. Ward and Moira M. Ward), 35, Moodyana Historical Room.

17. Harold W. Boon, "The Development of the Bible College or Institute in the United States and Canada since 1880 and Its Relationship to the Field of Theological Education in America" (Ph.D. diss., New York University, 1950), 42.

18. Christian Golder, *History of the Deaconess Movement in the Christian Church* (Cincinnati: Jennings and Pye, 1903), 488.

19. Copy of original incorporation papers, 12 Feb. 1887, Moodyana Historical Room.

20. James F. Findley, *Dwight L. Moody* (Chicago: University of Chicago Press, 1969).

21. Minutes of board meeting, April 1900, Moodyana Historical Room.

22. *CWM* 11 (Sept. 1910): 57.

23. Ibid., 11 (Feb. 1911): 442.

24. Ibid., 13 (Nov. 1912): 187.

25. Ibid., 16 (Aug. 1916): 977.

26. Ibid., 17 (July 1917): 907; 18 (Dec. 1917): 329. For Millar's other references, see *IT* 4 (Dec. 1903): 138; 4 (April 1904): 286; 5 (June 1905): 460; *CWM* 8 (Feb. 1908): 495; 8 (May 1908): 722.

27. *CWM* 12 (Sept. 1911): 223; 12 (March 1912): 504; 14 (Oct. 1913): 114; 14 (July 1914): 760; 15 (Jan. 1915): 323.
28. Ibid., 12 (Aug. 1912): 821; 14 (July 1914): 760.
29. Ibid., 14 (July 1914): 760; 15 (Jan. 1915): 323.
30. Ibid., 16 (May 1916): 723; 11 (June 1911): 899.
31. Ibid., 16 (March 1916): 63–64; 16 (July 1916): 876; 18 (Jan. 1918): 412; 18 (July 1918): 908; *MBIM* 21 (Jan. 1921): 244; 23 (Dec. 1922): 180.
32. *MBIM* 23 (Oct. 1922): 78.
33. *CWM* 14 (Sept. 1913): 49; 14 (Oct. 1913): 133; 14 (Nov. 1913): 178; 14 (June 1914): 697.
34. Ibid., 19 (Jan. 1919): 346; 19 (July 1919): 837; *MBIM* 21 (July 1921): 499.
35. Appendix 7 details other female evangelists listed in MBI periodicals.
36. Roberta Hueser, "Anna Larson—Woman of Many Talents" (reprinted from the *Rock Rapids Reporter*, n.d.).
37. The *Moody Alumni News* (*MAN*) began December 1926. In addition, the *IT, CWM, MBIM*, and *MM* also carried a section devoted to alumni news. See appendix 8 for listing of Moody alumnae and students (many studied but did not formally graduate) engaged in public ministries.
38. Letter from Wilson Wickman of Washington Island, Wisconsin, dated 23 May 1985.
39. *MBIM* 24 (June 1924): 537.
40. "A Woman Missionary in Idaho," *The American Missionary*, new series, vol. 5, no. 12 (March 1914): 730–31.
41. Virginia Healey Asher Collection, 197, biography, Billy Graham Center Archives, Wheaton, Illinois.
42. See appendices 9 and 10.
43. Articles found in order: *MBIM* 28 (Jan. 1928): 223; 37 (Sept. 36): 19–20; *CWM* 17 (Aug. 1917): 942–44; 19 (Jan. 1919): 474–475; *MBIM* 32 (June 1932): 437.
44. James Findlay, "Moody, 'Gapmen,' and the Gospel: The Early Days of Moody Bible Institute," *Church History* 31, no. 3 (Sept. 1962): 322.
45. Rev. Ada C. Bowles, "Women in the Ministry," *Woman's Work in America,* ed. Annie Nathan Meyer (New York: Henry Holt, 1891), 217.

Chapter 4

1. See Paul K. Jewett's addendum on "The Ordination of Women" in *Man As Male and Female: A Study in Sexual Relationships from a Theological Point of View* (Grand Rapids: Eerdmans, 1975), 160.
2. Benjamin St. James Fry of the Methodist Episcopal church wrote "Woman's Work in the Church" in 1892, taken from the *Proceedings of the Second Ecumenical Methodist Conference*. That document clearly expresses the variance of opinion among Wesleyan; Irish Methodist; United

Brethren; Primitive Methodist; Methodist Episcopal, South; African Methodist Episcopal; and Bible Christian conference participants.

3. Belle H. Bennett, president of the Woman's Home Missionary Society from 1896–1910 and Woman's Missionary Council from 1910–22, wrote "The History of the World-Wide Movement for the Liberation of Women," *The Methodist Quarterly Review,* Jan. 1912. See also Virginia Shadron, "The Laity Rights Movement, 1906–1918" in *Women in New Worlds,* ed. Rosemary Skinner Keller and Hilah F. Thomas (Nashville: Abingdon, 1982), vol. 1. For a full discussion, see John Patrick McDowell, *The Social Gospel in the South: The Woman's Home Mission Movement in the Methodist Episcopal Church, South, 1886–1939* (Baton Rouge: Louisiana State University Press, 1982).

4. See Janet Everhart, "Maggie Newton Van Cott: The Methodist Episcopal Church Considers the Question of Women Clergy" in Keller and Thomas, eds., *Women in New Worlds,* vol. 2.

5. Oliver argued that God had called her to the local pastorate, not evangelistic preaching. See Anna Oliver, *"Test Case" on the Ordination of Women Appealed from the New England Conference to the General Conference— A Statement by Her,* n.d.

6. William T. Noll, "Laity Rights and Leadership" in Keller and Thomas, eds., *Women in New Worlds,* vol. 1.

7. Ellen Coughlin-Keeler, *The Balance Wheel: A Condensed History of the Woman's Home Missionary Society of the Methodist Episcopal Church, 1880–1920* (New York: Woman's Home Missionary Society, 1920).

8. Fannie McDowell Hunter, *Women Preachers* (Dallas: Berachah Printing Co., 1905), 79.

9. See Mrs. Keister Hartford, "Women's Position in the Church," *The Quarterly Review of the United Brethren in Christ,* April 1894; Donald K. Gorrell, "A New Impulse" in Keller and Thomas, eds., *Women in New Worlds,* vol. 1; James E. Will, "Ordination of Women: The Issue in the Church of the United Brethren in Christ" in ibid., vol. 2; J. Bruce Behney and Paul H. Eller, *The History of the Evangelical United Brethren Church* (Nashville: Abingdon, 1979).

10. Daniel Berger, *History of the Church of the United Brethren in Christ* (Dayton, Ohio: United Brethren Publishing House, 1897), 527.

11. Called Portland Bible Institute in 1930 and merged with Seattle Pacific in 1969, this school appeared in the 1924 *Sunday School Times* ad and 1930 World's Christian Fundamentals Association ad. Anderson Bible Training School also appeared in the 1924 ad.

12. See sermon in Lee's *Five Sermons and a Tract,* ed. by Donald W. Dayton (Chicago: Holrad, 1975).

13. Seth C. Rees, *The Ideal Pentecostal Church* (Cincinnati: M. W. Knapp, 1897), 41.

14. Edward H. McKinley, *Marching to Glory: The History of the Salvation Army in the United States of America, 1880–1980* (San Francisco: Harper and Row, 1980), 20.

15. Norman H. Murdoch, "Female Ministry in the Thought and Work of Catherine Booth," *Church History* 53, no. 3 (Sept. 1984): 349.

16. Evangeline Cory Booth, *Woman* (New York: Revell, 1930), 27.

17. Mary Ella Bowie, *Alabaster and Spikenard: The Life of Iva Durham Vennard, Founder of Chicago Evangelistic Institute* (Chicago: Chicago Evangelistic Institute, 1947).

18. Chicago Evangelistic Institute appeared in the 1924 *Sunday School Times* ad, was renamed Vennard College and relocated to University Park, Iowa, in 1951.

19. Kenneth L. Robinson, *From Brass to Gold: The Life and Ministry of Dr. D. Willa Caffrey* (University Park, Iowa: Vennard College, 1971).

20. Ibid., 45

21. *The Sabbath Recorder,* Dec. 1907. Reprinted in "The Ministry of Women, Ordained to be Ministers," *The Sabbath Recorder* 202 (July 1980): 18.

22. Jerry R. Flora, "Brethren Women in Ministry: Century One," *Ashland Theological Seminary,* Fall 1982, 20.

23. Adolf Olson and Virgil A. Olson, *Seventy-Five Years, A History of Bethel Theological Seminary, 1871–1946* (Chicago: Conference Press, 1946), 86. Included in the paragraph on Esther Sabel, teacher of the seminary.

24. Ninety-four-year-old Esther Sabel lives in the Home for the Elderly in Downers Grove, Illinois. Two letters dated 8 March 1985 and 22 March 1985 provided most of the data for this biographical sketch. She never called her preaching by that name; she called it "speaking."

25. In 1913 Bethel Theological Seminary (founded by Swedish Baptists in Chicago in 1871) merged with Bethel Academy of St. Paul to form Bethel College and Seminary. Bethel Institute (listed in the 1924 *Sunday School Times* ad) opened in 1920; the Bible and Missionary Training School operated from 1922 until 1935, training young people to do lay ministry in local churches.

26. Minnie S. Nelson, "The Story of One of Our Women Preachers as She Herself Tells It," *The Standard,* 20 Sept. 1946, 8. See also 8 Nov. 1946, p. 6; and 13 Dec. 1946, p. 6, for the story of pastors Hilda Ljungquist and Ethel Ruff.

27. Leon McBeth, *Women in Baptist Life* (Nashville: Broadman, 1979), 111.

28. "Once For All," *Biblical Recorder,* 10 Feb. 1892.

29. Patricia S. Martin, " 'Keeping Silence': Texas Baptist Women's Role in Public Worship, 1880–1920," *The Journal of Texas Baptist History* 3 (1983): 15.

30. Montgomery explained Paul's 1 Corinthians 14:34 prohibition as a quotation of the Judaizers' oral law.

31. See Jesse A. Hungate, *The Ordination of Women to the Pastorate in Baptist Churches* (Hamilton, N.Y.: James B. Grant, 1899). When asked to sit on a woman's ordination council, Baptist minister Hungate mailed questions to other Baptist clergy and compiled their responses in his book.

32. See appendix 12, based on American Baptist Yearbook ordination lists. Of those fifty, the vast majority (forty-four) received ordination after World War I, thirty-one were married, and six of those were ordained jointly with their husbands. Eighteen women lived in New England and seventeen in the mid-Atlantic states of Pennsylvania (9), New York (7), and New Jersey. Another thirteen came from the midwestern and central states — Iowa (4), Illinois (3), Michigan, Idaho, Wisconsin, and Minnesota. One minister lived in California and one in New Mexico.

33. Thirty-four libraries in the towns where those Baptist women were ordained responded to my inquiry for historical information. Fourteen of those responses contained biographical data beyond what the yearbook listed. For three of fourteen women, facts about their lives point to clear identification with Evangelicals or conservative Baptists. Accounts of the rest at least provide insight into the pastoral experience of women clergy of that era.

34. In correspondence with John Lundvall (age 78), whom Rev. Park baptized as a boy in 1921, I discovered that Park's autobiography *The Fool and I* was located at the Franklin Trask Library of Andover Theological School, Newton Centre, Mass.

35. Letter of Edward H. Carlson of Kents Hill, Maine, dated 27 Dec. 1984.

36. 29 July 1921 newspaper clipping provided by Hudson Historical Society, Hudson, Massachusetts, entitled "Will Become Missionary — Rev. Gertrude Teele Sails for Burma, August 20."

37. Letter of H. Hale Nye (age 85) of Captiva, Florida, dated 10 Jan. 1985.

38. 1924 church minutes of the Austin Square Baptist Church, Lynn, Massachusetts.

39. See appendix 13 based on Congregational Yearbook lists of ordained ministers and necrology accounts. Since many deceased female ordained ministers described in the necrologies did not appear earlier on the ordination lists, these records were obviously incomplete. Compared to the post-World-War-I increase in ordained Baptist women, the Congregationalists ordained more women in the decade before 1900 (33) than from 1900 to 1909 (19) or 1910 to 1919 (23). Whereas most ordained Baptist women lived in the northeastern States, the Congregationalists centered in midwestern and central plains states such as South Dakota (8), Iowa (7), and Nebraska (4). For 78 ordained Congregational women I sent 65 inquiry letters and received 37 responses, 12 containing significant information.

40. Mary E. Drake, *Fanny* (1894), Historical Resource Center, Pierre, South Dakota.

41. Carol K. Kammen, "The Problem of Professional Careers for Women: Letters of Juanita Breckenridge, 1872–1893," *New York History* 55, no. 3 (July 1974): 280–300. See collection of letters in the Olin Library, Regional History Collection, Cornell University.

42. Historical Committee of the Congregational Church of Littleton, record book, p. 18.

43. James William Lenhoff, "Gold Town Church" (Oroville, Calif., n.d.).

44. Barbara Kellison, "Rights of Women in the Church" (Dayton, Ohio: Herald and Banner Office, 1862). See excerpt in *Women and Religion in America: The Nineteenth Century,* ed. Rosemary Radford Ruether and Rosemary Skinner Keller (San Francisco: Harper and Row, 1981), vol. 1, ch. 5, "The Struggle for the Right to Preach," document 5. Vol. 2 of this documentary history, published in 1985, covers the colonial/revolutionary period.

45. *1952 Yearbook of the Congregational Christian Churches,* "Necrology."

46. "The Ritual of the Ordination Service," 19 May 1929.

47. Hunter, *Women Preachers,* 70.

48. "History of the Grenola Christian Church," 26 Aug. 1984.

49. Robert J. Leach, *Women Ministers—A Quaker Contribution* (Wallingford, Pa.: Pendle Hill, 1979).

50. Arthur O. Roberts, *The Association of Evangelical Friends: A Story of Quaker Renewal in the Twentieth Century* (Newberg, Oreg.: Barclay, 1975).

51. Cleveland Bible Institute (Malone College) appeared in both the 1924 *Sunday School Times* ad and 1930 World's Christian Fundamentals Association ad. See Byron Osborne, *The Malone Story* (Newton, Kans.: United Printing, 1970).

52. Charles H. Brackett, "The History of Azusa College and the Friends, 1900–1965" (M.A. thesis, University of Southern California, 1967), Azusa College Library.

53. "Catalogue and Prospectus of the Training School for Christian Workers," 1900–01, Azusa College Library.

54. "Second Annual Catalogue, 1918–1919," under Aim of the School.

55. Mary Lou Cummings, ed., *Full Circle: Stories of Mennonite Women* (Newton, Kans.: Faith and Life, 1978), 8.

56. Ibid., 181.

57. Mary Miller, *A Pillar of Cloud: The Story of Hesston College 1909–1959* (North Newton, Kans.: Mennonite Press, 1959). Hesston appeared in the 1924 *Sunday School Times* ad.

58. Letter dated 4 May 1984 from Margaret Wiebe, Hesston College Librarian. Elaine Sommers Rich, in *Mennonite Women—A Story of God's Faithfulness* (Scottdale, Pa.: Herald, 1983), makes no reference to any preaching, pastoral ministry.

59. Advent Christians, distinguished from Seventh-Day Adventists by their Sunday worship, held to the conditional immortality doctrine in regard to the unsaved after death. Premillennial but not dispensational, Advent Christians believed in the verbal inspiration of Scripture. See also J. G. Beach, *Women in the Seventh-Day Adventist Church* (Nashville: Southern Publishing Association, 1976).

60. Harold Wilson, *Seventy-Five Years: Berkshire Christian College 1897–1973,* n.d. Now Berkshire Christian College in Lenox, Mass., this school appeared in the 1924 *Sunday School Times* ad and 1930 World's Christian Fundamentals Association ad. Brereton in "Protestant Fundamentalist Bible Schools" calls it typical of "Denominational Fundamentalism" and Methodist holiness in flavor.

61. *Boston Bible School and Ransom Institute,* 3–4. This first college catalogue (1902–03) is located in the Berkshire Christian College Library Archives.

62. Elisha Z. Ellis, "With the 'Old Hands'—Anna Eliza Smith," *World's Crisis,* 1904, 2.

63. See Shirlee M. Bromley, "Female Preachers in the Advent Christian Denomination," 25 April 1978, Berkshire Christian College research paper.

64. "Adventists Delay Women's Ordination," *The Woman's Pulpit* April–June 1985, 1, 8.

65. Rev. A. E. Oldroyd, *The Place of Women in the Church* (London: Office of the English Church Union, 1917), 7.

66. Hunter, *Women Preachers,* 86.

67. Ibid. 199.

68. F. P. Mayser, "Shall Women Vote in the Church?," *The Lutheran Church Review,* July 1899, 482.

69. Ernst P. H. Pfatteicher, "Woman as a Congregational Voter," *The Lutheran Church Review,* July 1899, 478; Theodore E. Schmauk, *St. Paul and Women and the Epistle to Timothy and The Woman Question* (Philadelphia: Evangelical Lutheran Theological Seminary, 1899), 534.

70. See James W. Albers, "Perspectives on the History of Women in the Lutheran Church-Missouri Synod During the Nineteenth Century," *The Lutheran Historical Conference* 9 (1982): 137–83.

71. James O. Henry, *For Such a Time As This: A History of the Independent Fundamental Churches of America* (Westchester, Ill.: Independent Fundamental Churches of America, 1983).

Chapter 5

1. Dr. Thomas A. McDill, "General Conference Preview," *The Evangelical Beacon,* 15 May 1983, 6.

2. U.S. Congress, House, *Reports of the Industrial Commission of Immigration,* vol. 15, doc. 184 (1901), 261. See also chart on "Immigrants, by Country, 1820–1970" in U.S. Department of Commerce, Bureau of the Census, *Historical Statistics of the United States—Colonial Times to 1970,* pt. 1 (1975), 105.

3. U.S. Department of Commerce, Bureau of the Census, *Tenth Census of the United States, 1880; Occupations,* table 31 "Clergymen," 727. These

Scandinavian ministers clustered in the upper-midwestern states of Minnesota (159), Illinois (85), Wisconsin (80), and Iowa (76).

4. U.S. Department of Commerce, Bureau of the Census, *Eleventh Census of the United States, 1890*, vol. 1, pt. 2, table 109, "Foreign Born Clergymen," 484.

5. Frederick Hale, *Trans-Atlantic Conservative Protestantism in the Evangelical Free and Mission Covenant Traditions* (New York: Arno, 1979), 22, 134.

6. H. Wilbert Norton et al., *The Diamond Jubilee Story of the Evangelical Free Church of America* (Minneapolis: Free Church Publications, 1959), 71.

7. Frank T. Lindberg, *Looking Back Fifty Years* (Minneapolis: Franklin Printing Co., 1935), 51.

8. E. A. Halleen et al., *The Golden Jubilee—Reminiscences of the Swedish Evangelical Free Church Work 1884–1934* (Minneapolis, 1934), 27.

9. *Centennial: Evangelical Free Church 1884–1984* (Minneapolis: Free Church Press, 1984).

10. Norton, *Diamond Jubilee*, 142.

11. Hale, *Trans-Atlantic Conservative Protestantism*, 308.

12. In *Fundamentalism and American Culture: The Shaping of Twentieth-Century Evangelicalism 1870–1925* (New York: Oxford University Press, 1980), George M. Marsden first mentions the Free Church on page 195 in the section covering 1925–40. Marsden claims the Free Church lost much of its Scandinavian identity and became Americanized by taking on Fundamentalist characteristics. Yet many Free Church Scandinavians brought their dispensational and biblicist ideas *with* them to America.

13. See Edvard P. Torjesen's *Fredrik Franson—A Model for Worldwide Evangelism* (Pasadena: William Carey Library, 1983), based on Torjesen's compilation of writings by or about Franson, in the microfilm collection "Papers of Fredrik C. Franson, 1872–1909" (CN87), Billy Graham Center Archives, Wheaton, Illinois.

14. Torjesen, *Franson*, 48.

15. The appendix in Torjesen's *Franson* lists organizations founded either through Franson's direct personal influence or from a revival movement of which he was a part.

16. H. Neviandt, *The Salvation Army and the Work of Swedish Evangelist Franson Briefly Illumined According to the Holy Scriptures* (Barmen, Germany: von Haarhaus and Co., 1890), Fredrik C. Franson Papers.

17. "Franson and the Work of Women Evangelists," *Vapaarkirkollinen* no. 2, 1934, pp. 23–24. This handwritten English translation in the Franson Papers contained numerous grammatical errors corrected to make the passage understandable.

18. Published originally in German as *"Weissagende Tochter"* in *Gemeinschaftsblatt* in 1889 or 1890, and as a booklet at Emden in 1890. Franson translated it himself into Swedish in 1896, published in St. Paul by the Bible Women's Home Publishers. Eighty years later the pamphlet was finally translated into English by Sigurd F. Westberg in *The Covenant Quarterly* 34 (Nov. 1976): 21–40.

19. Della E. Olson, *A Woman of Her Times* (Minneapolis: Free Church Press, 1977), 34. See "Catherine Juell: The Bible Woman from Oslo" by Emil Larsen in *Tro og Liv*, 1 Jan. 1883, Copenhagen, Franson Papers.
20. Olson, *Woman of Her Times*, 24.
21. Ibid., 21.
22. Lindberg, *Looking Back*, 16.
23. Halleen, *Golden Jubilee*, 40.
24. Olson, *Woman of Her Times*, 60.
25. Della Olson, " 'Certain Women Also,' " *The Evangelical Beacon*, 1 Oct. 1984, 10–12.
26. Olson, *Woman of Her Times*, 77.
27. Halleen, *Golden Jubilee*, 41.
28. Olson, *Woman of Her Times*, 50.
29. Ibid., 64–70.
30. Ibid., 69.
31. Hale, *Trans-Atlantic Conservative Protestantism*, 275.
32. Lindberg, *Looking Back*, 58.
33. Olson, *Woman of Her Times*, 72.
34. Ibid., 74.
35. Arnold T. Olson, *This We Believe* (Minneapolis: Free Church Publications, 1961), 437.
36. Olson, *Woman of Her Times*, 79.
37. Ibid., 81.
38. Marian G. Price, "A Study of Some of the Effects of Nineteenth Century Revivalism on the Status and Accomplishments of Women in the Evangelical Covenant Church of America" (Ed.D. diss., Boston University, 1977), 103–4.

Chapter 6

1. See Brown's article "Exegesis of 1 Corinthians 14:34, 35 and 1 Timothy 2:11–12" in the July 1849 *Oberlin Quarterly Review*.
2. Rev. George Francis Wilkin, *The Prophesying of Women* (Chicago: Revell, 1895), 18.
3. Janette Hassey, "The Female Revivalist in America: A Case Study of Phoebe Palmer and Aimee Semple McPherson" (University of Chicago course paper in "Revivalism: Church and Ministry" class, submitted 3 March 1983).
4. Harold E. Raser, "Phoebe Palmer's Theology of Christian Holiness," *The Nazarene Theological Seminary Tower*, Spring 1983.
5. Phoebe Palmer, *Promise of the Father; or, A Neglected Speciality of the Last Days. Addressed to the Clergy and Laity of all Christian Communities.* (Walter C. Palmer, 1859; reprint, Salem, Ohio: Schmul), 50. Nancy A. Hardesty's

"Minister As Prophet? Or As Mother?" in *Women in New Worlds*, ed. Rosemary Skinner Keller and Hilah F. Thomas (Nashville: Abingdon, 1982), vol. 1, analyzes and compares Palmer's book with Frances E. Willard's *Woman in the Pulpit* (Chicago: Women's Temperance Publication Association, 1889; reprint, Washington, D.C.: Zenger, 1978). Hardesty describes Palmer's model of the woman preacher as the Pentecostal prophet and Willard's picture of the female minister as Mother, based on the cult of true womanhood.

6. Palmer, *Promise of the Father*, vii.

7. Ibid., 13.

8. Timothy L. Smith, *Revivalism and Social Reform* (Gloucester, Mass.: Peter Smith, 1976), 133.

9. Catherine Booth, "Female Ministry; or, Woman's Right to Preach the Gospel" (London, 1859; reprint, New York: The Salvation Army Supplies Printing and Publishing Department, 1975), 19–20.

10. Catherine Booth, "Female Teaching: or, The Rev. A. A. Rees versus Mrs. Palmer, being a reply to a pamphlet by the above gentleman on the Sunderland Revival" (London: G. J. Stevenson, 1861; photocopy, Ambrose Swasey Library, Rochester, N.Y.), 22.

11. See Nancy A. Hardesty, *Women Called to Witness: Evangelical Feminism in the 19th Century* (Nashville: Abingdon, 1984), ch. 1, on Willard, her "Woman of the Century." Hardesty's appendix provides a partial chronological listing of defenses of women's ministry.

12. Less than one-third of *Woman in the Pulpit* contains Willard's own writings. Chapter 2, "The Spirit Giveth Life," first appeared in the December 1887 *Homiletic Review* at the editor's request. Dr. Van Dyke's rebuttal to that article constitutes chapter 6. Professor Townsend's counter-argument appears as chapter 7, while in two other chapters Willard compiled the testimonies of male and female preachers.

13. Willard, *Woman in the Pulpit*, 34.

14. Ibid., 167.

15. Palmer and Booth, happily married to husbands supportive of their public ministry, apparently viewed the issue of subordination through different lenses than did Willard.

16. Benjamin Titus Roberts, *Ordaining Women* (Rochester, N.Y.: Earnest Christian Publishing House, 1891), 68. In addition to the ATLA microfiche copy, see *Holiness Tracts Defending the Ministry of Women*, Donald W. Dayton, ed. (New York: Garland, 1984), for a reprint of *Ordaining Women*.

17. Ibid., 44.

18. A. J. Gordon, *How Christ Came to Church* (Philadelphia: American Baptist Publication Society, 1895), 129–30.

19. See Bruce Shelley, "A. J. Gordon and Biblical Criticism," *Foundations* 14 (Jan.–March 1971): 69–77. On another controversial topic, Gordon argued for the type of healing practiced in apostolic times in his 1882 *Ministry of Healing*.

20. Northern conservative Baptists apparently approached Scripture with more flexibility than the northern Presbyterians. See Norman H. Maring, "Baptists and Changing Views of the Bible, 1865–1918," *Foundations* 1 (July 1958): 52–75; (Oct. 1958): 30–62.

21. Gordon, "May A Woman Prophesy?" *Christian Herald and Signs of the Times*, n.d., 1.

22. Gordon, "The Ministry of Women," *Missionary Review of the World* 7 (Dec. 1894), 918.

23. Ibid., 919.

24. Donald Dayton, in his unpublished paper "Evangelical Roots of Feminism" (p. 12), claimed that Gordon did not ground his argument for the ordination of women upon Galatians 3:28 and a doctrine of the equality of women, but upon his doctrine of the Holy Spirit. Gordon's essay did *not* argue for ordination but rather for women's right to preach. If anything, Gordon implicitly opposed women's ordination, finding no New Testament precedent.

25. Franson, "Prophesying Daughters," 35 (Westberg translation, in *The Covenant Quarterly* 34 [Nov. 1976]).

26. Ibid., 40.

27. Katharine Bushnell, *God's Word to Women* (Piedmont, Oakland, Calif.: published by the author, n.d.; reprint, ed. Ray B. Munson, Box 52, North Collins, N.Y., 1976). Containing no page numbers, *God's Word to Women* will be cited according to paragraph numbers.

28. Ibid., author's note.

29. Ibid., para. 363.

30. Ibid., para. 738.

31. Jessie Penn-Lewis, *The Magna Charta of Woman* (Bournemouth, England: The Overcomer Book Room, 1919; reprint, Minneapolis: Bethany Fellowship, 1975).

32. Ibid., 9.

33. Lee Anna Starr, *The Bible Status of Woman* (New York: Revell, 1926).

34. Ibid., 7.

35. Ibid., 276.

36. Ibid., 285.

37. In chapter 11, concerning Paul's 1 Corinthians 7 teaching on marriage, Starr revealed an approach significantly different from all previous authors. When Paul says in 7:12, "to the rest I say this (I, not the Lord)," and in 7:25 ("I have no command from the Lord, but I give a judgment"), he refused to speak with apostolic authority. In that case, Starr explained, Paul, though inspired, was not infallible in that particular personal opinion. Since Paul does not call his teaching in 1 Corinthians 14 and 1 Timothy 2 uninspired, Starr accepted those passages as inerrant.

38. John Roach Straton, *Does the Bible Forbid Women to Preach and Pray in Public?* 1926. See appendix 11.

39. See Robert George Delnay's "A History of the Baptist Bible Union" (D.Th. diss., Dallas Theological Seminary, 1963). Canadian T. T. Shields joined American Fundamentalists to form the Union in 1923. Shields' secretary Edith Rebman served on the BBU executive committee and held great authority for a time at Des Moines University.

40. Ferenc M. Szasz, "Three Fundamental Leaders: The Roles of William Bell Riley, John Roach Straton, and William Jennings Bryan in Fundamentalist-Modernist Controversy" (Ph.D. diss., University of Rochester, 1969), 132.

41. Dr. Robert C. Anderson of Western Conservative Baptist Seminary (Portland) has researched Utley in connection with his study of turn-of-the-century female evangelists. Utley wrote *Why I Am a Preacher* (New York: Revell, 1931) and edited *Petals From the Rose of Sharon.* Converted at age eight under Aimee Semple McPherson's ministry in California, Utley eventually left Baptist circles and was licensed a Methodist preacher. See articles about Utley in *Time,* 30 Dec. 1935 and 10 Jan. 1938; *Newsweek,* 28 Dec. 1935; *New York Journal,* May 1927.

42. Straton quoted no commentators. Franson utilized Theodoret, Chrysostom, Theophilus, and Luther. Gordon used several, including Canon Garratt's "Ministry of Women."

43. Penn-Lewis, *The Magna Charta of Woman,* 33.

44. Adam Clarke, *The New Testament,* vol. 6 "Romans-Revelation" (1851; reprint, New York: Abingdon-Cokesbury, n.d.), 278.

45. George P. Hays, *May Women Speak? A Bible Study By a Presbyterian Minister* (Chicago: Women's Temperance Publication Association, 1889).

Chapter 7

1. Rosemary Skinner Keller, "Lay Women" in *Women and Religion in America: The Nineteenth Century,* ed. Rosemary Radford Ruether and Rosemary Skinner Keller (San Francisco: Harper and Row, 1981), vol. 1.

2. Donna A. Behnke, "Forgotten Images: Women in American Methodism"; and Rosemary Skinner Keller, "The Deaconess: 'New Woman' of Late Nineteenth Century Methodism" in *Explor* 5:1 (Spring 1979): 23–32, 33–41.

3. Mary Agnes Doughterty, "The Methodist Deaconess: A Case of Religious Feminism," *Methodist History* 21:2 (Jan. 1983): 95.

4. Madeleine Sweeny Miller, *New Testament Women and Problems of Today* (New York: The Methodist Book Concern, 1926), 164.

5. Lucy Rider Meyer, *Deaconesses: Biblical, Early Church, European, American* (Chicago: The Message Publishing Co., 1889).

6. Catherine Prelinger and Rosemary Keller explain the relative success of the Methodist deaconesses compared to Lutherans in America in "The

Function of Female Bonding: The Restored Diaconessate of the Nineteenth Century" in *Women in New Worlds,* ed. Rosemary Skinner Keller and Hilah F. Thomas (Nashville: Abingdon, 1982), vol. 2.

7. George Francis Wilkin, *The Prophesying of Women* (Chicago: Revell, 1895), 297.

8. Jesse A. Hungate, *The Ordination of Women to the Pastorate in Baptist Churches* (Hamilton, N.Y.: James B. Grant, 1899), 137.

9. Bishop Alma White, *Woman's Ministry* (London: Pillar of Fire, n.d.), 2.

10. Edvard P. Torjesen, *Fredrik Franson—A Model for Worldwide Evangelism* (Pasadena: William Carey Library, 1983), 47.

11. Melvin Easterday Dieter, *The Holiness Revival in the Nineteenth Century* (Metuchen, N.J.: Scarecrow, 1980), 42.

12. Uldine Utley, *Why I Am A Preacher. A Plain Answer to an Oft-Repeated Question* (New York: Revell, 1931), 77.

13. Torjesen, *Franson,* 62.

14. Charles H. Pridgeon, "The Ministry of Women" (Gibsonia, Pa.: The Pittsburgh Bible Institute, n.d.), 26–28. Pridgeon (1863–1932), a Presbyterian minister, worked as an evangelist with D. L. Moody, had contact with A. B. Simpson, and experienced sanctification in 1892. He founded Pittsburgh Bible Institute with his wife Louise Shepard Pridgeon in 1901.

15. T. DeWitt Talmage, *Woman: Her Power and Privileges* (New York: J. S. Ogilvie and Co., 1888), 16.

16. Christian Golder, *History of the Deaconess Movement in the Christian Church* (Cincinnati: Jennings and Pye, 1903), 528.

17. P. D. Stephenson, *The Woman Question* (Charlotte, N.C.: Presbyterian Publishing Co., 1899), 227.

18. "Editorial Response," *Western Recorder* 8 Feb. 1923, 8.

19. Timothy P. Weber, "The Two-Edged Sword: The Fundamentalist Use of the Bible" in Mark Noll and Nathan Hatch, eds., *The Bible in America* (Oxford: Oxford University Press, 1982), 6.

20. Mrs. George C. Needham, *Woman's Ministry* (New York: Revell, 1895).

21. Oswald J. Smith, *Can Organized Religion Survive?* (Toronto: Toronto Tabernacle Publishers, 1932), 211.

22. Vincent H. Gaddis and Jasper A. Huffman, *The Story of Winona Lake— A Memory and A Vision* (Winona Lake, Ind.: Rodeheaver, 1960).

23. Viola D. Romans, "The Nation's Call," *Winona Echoes,* Aug. 1914, 349–50.

24. Rufus Jones, "The Changing Role of Women" (paper presented at the Denver Seminary Senior Colloquium, 1979), 2.

25. Stanton Coit, *Women in Church and State* (London: West London Ethical Society, 1910), 27.

26. Barbara Leslie Epstein, *Politics of Domesticity: Women, Evangelism, and Temperance in Nineteenth-Century America* (Middletown, Conn.: Wesleyan University Press, 1981); Susan Dye Lee, "Evangelical Domesticity: The Woman's Temperance Crusade of 1873–74" in *Women in New Worlds,* Keller and Thomas, eds., vol. 1.

27. Ruth Bordin, *Woman and Temperance: The Quest for Power and Liberty, 1873–1900* (Philadelphia: Temple University Press, 1981); Carolyn DeSwarte Gifford, "For God and Home and Native Land" in *Women in New Worlds,* Keller and Thomas, eds., vol. 1.

28. Mary Henry Rossiter, *My Mother's Life—The Evolution of a Recluse* (Chicago: Revell, 1900).

29. Mrs. John H. Chapman, "Reflections of a Fundamentalist," *The Baptist* 5, no. 8 (22 March 1924): 182.

30. S. G. Anderson, *Woman's Sphere and Influence* (Toledo, Ohio: West Presbyterian Church, 1898), 22.

31. The chapter on "Women and Revivalism" in *Women and Religion in America,* ed. Ruether and Keller, vol. 1, discusses the early-nineteenth-century setting. The major exceptions to the rule were the revivalistic churches in the South.

32. Dana Lee Robert, "Arthur Tappan Pierson and Forward Movements of Late-Nineteenth-Century Evangelicalism" (Ph.D. diss., Yale University, 1984), 308–10.

33. Arthur T. Pierson, *Catherine of Siena, an Ancient Lay Preacher* (New York: Funk and Wagnalls, 1898).

34. Ibid., 5.

35. David Mitchell, *The Fighting Pankhursts—A Study in Tenacity* (New York: Macmillan, 1967).

36. Rudolf A. Renfer, "A History of Dallas Theological Seminary" (Ph.D. diss., University of Texas, 1959).

37. Though women in 1986–87 can finally enter the Th.M. and S.T.M. programs for the first time, that is not to prepare them for ordination, pulpit ministry, or senior pastorates. According to Dallas, 1 Timothy 2 excludes women from the pastor/teacher/elder role. Faculty member Charles C. Ryrie's *The Role of Women in the Church* symbolizes the traditional Dallas restrictions on women. Dallas also at first refused to admit black students. Did the existence of racist policies and practice possibly parallel sexist attitudes in some evangelical circles?

38. Lewis Sperry Chafer, "Effective Ministerial Training," *Evangelical Theological College Bulletin,* May 1925, 9.

39. An examination of the educational background of the men who teach Bible and Theology on MBI's faculty listed in the 1985–86 catalogue illustrates the phenomenal impact of Dallas. Thirteen of the nineteen Bible and theology professors graduated from Dallas. The dean of education and chairs of five departments—Bible, Theology, Pastoral Studies, Evangelism, and Christian Education—also graduated from Dallas.

40. See David Moberg, *The Church as a Social Institution* (Englewood Cliffs, N.J.: Prentice-Hall, 1962); and H. Richard Niebuhr, *The Social Sources of Denominationalism* (New York: H. Holt and Co., 1929) on the institutionalization process in religious groups.

Afterword

1. "The Role of Women in Ministry," *Alliance Witness*, 5 Aug. 1981, 27.
2. Richard W. DeHaan, "The Woman God Made—Her Creation, Submission, Equality, and Behavior" (Grand Rapids: Radio Bible Class, 1980), 29.
3. "The Biblical Woman: But What Can She Do?" *Moody Monthly*, Feb. 1983, 12–15.
4. Susan T. Foh, "Women Preachers, Why Not?" *Fundamentalist Journal*, Jan. 1985, 17–19.
5. Katharine Bushnell, *God's Word to Women* (Piedmont, Oakland, Calif.: published by the author, n.d.; reprint, ed. Ray B. Munson, Box 52, North Collins, N.Y., 1976), para. 734.
6. Lee Anna Starr, *The Bible Status of Woman* (New York: Revell, 1926), 387.
7. Jessie Penn-Lewis, *The Magna Charta of Woman* (Bournemouth, England: The Overcomer Book Room, 1919; reprint, Minneapolis: Bethany Fellowship, 1975), 15.

BIBLIOGRAPHY

I. *Women and the Church in America: Microfiche Collection* (Beltsville, Md.: NCR Corporation for the American Theological Library Association Board of Microtext, 1977).

*ATLA later publications in 1978 and 1981 are designated and all microfiche numbers are in brackets.

Anderson, Samuel G. "Woman's Sphere and Influence." Toledo, Ohio: Franklin Printing, 1898. [#104]

Bowles, Ada C. "Woman in Ministry." In *Woman's Work in America,* ed. by Annie Nathan Meyer. New York: Henry Holt, 1891. [#179]

Dever, Mary. "Woman in the Pulpit." *The Lutheran Quarterly,* April 1904, 284–87. [1978 F 2010]

Dix, Morgan. *Lectures on the Calling of a Christian Woman and Her Training to Fulfil It.* New York: D. Appleton and Co., 1883. [#107]

"The Eligibility of Women Not a Scriptural Question." *The Methodist Review* 73 (March 1891): 287–91. [1978 F 2012]

Fry, Benjamin St. James. "Woman's Work in the Church" from *Proceedings of the Second Ecumenical Methodist Conference.* New York: Hunt and Eaton, 1892. [1981 #464]

Hartford, Mrs. Keister. "Women's Position in the Church." *Quarterly Review of the United Brethren in Christ,* April 1894. [1981 F 2156]

Harvey, William Patrick. *Shall Woman Preach?* Louisville: Baptist Book Concern, 1905. [#298]

Hays, George P. *May Women Speak? A Bible Study By a Presbyterian Minister.* Chicago: Women's Temperance Publication Association, 1889. [#112]

Holland, Frederic May. *Our Clergy Women.* Chicago: Open Court Publishing Co., 1892. [#168]

Hungate, Jesse A. *The Ordination of Women to the Pastorate in Baptist Churches.* Hamilton, N.Y.: University Book Store, 1899. [#166]

Hunter, Fannie McDowell. *Women Preachers.* Dallas: Berachah Printing Co., 1905. [#167]

Marvin, Frederic R. *Consecrated Womanhood.* New York: J. D. Wright and Co., 1903. [#119]

Mayser, F. P. "Shall Women Vote in Church?" *Lutheran Church Review,* July 1899. [#165]

Meyer, Lucy Rider. *Deaconesses: Biblical, Early Church, European, American.* Chicago: The Message Publishing Co., 1889. [#120]

Needham, Mrs. George C. *Woman's Ministry.* New York: Revell, 1895. [#59]

Oliver, Anna. "Test Case" on the Ordination of Women Appealed from the New England Conference to the General Conference. A Statement by Her. [1981 F 2208]

Pfatteicher, Ernst P. H. *Woman as a Congregational Voter.* Philadelphia: Evangelical Lutheran Theological Seminary, 1899. [#124]

Roberts, Benjamin Titus. *Ordaining Women.* Rochester, N.Y.: Earnest Christian Publishing House, 1891. [1981 F 2183]

Schmauk, Theodore E. *St. Paul and Women and the Epistle to Timothy and The Woman Question.* Philadelphia: Evangelical Lutheran Theological Seminary, 1899. [#159]

Shaw, Rev. Anna Howard. *Women in the Ministry.* Meadville, Pa.: T. L. Flood, 1898. [#163]

Stephenson, P. D. *The Woman Question.* Charlotte, N.C.: The Presbyterian Publishing Co., 1899. [#129]

Sunderland, J. T. *The Liberal Christian Ministry.* Boston: G. H. Ellis, 1889. [#183]

Wilmarth, James W. "Woman's Work in the Church." *Baptist Quarterly Review* 10 (Oct. 1888). [1981 #232]

Woosley, Louisa M. *Shall Woman Preach? or, The Question Answered.* Caneyville, Ky., 1891. [1981 F 2195]

II. *History of Women: Microfilm Collection* (New Haven, Conn.: Research Publications, Inc., 1976–79).

*All microfilm reels and numbers are in brackets.

Baker, Hatty. *Women in the Ministry.* London: C. W. Danie, 1911. [Reel 790, #6307]

Bancroft, Jane Marie. *Deaconesses in Europe and Their Lessons for America.* New York: Hunt and Eaton, 1889. [Reel 481, #3602]

Bashford, James Whitford. "Does the Bible Allow Women to Preach?" 1879/80. [Reel 939, #8263]

Coit, Stanton. *Woman in Church and State.* London: West London Ethical Society, 1910. [Reel 717, #5737]

Dietrick, Ellen Battelle. *Women in the Early Christian Ministry.* Philadelphia: Alfred J. Ferris, 1897. [Reel 532, #4084]

Easton, Peter Zaccheus. *Does Woman Represent God?* New York: Fleming H. Revell, 1895. [Reel 935, #7942]

Gage, Matilda Joslyn. *Woman, Church, and State.* Chicago: C. H. Kerr and Co., 1893. [Reel 545, #4202]

Golder, Christian. *History of the Deaconess Movement in the Christian Church.* Cincinnati: Jennings and Pye, 1903. English translation from German. [Reel 656, #5224]

Goudge, Henry Leighton. *The Place of Women in the Church.* Milwaukee: The Young Churchman, Co., 1917. [Reel 894, #7402]

Grover, A. J. *The Bible Argument Against Woman—Stated and Answered From a Bible Standpoint.* Chicago: Executive Committee of the Cook County Woman's Suffrage Association, 1870. [Reel 385, #2720]

Hayden, M. P. *The Bible and Woman.* Cincinnati: The Standard Publishing Co., 1902. [Reel 659, #5255.1]

Hodgkin, Jonathan Backhouse. *Woman's Place in the Church.* London: Published by the editor of the "Friendly Messenger," 1907. [Reel 939, #8269]

Keeler, Ellen Coughlin. *The Balance Wheel: A Condensed History of the Women's Home Missionary Society of the Methodist Episcopal Church.* New York: Women's Home Missionary Society, 1920. [Reel 901, #7484]

Oldroyd, A. E. *The Place of Women in the Church.* London: Office of the English Church Union, 1917. [Reel 939, #8275]

Richardson, Aubrey. *Women of the Church of England.* London: Chapman and Hall, Ltd., 1907. [Reel 760, #6094]

Robinson, Cecilia. *The Ministry of Deaconesses.* London: Methuen and Co., 1898. [Reel 595, #4707]

Rossiter, Mary Henry. *My Mother's Life—The Evolution of a Recluse.* Chicago: Fleming H. Revell, 1900. [Reel 597, #4723]

Spencer, Mrs. H. C. *Problems on the Woman Question, Social, Political, and Scriptural.* Washington: Langran, Ogilvie and Co., 1871. [Reel 410, #2974]

Talmage, T. DeWitt. *Woman: Her Power and Privileges.* New York: J. S. Ogilvie and Co., 1888. [Reel 491, #3690]

"Theological Training for Women." Hartford: Hartford Theological Seminary Publications, 1892. [Reel 939, #8265]

Thompson, Henry Adams. *Women of The Bible.* Dayton, Ohio: United Brethren Publishing House, 1914. [Reel 862, #7060]

Wheeler, Henry. *Deaconesses Ancient and Modern.* New York: Hunt and Eaton, 1889. [Reel 495, #3740]

White, Alma. *Woman's Ministry.* London: Pillar of Fire, n.d. [Reel 939, #8282]

Wilkin, George Francis. *The Prophesying of Women. A Popular and Practical Exposition of the Bible Doctrine.* Chicago: Fleming H. Revell, 1895. [Reel 619, #4931]

Wittenmyer, Annie. *Women's Work for Jesus.* Philadelphia: published by author, 1871. [Reel 419, #3061]

Yates, Elizabeth Upham. "The Admission of Women to the Methodist General Conference." New York: National American Woman Suffrage Association, 1900. [Reel 939, #8267]

SUBJECT INDEX

SCRIPTURE INDEX